S0-AHA-207

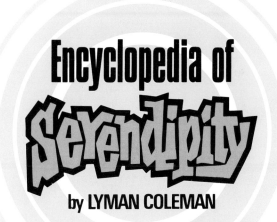

Encyclopedia of Serendipity

by LYMAN COLEMAN

designed and prepared by Bob and Lois Blewett

© 1976 Serendipity House. All rights reserved. Printed in U.S.A.

You are invited
to experience
for yourself
serendipity*—
to stretch,
grow,
become,
the new thing
God has for you . . .
to discover
your fantastic gifts
and to find
a fresh,
new approach
to spiritual growth
and
religious education
through
Serendipity
programs.

*Serendipity is the
facility of making happy
chance discoveries.
— Horace Walpole, 1754

The author wishes to acknowledge those who have had a part in making this program a reality: ☐ Father Don Kimball for his help in the planning ☐ Dave Stone for assisting in the research ☐ Lois Blewett for the copy editing ☐ Bob Blewett for the art and design ☐ Gene Wieland Jr., Joel Strasser, Wally Howard, Paul Shrock and Bob Blewett for the photos ☐ Stan Yoder, Peter Yoder and the Mennonite Publishing House for the production of the books ☐ The Oxford and Cambridge University Press for permission to use passages from *The New English Bible,* ©The Delegates of the Oxford University Press and the Syndics of the Cambridge University Press, 1961 and 70. All rights reserved. ☐ American Bible Society for their permission to quote from *Good News for Modern Man, Today's English Version,* ©1966, American Bible Society.

BASIC AREAS OF REFERENCE

This Encyclopedia is our gift to the Serendipity family—you who are one with us in a beautiful dream; the dream of a church renewed in the Spirit of God, given to people, binding up the wounds of loneliness and broken relationships in small caring groups.

We give you the best material that we have. It will be an invaluable resource tool in your ministry.

The Encyclopedia has a section for each kind of group activities. The color-coding in the center of the book matches that of the four tracks of the new youth programs.

The next few pages will give you the story behind Serendipity—how the Serendipity group process has evolved over the years. It will continue to evolve as we find new ways of bringing people into a personal relationship with Christ and one another.

I want to thank some of the people who have shared over the years in Serendipity: Bob and Lois Blewett for their art, design and editorial work; Stan Yoder, Pete Yoder, Marilyn Swartzentruber and all of the other beautiful people at the Mennonite Publishing House for the production and office work for everything we do; and, most of all, Margaret, my wife, for sharing the dream and struggle and keeping the home front warm and supportive through all these years.

Join us in this scary adventure. In the years ahead the church will turn more and more to "people" ministries, and the need for trained and qualified leaders will be a priority. We are counting on you to fill that need.

Yours in His serendipity,

Lyman

The Serendipity Years

Serendipity, as we use the word, is a fusion of group-building exercises, self-discovery Bible study and spiritual community. It takes place in a riot of interpersonal relationships that are mischievously revealing and outrageously healing. It is childlikeness and Christ-likeness, laughter and tears, all mixed up together. It is frogs and frog-lovers, losers and sinners, caterpillars and Dulcineas on their way to becoming the people of God.

It is the super cool teenager and the little old lady finding out about each other. It is the joy that comes from personal discovery, the inner warmth that comes from honest, sincere praise.

It is mother and daughter, father and son, finding they are not so much apart. It is a fellowship of strugglers, sharing, caring, growing and discovering the new thing that God has for them.

It is the high-collared clergyman and the low-collared layman discovering that down deep inside each is a scared little boy wanting to be known—but afraid to be found out.

It is a handful of people honestly wrestling with the purpose and meaning of their lives, open to the Spirit and the Bible, without fear of being stupid or wrong. It is the cup of cold water offered as fellow ministers of Christ, calling forth the best in one another.

It is the call in the middle of the night, the touch of an understanding friend, the mysterious, unexplainable bond that draws people together in Christ.

It is the serendipity of the Holy Spirit, setting us free to be the persons we were meant to be. One in the Spirit—holy, holey, wholly FREE.

Serendipity is the outgrowth of the struggles in my life and ministry. I was raised in a strongly religious family where the Bible was read and Christ was honored. I was trained in a warm Methodist church and attended good, conservative schools. If anyone should have stayed in the Southern tradition, I should have. But somehow, it didn't work that way. There was a haunting, grating discontent in my life. Maybe it is here that the roots of Serendipity can be found. For as I fidgeted through endless hours of family devotions, religious instruction and Bible lectures, I had a gnawing feeling that there must be a better way. Surely the greatest story ever told could be a little more exciting. Then in my last year of college I took a course that really turned me on, but it was not in the religion department.

At every "Integration of Ability" class we were given a creative exercise to get in touch with an area of our creative self. Once we took our initials and doodled until we had the makings of an expressionistic design. Then we walked out our doodles in our imagination and wrote a free verse poem. Finally we developed the doodles into a symbolic self-portrait by coloring our feelings. We even played our feelings on the piano with our arms and elbows.

Back in 1954 this was radical. (The professor was fired two years later.) And for me, it was doubly radical. But it opened up something in me that I didn't know. I was a creative being with vast reservoirs of untapped potential and God-given gifts.

In my own private study of Scripture, I started to "feel" the passage. I put my meditations in diary form, adding color and texture and sound. In my years in seminary I tried to help my Young Life kids discover the Scriptures through the creative techniques. And with one professor (Howard Hendricks), I turned in crazy, expressionistic drawings for Bible interpretations, and he was crazy enough to accept them.

But the years had much trial and error, with many more failures than successes. Most of my teachers and a great many of my associates thought the ideas a little weird and even dangerous. And maybe they were, but that's the way Serendipity started out.

My brother, a teacher at Asbury Seminary, asked me to write a booklet that people in the "Prayer Cell Movement" could use in their private devotions. The result was "Do It Yourself In Devotions" and "Teen Time Devotions." Margaret, my wife, hand-lettered the first edition, and for

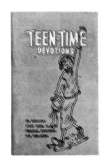

illustrations we obtained permission to use a cartoon strip. My brother printed them on a tiny offset press in the basement of the seminary and sold them for 25 cents each. Then Billy Graham picked them up and used them for give-a-ways on his first two television crusades.

1959-61   The Searching Years

ate themselves and their needs.

Growth by Groups is significant in the evolution of the Serendipity process. It was the first time I had attempted to wed Bible study and group experience. In addition to discussion, I built in several principles that I feel are crucial to having an effective group: (a) the contract for all members to sign, (b) the commitment to mutual support, (c) a system for evaluation and multiplication.

It would be another 10 years, however, before we discovered that group building must come before content discussion to help people form a "group."

In the late 50's the Church Renewal movement was coming in, causing a lot of us getting out of seminary to see a ray of hope for the years ahead. John Castell in his book, *Spiritual Renewal through Personal Groups,* told about six churches that started small sharing groups for people who wanted to grow in their faith. I remember feeling that I had found a niche in the church where I could give myself.

I was looking for a project for a doctoral dissertation and decided on group dynamics. Unfortunately, it was still an uncharted discipline. Most of the emphasis at the time was upon behavior analysis and very little upon group building and growth. We would sit in groups and study how each person was reacting. Frankly, I found this experience unconstructive. We learned a lot about ourselves, but very little about helping each other to change. The group was primarily a "buzz" system to discuss a topic of another's choosing.

The only group I found effective was Alcoholics Anonymous, so I patterned my project after its concepts of mutual dependence and discipline. I called it

Growth by Groups. I laid down a discipline for a person to follow in his devotional life for one year as a basis for membership in a support group. Each person had to sign the contract, and the group had to stay together for a year while they went through the program.

The study material offered an inductive method for studying each kind of literature in the Bible: (a) paraphrase and summary for the Epistles, (b) survey and analysis for the Gospels, (c) rapid reading and synthesis for the Historical Books, (d) subjective analysis for the Psalms.

Leadership rotated within the group each week. Attendance was expected, except in case of an emergency. There was also an elaborate system of dividing and multiplying groups within the church from year to year. This program is still in operation under a separate corporation, Christian Outreach, Inc.

I feel now that the program is quite heavy. Too, the discipline of studying the Scriptures can be an escape from the *real* needs in the group. In an effort to remedy this, I later added some questionnaires for participants to evalu-

"Growth by Groups" started out as a doctoral project and ended up as a family project. And it just about killed us. No one wanted to print the thing when I finished it, so Margaret and I printed it ourselves—a thousand copies—and stored them in our extra bedroom. When the second baby came along, we moved the office to the dining room (which wasn't that big in the first place) and shipping and invoicing was done from the kitchen counter and the attic. Before long, the whole house was taken up with boxes of Bible studies in various stages of collating. Our friends were afraid to come over for fear of what they might be recruited for.
This went on for five years—until friends volunteered to take over the mess and give their lives to it, which they have done to this day. If it had not been for Bud and Vera Eastburn, I don't know what we would have done.

1962-65 The Experimental Years In Youth Work

Armed with our *Growth by Groups* program that was surely going to cure every problem in the church, I announced to the world that I was available to go into any area and teach how to accomplish Church Renewal.

To my amazement, we had few takers. In fact, in the first year we had a grand total of three invitations. We finally sold our home to make ends meet and used the extra time to read everything possible in the personal growth and motivation field, all the way from Dale Carnegie to Napoleon Hill.

These were the years of the hootenanny. Bob Dylan was the idol of the teen world, and the guitar was its new-found toy. Since I had nothing else to do, I started creating exercises to help young people relate Scripture to the folk generation.

That summer a Baptist camp in New Jersey asked me to lead the Senior Highs in Bible study for a week. I tried our "folk expression" technique. Each morning the kids explored a passage in Scripture and put their responses into a simple creative piece—a drawing, a free verse poem or a diary. In the after-

noons, they put their thing into a folk medium—wall poster, pop sculpture, ballad, reading or interpretive dance. Each evening, we staged a hootenanny with the kids performing their masterpieces.

It worked! Kids who had been turned off to the Bible suddenly were engrossed. A sense of community slowly emerged. And the evening hootenannys, while not very professional, were beautiful times together.

The word spread. Invitations started to come in, and Gene Herr, Youth Secretary for the Mennonite Church, asked me to write up the program for their denomination. It grew into a full-scale pictorial study book. We sold our house again to get the money to print it and came out with our first Serendipity book, *Acts Alive*.

The book had a mixed reception, particularly in the Mennonite Church. One of the bishops called the book a "heap of educational garbage."

The next few years were exciting but hard-going. At some meetings I would be met with great hostility and opposition; at others people accepted the ideas.

The rhythm of the Serendipity process started to take shape; the wedding of self-discovery and self-expression with Scripture, the short creative exercise to prime the pump, a continuing support group to share results, and the occasional special program to share with the larger community.

"Acts Alive," based on the Book of Acts, is a series of fast-moving creative exercises in folk expression. Exploring many of the key passages in the book, the student tries his hand at creative doodling, creative writing, pop art and impressionistic pantomime. Each unit has a workshop and a folk night program. It's excellent for youth camps and conferences where special resource personnel are available.

1966-68   The Wild Coffee House Years

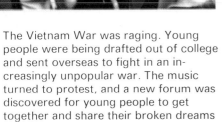

The Vietnam War was raging. Young people were being drafted out of college and sent overseas to fight in an increasingly unpopular war. The music turned to protest, and a new forum was discovered for young people to get together and share their broken dreams with each other—the coffee house.

Many saw the coffee house as a den of iniquity, but a few churches (like the Church of the Savior in Washington, D.C.) were proving that the coffee house was an effective marketplace for the church to minister in the world, earning the right to share their faith in Christ.

I started to put on workshops for youth groups to prepare for their mission to the community. The group skills of listening and caring were perfectly suited to coffee house dialogue, and the creative techniques were great for developing good folk entertainment.

We started to experiment with multimedia. We called the sessions "happenings," drawing upon the "instant art" craze on the college scene. After a few minutes of researching a Bible passage, the young people divided into teams to produce an art, music or multi-media piece.

These were the wild years in my own development. It was as though I had to get something out of my system—to prove something. The elders in the church often got upset by the way-out ideas, and I took a weird sort of satisfaction in upsetting them. I regret this now.

Nevertheless, this period was crucial in my own spiritual development as well as in the Serendipity process. During those years, we developed the creative exercise into the show-and-tell techniques that were to become more and more introspective and therapeutic.

If it is true that every person goes through a time of rebellion, these years could be considered my most rebellious, but they were also the prelude to a spiritual breakthrough just around the corner.

"The Coffee House Itch" is a training program for a youth group that wants to start a ministry in the community. You may call it something other than a coffee house, but the step-by-step development is the same. The important thing is to build a core group that is dedicated to a common mission, and the program accomplishes this.

"Man Alive," a sequel to "Acts Alive," is based on the life of Christ. The fast-moving creative exercises work with the same Scriptures that Handel used in composing "The Messiah." Special instructions are provided for folk art, music, creative writing and multi-media workshops. The Finale is your own Messiah production and an exhilarating experience.

"Kaleidoscope" is probably the most far-out of the Serendipity Books. It provides a series of exercises that enable young people to "do their thing" in multi-media, pop art and sculpture, interpretive pantomime. Selected Scriptures involving the creation, fall, and re-creation are used to help young people see their own pilgrimage. Good for camps and conferences where extra resource help is available.

"Festival" came out later, but belongs to this era. It is a short course in film-making, with group building and Scripture research as an integral part of the process. Excellent for bored youth groups who are looking for a challenge and are interested in "making films." No professional equipment or personnel are needed. Several churches can work on the project and stage a Film Festival at the close.

11

In the late 60's, a new movement in group experience started to sweep across the country. It was variously called sensitivity training, Encounter Groups, or the Human Potential Movement. I was frightened by the emphasis upon physical touch. I had been trained in seminary to keep a safe distance from people, and I was naturally reserved. Even in a group situation, I hid behind a professional air for fear that someone might "get to me" if they got too close. Like a pro, I knew when to excuse myself from a group and busy myself when things started getting deep.

In these years, the big, bluff exterior started to crumble and I discovered a whole new dimension to group experience that radically changed my life and the programs I was writing.

I was in Atlanta for a conference, the first of a series being put on by a team I was a part of. Lloyd Ogilvie said the team would meet together at least once a day to report in on how we were feeling—and that we would plan the agenda around our own needs. This scared me to death. The thought of revealing my needs to my peers was bad enough—I had had a bad "team" experience before—but the idea of going before the whole world "in weakness" was worse. (I had explained away the words from the Apostle Paul about that as psychologically unsound.)

The first day or two when we met together as a team, I faked it. I said something about my frustrations in the ministry—a subject that was safe to talk about. But some of the men opened up about their personal needs. They really got to me.

On the last morning of that conference, I was to lead the morning worship. This was my professional bag, but I was not ready for worship that morning—and I decided not to fake it. So I refused, and Ralph Osborne took over.

After the session I got together with Ralph and said, "I'm sorry, but I just can't pretend that everything is fine with me. This idea about being a team and ministering to each other is tearing me up because I was on a team once that wasn't a team and I just don't want to go through that again."

I talked and talked and Ralph just sat there. When I was completely talked out he said, "Lyman, how would you like for me to pray that God will erase those memories and give you a new start in building some deep relationships?"

My first thought was, "These guys are a bunch of fanatics!" But after a moment, I said yes. He stood up, laid his hands on my head and prayed that God would erase the hurt and pain of my bad experience and give me a clean

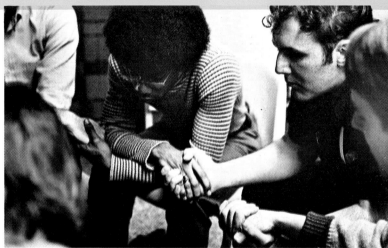

start. And...do you know what? It worked. It worked!

The next 27 days in conferences was something else. I was like a little child, starting all over again. I led the same *Discovery* games and I talked about the same in-depth relationships in small groups, but I did it as a learner instead of a teacher. Leading from weakness and being vulnerable were more than theories. They were a whole new lifestyle of leadership for me.

When I got home I had some homework to do before I could finish the book. I had always looked upon small groups as an educational tool for a learning activity, but now I had discovered that a small group can be much more if the members are willing to give themselves completely to each other. When Jesus refers to the church he is saying that people who are lonely and hurting can get together and really find healing for their hurts.

"Serendipity" and "Discovery" were partially typeset when I called the printer and asked for the books back. I reshaped them around much more personal sharing. And I had the group respond to each other's needs as ministers of Christ. I feel these are two of the best in the Serendipity series.

"Rap" and "Groups In Action" are popular versions of the original "Growth by Groups" program. Each has a basic program for a "koinonia" study group. "Rap" is based on the Sermon on the Mount and designed especially for teenagers. "Groups In Action" is based on the Book of Acts and is designed for adults. Special instructions explain how to start small groups in your church, how to lead groups, etc. There are special articles by leaders in church renewal.

If you have never tried a small-group program, I would suggest these two.

1971-73   Putting It Together

For me, spiritual growth has been a series of extremes, like a pendulum gone wild. For most of my years, I was a people isolationist, a group con artist with a bag of tricks for every occasion, as long as it didn't involve me. Then the dam broke and I swung completely in the opposite direction. For two years, I gave myself so much to people that I was emotionally spent.

In *Beginnings*, I wrote that the Human Potential Movement opened me up to my own feelings for the first time in my life. I learned to laugh and cry—to reach out and touch, to show my feelings and to feel for others. I experienced the joy of sharing with fellow-strugglers, of our caring for the hurts and needs of each other—in a community of love, trust and acceptance. Beautiful things happened to me that changed my life...and my lifestyle.

When I discovered this relational life-style, I went hog-wild on relationships. I tried to give myself away to every person with whom I came in contact. Every weekend I was in a new city, starting all over with a new group—before the hurt and the pain of the previous weekend's

good-byes had been healed.

Suddenly, I found myself feeling a terrible loneliness in the midst of caring people, and I didn't know why....

What had happened to me? Where did Christ fit into all of this? These were the questions that troubled me in these years as I sought to get myself together —as a whole person with a whole Gospel for the whole world.

I remember going to a theologian that I respected and asking him to explain what had happened to me. He referred me back to the ministry of Christ and the "incarnational" way in which he shared himself with people.

The Gospels became very precious and comforting to me. I discovered that Jesus talked very little *about* theology, but constantly invited people to reach out, touch, experience Him. And it was very often a non-theological experience. In fact his followers would probably have flunked the average catechism test given in the church today.

I put together a rationale for group experience. I described it as going around a baseball diamond, with home plate being depth Christian community. In the

first stage (first base) I went along with the Human Potential Movement in saying a group must begin with History Giving. Members of a group need to get to know about one another.

For the second stage (second base) in the development of a group, I broke with the clinical ideas of feedback in the Encounter program and substituted the word Affirmation (positive feelings). The use of confrontation or attack as a group technique may be all right in a contract group with a qualified leader, but for amateurs to use such methods on unsuspecting people is almost criminal.

To be honest to my own experience, I had to incorporate a deeper dimension in a group-building process for the time when the members are willing to minis-

ter to each other through the presence and power of the Holy Spirit. I called this step, Goal Setting, and symbolized it with a cross in the center of the group.

These two distinctions, (a) affirmation instead of confrontation, and (b) ministry to each other through the Holy Spirit,

were to become the foundation of the Serendipity model.

The real story of these years is that of my spiritual homecoming. For many years I had been living in a spiritual "no man's land" of secular humanism. I had abandoned my conservative up-bringing as stuffy and uncomfortable and not found anything to take its place.

Secular humanism has a lot of integrity to it, so I owe a great deal of my personal growth to it. But down deep inside, I found an inner hunger for spiritual wholeness that could not be satisfied on the human level.

I have come almost full circle in my spiritual pilgrimage, but this time, it is my own experience...and it feels right.

"Breaking Free" is my autobiography in a study course form. I took the major areas of my life where I needed help and found a Bible passage for each one. Then I wrote a creative exercise to help me deal with each area: fear, inadequacy, worry, resentment, regret and despair. The course is great for a group after they have already gone through one of the other programs.

"Celebration" has sensory exercises in self-awareness delicately balanced with Scripture study for understanding your experiences in the light of Scripture. This program is probably the most far out of the Serendipity series; yet, it also has a good Bible base for guidance. I recommend this for camps and conferences.

"Beginnings" is my favorite of the original Serendipity books, because it touches where I am right now. I have dealt with my own inner needs for spiritual depth, working with the mystery passages that talk about the Holy Spirit's ministry in our lives. You can discover what it means to be truly "self-actualized" and totally fulfilled.

My children were growing up. Tudor was 12, Anna was 11 and Kevin, 5. Suddenly I realized that we had a long way to go in making our own family into a Serendipity community and I vowed to do something about it.

I was already working on some programs for intergeneration groups—putting youth and adults together for Sunday school classes. In a moment of insanity, I decided to extend the age to include children as well.

Each evening, as a family, we would try out my new ideas from the day's writing. We had to stretch for something for Kevin. The various Scripture exercises were reduced to childish discussions. That turned off the older kids.

The only design we all agreed on was the multiple-choice questionnaire that had plenty of options. We would start out with very simple ideas and go on to an open-ended question or a creative exercise. It really worked—for each age.

We decided to put the questionnaires on placemats for dinner table conversation, hoping to coax families to use the time in the day they had to be together anyway.

We started to branch out in our thinking to the young adults and young couples in the church—where nothing had seemed to work. Keith Miller offered a series of talks that he had recorded for NBC Radio and we used them with self-reflection questionnaires.

Putting all of these ideas together into the Personal Growth Programs was a real challenge. The result was modular units for (a) study groups (b) family units, (c) coffee get-togethers. Each has its own material which interlocks with material of the other parts, forming an exceptionally versatile kit. One small group can benefit, or an entire church, or the whole community. The sky's the limit. It was a start in the new desperately needy area of intergeneration programming. In the years to come, we intend to keep working to find more and more ideas that work.

"Come Fly," "Hassle," and "Destiny" are the three Personal Growth Programs.

"Come Fly" is basic. It deals with lifestyle. What the Christian life feels like, tastes like, smells like. The multiple-choice questionnaires for each session are uncomplicated. If you have never tried a Personal Growth program for your Sunday school class, use this course first.

"Hassle" is a mischievously safe way to deal with the touchy area of family

relationships. The questionnaires are designed to help us laugh about our foibles with each other and with others in the same predicament. An intergeneration Sunday school class with teenagers and their parents could use this and everyone would gain from it. Or you could have all teenagers—or all parents. The program is low key. No attempt is made to solve knotty problems, but a lot is accomplished indirectly by building lines of communication in a fun-loving way.

"Destiny" is about Don Quixote and impossible dreams—and your own dreams! The questionnaires are designed to help you discover your uniqueness—your gifts—and to set some goals for yourself. The group you are in is responsible to help you reach your goals. All this is done on a basic level that allows all ages and all kinds of people to be in the same group. Through this program you can accomplish amazing things, especially if you've used "Hassle" or "Come Fly" first. Your group will find out the new thing God is up to in their lives!

17

George Bernard Shaw said, "Other people see things and say, 'Why?'...but I dream things that never were—and I say, 'Why not?'" As we look ahead, we invite you to join us in asking, "Why not?"

The need in the church for relational, caring approaches in religious education is greater today than ever before. Everywhere, we hear agonizing cries for help concerning marriage, family, singles, young adults, senior citizens, youth, parents, community relations—you name it—and also a corresponding need to go deeper into Scripture to find spiritual depth.

As the pace of life accelerates, the church has to continue to offer a place for caring, depth relationships—where people can belong and feel wanted.

We hope to provide a series of one-day Serendipity kits for new "rally days" in the church, patterned after our work-shop model. We hope to enlist a thousand teammates to share in the Serendipity family, plus a small army of people who are willing to give themselves to the Serendipity dream.

If the next 20 years are anything like the first, we are probably in for a great many surprises. For after all, this is what Serendipity is all about!

"Evenings for Parents," "More Evenings for Parents," "Evenings for Couples" and "More Evenings for Couples" are four separate programs written by Chuck Gallagher and the Marriage Encounter Resource Community for building better relationships. Each program has material for four evenings, with a step-by-step guidebook for presenting them in your parish or school district.

The format for each evening is simple: (a) a short presentation by a couple, (b) a simple questionnaire for everyone to fill out, (c) a dialogue for 10 minutes with your spouse concerning the questionnaire, (d) a discussion in a group of three or four couples, (e) a short wrap-up.

We are honored to have a part in designing and producing these programs for the larger Christian community.

"Breaker 1-9," "10-4, Good Buddy," and "Movin' On" are our answer to the young scene today for a study series on the basics of the Christian life. These programs are adapted from the series we wrote for the Fellowship of Christian Athletes. "Breaker 1-9" is for getting your life together; "10-4, Good Buddy" is for building relationships; "Movin' On" is for developing moral character. Each program has 16 sessions, with leader's instructions in a separate book.

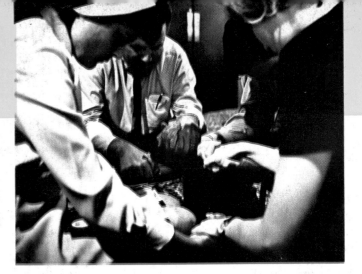

Philosophy

OF GROUP PROCESS

1. YOU are created in the image of God and endowed with unlimited potential.

2. Your POTENTIAL can best be realized through Jesus Christ, in the company of a supportive Christian community.

3. To become a real SUPPORTIVE CHRISTIAN COMMUNITY, you need to get to know one another in depth...and this takes time, effort and a common commitment to life together.

4. Personal GROWTH begins with inner change — as you respond to the invitation of God for newness of life.

5. The HOLY SPIRIT has endowed you with SPIRITUAL GIFTS for ministry to others — within your supportive community and through the community to the church at large.

6. SCRIPTURE is the living account of God's redemptive activity and the best guide to his will for right now.

7. Spiritual WHOLENESS includes your whole being — your emotions, your relationships, your values and your lifestyle.

8. CELEBRATION happens naturally and spontaneously when you are set free in a supportive Christian community to discover and express the beautiful person you are in Christ.

Group Theory

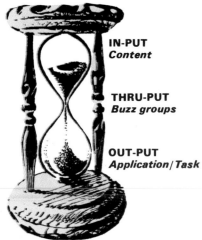

IN-PUT
Content

THRU-PUT
Buzz groups

OUT-PUT
Application/Task

Hour Glass Theory *Talk-it-over*

SESSION	CONTENT
	GROUP BUILDING
	APPLICATION/TASK

1   2   3   4   5   6   7   8

There are several ways to look at small-group experience. The buzz or talk-it-over group of early "group dynamic" days can be visualized with an hour glass. A presentation of some kind is made first and then groups discuss the content.

The material is often controversial in nature, designed to polarize the feelings of the group members for a lively discussion. A discussion is usually considered to be good if members fight for their points of view. I can remember the days back in graduate school when we made little circles to represent the group member and then drew arrows between the members to indicate who was fighting whom.

The idea is for the group to move eventually into some kind of catharsis or synthesis or agreement on a middle position. But in my own experience, this seldom occurred. Instead, each person became more hardened in his position. And, worse, the fighting hurt people.

In a real sense, the group experience was used by the teacher to deal with the subject matter; and the group members were used as dialogical pawns. Fortunately this style of group went out about fifteen years ago.

Now, in what I call "group process," the members are looked upon as human beings, with a value all their own—apart from the "use" they might have in discussing a particular subject matter. The primary purpose for people coming together in a group is to become an enabling community: that is, to help one another develop his own special gifts and resources. There is still a place for content, but it is introduced *after* the group members have become acquainted, so they have a chance to *understand* one another.

I call this the Ribbon Cake Theory, because the slices of cake have varying proportions of mix. The first slice (the first session) is spent mainly with group building—getting to know each other. There may be a little content in the beginning and a little task, or goal, brainstorming at the end, but most of the time is spent in building the group. In the second slice (the second session), most of the time is again spent on group building.

With the third, fourth and fifth slices, there is more and more content and application. In the overall picture as much time is given to content and the application/task as in the Hour Glass Theory, but they are introduced after the group is able to deal with the subject matter as fellow-seekers after the truth.

Let's assume that Johnny is a rabid liberal in his thinking, and Mary is an arch conservative. In the Hour Glass group experience, they will probably end up destroying each other. But in the Ribbon Cake group, they will find out, more likely than not, that they are both scared, insecure, fellow-strugglers, hiding behind a mask of intellectual sophistication. They realize their role of helping each other "come out of the shell" with openness and honesty in a common search.

When this happens, real learning takes place—a learning based upon self-discovery, mutual support and encouragement.

Ribbon Cake Theory *Group Building*

The Method Behind the Madness

A Christian community where real healing takes place, where support for one another is found, where the Spirit of Christ is experienced — not just talked about — is what we all yearn for, but seldom experience. When we do experience it, we don't understand why. We glibly say, "The Holy Spirit brought us together," but we assume the reason *why* and *how* is beyond comprehension. This is unfortunate, because there are very simple principles involved in "becoming a Christian community," and it could "happen" anytime, whenever they are followed.

Like a baseball diamond

To understand what is involved, picture a baseball diamond. Home plate might be compared to "depth Christian community" for a small group. It is the goal we are seeking to arrive at in the group experience. In the New Testament, the word "koinonia" is used to express it — a marriage-like relationship with one another in which there is total openness and freedom to be yourself, where you can share with each other your pain and sorrow as well as your hopes and dreams without fear of condemnation, and to support each other in perfect love.

1st base / History-giving

To get to home plate, you have to go around the bases, which is another way of saying there is a process to becoming a group. First base in this process might be called *history-giving.*

In this first phase, the members of a group need to take the time to tell about themselves. You need to share: (a) *your past* — where you came from, your background, something about your family relationships, good times, hard times, your childhood dreams and aspirations, the significant people in your life, your religious roots and your spiritual pilgrimage up to the present; (b) *your present* — where you are right now, your job, your hobbies, what concerns you, what bugs you, what you do for kicks, what keeps you up at night, where you are right now in your faith,

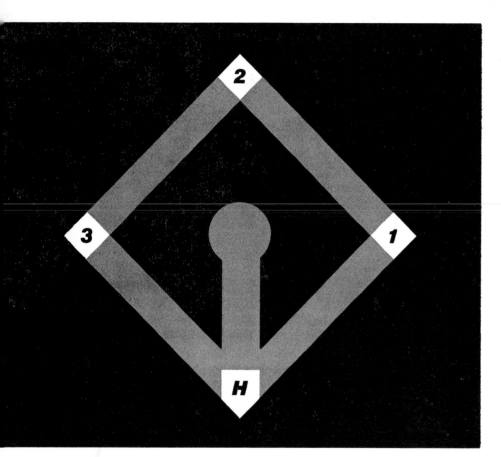

2nd base / Affirmation

After three or four sessions of history-giving, go on to second base. Let the members of the group respond to each other. There are two ways this can be done. One is called "confrontation"; the other, "affirmation." In the Serendipity Books we do not use the confrontation tactics because they can be dangerous. In the confrontation approach, you allow (or encourage) the members of the group to attack each other with any "feelings" they have. ("I get the feeling that you are a little up-tight. Am I correct?" "I get the feeling that you resent me. Is that right?" "I feel that you are being a phoney" etc.) This approach can be very effective in breaking down barriers, stripping away the polite niceties and getting down to brass tacks with each other. But it can do much harm, particularly with unstable people or untrained leadership in the group.

This gives us *affirmation*. You "enable" each other by pointing out the positive traits you have observed. Then, in the atmosphere of warmth and affirmation, each person shares the thing that he would like to change about himself.

In a parable, this might be termed the process of "kissing the frog" and then the frog's pointing out his own wart. Not only is this approach less dangerous, but it is also more biblical. In a sense, affirmation is the process by which we can do for each other what Jesus Christ did for Simon (that vacillating neurotic)

what the growing edge is in your spiritual life and what you need to work on; (c) *your future* — where you want to be five years from now, the scary thing you would like to try, what you feel God is telling you to do.

It takes a long time for each member to give this kind of information, but it is absolutely crucial if your small group is really going to become a healing community. The more information you

collect on each other, the more you will be able to minister to each other when you get to the deeper levels of group experience.

To make the process of history-giving more exciting, Serendipity Books provides a series of fast-moving, fun-centered communication games. The subject matter of these games is your own life — you get to know each other without even trying!

when He said, "Simon, you shall be called Peter, a rock."

This process can be facilitated through communication games that are designed to allow group members to recognize positive strengths in each other.

3rd base / Goal-setting

In the atmosphere of warmth and acceptance that has been created in the affirmation phase, you move on. The members of the group have been released to a new and deeper level of sharing, based on mutual love and trust. At third base the process looks much like the process on first base. Each person gives information, but this time, the information is far more personal: where you are hurting at the moment; where you need to grow in your relationships with yourself, your wife or husband, your children; where you need to be healed; where you need the ministry of Jesus right now, etc.

If you had asked these kinds of questions at the first sessions, you would have scared everyone and probably killed the group. You just don't talk about your needs to strangers. However, when you have established a trust and confidence in each other, it is only natural to share these things. In fact, if you keep these areas hidden from each other, the group will spiritually die...because you will be robbing it of its basic purpose for existence — to become a healing community where the Holy Spirit ministers through the gifts he has distributed among his people.

This phase can also be facilitated through communication games with each person going deep into his own life, sharing areas where he wants and needs to change. Fantasy games are especially good at this point, because they allow the "little boy" inside to talk about his hopes and dreams. It also allows the group to hear and to minister to the "little boy." You can confirm the dream, administer tender love and forgiveness where it is needed, reinforce the goal that the person has set for himself and hold him accountable for his best...through the power of Christ.

Home plate / Koinonia support system

This brings us to home plate — *Koinonia:* the uniting of the group members not only to one another, but also to Jesus Christ. And it is Jesus Christ who has made the unity possible by endowing each one with special gifts of ministry "for the building up of the whole body."

There are no communication games for this phase, because no games are needed. In a sense, the facilitation of the group has shifted from an outside control, to a mysterious new control system where the Spirit is free to move in and through the members of the group.

When you reach this point in your group process, you will know it. And until you have experienced it, there is no way to explain it. Maybe the closest description might be the phrase in the best sense of the term — a spiritual marriage.

Group Structures

Certain communication exercises work best in groups of two; others in groups of four; and others in eights. This is the reason for the suggestions given for the structuring of each group session. (Note the sessions on pages 109 - 211.)

We have suggested groups of two, when a group is new or not well-acquainted, because most people are less inhibited with one person than with several. We recommend groups of four when the material calls for discussion, because everyone can participate without the group lasting forever. When it comes to celebrations, team projects and depth affirmation experiences, we turn to the group of eight, because it is good for nonverbal experiences, or where a team approach is needed.

Below is a rough outline of the various configurations we use in the Serendipity programs and a reason for each structure.

	CONFIGURATION	BEST USE	RATIONALE
	TWOSOME Face-to-face	**Beginnings** **Introductions** **Conversation starters** **Interviews** **Depth revelations**	With one other person, most people are fairly relaxed and self-confident. Listening is easy. Feeling is close.
	FOURSOME Kneesie-nosey	**Getting acquainted** **Discussions** **Affirmation**	Everybody has a chance to talk. No moderator is necessary.
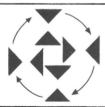	**WAGONWHEEL** Four back to back in center. Four on outside, rotating every two minutes.	Quick, multiple introductions Conversation starters	An already formed group of eight or ten can keep together, yet be on a one-to-one ratio while getting acquainted.
	EIGHTSOME Circle of eight	**Nonverbal exercises** **Celebrations** **Affirmation** **Team spirit** **Group projects** **Worship/Commissioning**	People work together in a support system over a long period of time. Will feel safe, protected and go into real depth.

Tips for the Leader

1. In three of the Serendipity Books *(Groups in Action, Rap, Beginnings)*, there is no single leader. The leadership rotates within each small group from week to week.

In the other books, the leader functions as a convener and overseer. He begins each meeting and explains the instructions. After the preliminary exercise, he sets the pace for openness and honesty by sharing with the entire class how he would answer the first question or so. Then he joins one of the groups and participates as one of the group members.

2. The secret to a closely knit, depth support group is a voluntary commitment on the part of each group member to really take part. This commitment should be spelled out beforehand in the form of a contract so that everyone knows what he is getting into.

If the program is going to be used at a conference or retreat, the nature of the program should be explained so that only those who want to be involved sign up.

3. Everyone in the course will need a workbook. To try to get along without books will cheapen the program and destroy the sense of excitement in the venture. Also, a person should be asked to pay for his workbook. If a person does not want to invest anything in the workbook, the chances are he is not too interested in belonging to a depth support community.

4. When small groups are formed at the first session, try to split up close friends, couples and church cliques. Once groups are formed, keep the same ones for the rest of the course. This permits the members of a group to get to develop a trust and confidence in each other.

5. If new people join the course after the groups have been formed, you can form a new group or try to fit them into existing groups. You will have to decide which is best in your own situation. Actually, if a group has really discovered "community," they will welcome a new member...because love cannot be confined.

6. If you are going to use Serendipity with an already existing group (that has never learned to trust each other in the many years they have been together), try to begin the course with a protracted time together and in a setting outside of the regular routine.

For instance, try to schedule an overnight retreat, a day-long meeting or an evening of four to six hours together. Ask for a commitment from the ones who want to come. They are to be prepared to risk themselves to an experiment in Christian community. If they sign-up, they are pledging themselves to a "Serendipity...a riot of interpersonal relationships that are profoundly childlike and outrageously spiritual."

Many times a group that has never reached "first base" with each other can break through to a new level of relationship with a day-long experience — much like the Serendipity Workshop.

Then they can go back to their regular setting...and continue as a support community in depth.

7. If at all possible, change the routine from time to time by inserting some Special Group Activities (page 213). For instance, the Discussion Designs would work beautifully in a retreat or conference setting in the afternoons. A social could be scheduled after one of the regular evening programs, and one of the worship services could be part of the closing night.

Once you have started to discover the secret of Serendipity, you will want to find ways of sharing your experience with others. As a group, you could give others a taste of Serendipity. Who knows where your dreams might lead!

The secret behind a Serendipity group is the supportive community. Such a group enables the best in each other to come forth in an atmosphere of love, trust and acceptance.

For this to happen, everyone who enrolls must be committed to a common discipline.

MY CONTRACT WITH GOD AND THE MEMBERS OF MY GROUP

For the next few weeks I agree to take part in an experiment in Christian community with the others in this group. I pledge to give priority to the group meetings, to share responsibility for the leadership, and to give my support to the others in the group.

Signed: _____

Date: _____

How to Start a Group

A group can consist of any combination: all men, all women, couples, young people, youth and adults together. In the same group, you might have the young and the old, the educated and uneducated, the "way out" and the "way in." In fact, radical differences in background, philosophy and life-style in the makeup of a small group can be an asset as long as there is a basic commitment to each other for the duration of the course.

The course provides the opportunity for the group to get to know each other in the first few sessions. Half of the fun is in discovering each other as fellow human beings — in search of God.

To begin, here are a few suggestions:

1. Start with yourself

The hardest person you will have to convince is yourself. After you are thoroughly convinced that you need a small group to belong to, you will be able to find others. There is something contagious about a person who is honest enough to admit his need for others.

2. Enlist a friend

The chances are that you know of someone else who would be interested in belonging to a small group. Get together with this person and share your own need for a group. Show him this book. Ask him if he has the same need. All it takes is for someone to say, *Hey, I'm hurting for a group of people where I can relate and belong! How about you?*

3. Plan a "get together"

Invite anyone who might be interested to a "coffee" in your home. Use some communication exercises to get them talking in groups of four. Without even realizing it, the guests will find themselves "caught up" in the warmth of a community of love — enjoying the fellowship and experiencing a little bit of the meaning of "koinonia."

4. Explain the course

Once a person has experienced a taste of "koinonia," he is going to want more. This will give you the opportunity to explain the various possibilities in the course.

Don't shortchange the group by

making it just another social club where people can come or go as they please. One of the prerequisites of a group is "togetherness." This means wedding yourselves together as a team for a specific period of time and helping each other reach a common objective.

You owe it to the prospects to clearly lay out the minimum conditions in the course. Namely,

(a) You will meet together once a week or once every other week for six to eight weeks. (After this, you have the option of continuing as a group for another twelve weeks if you want to.)

(b) You will select your own agenda for each session from the various options that are available. Track One offers you group-building sessions. Track Two offers you spiritual growth labs. Tracks Three and Four offer you inductive Bible study exercises. You can stick with one track or switch back and forth.

(c) There is no outside reading or homework required, but the first part of each session starts off with a brief creative exercise to get you involved in the content of the session.

(d) You can rotate the leadership within the group, each person taking his turn.

(e) Everyone will need a workbook to belong to the group. It is highly recommended that each person pay for his own book.

5. Decide on a time and place

The group can meet any time in the week and any place in the community. Men's groups often meet for breakfast. Ladies' groups for tea. Couples' groups for coffee in the evening. Some groups meet during the regular meeting hour of Sunday School — or after church at one of their homes. The only condition is a minimum of 60 minutes for the preliminary exercise and sharing time, followed if possible by a free period in which the small groups can continue if they want to.

The place can be a local restaurant, an office, one of your homes or a different home each week, or even one of the rooms at church. The only condition is to have chairs that can be arranged in small clusters for the sharing period at each session. (This is especially important if you have more than six in your group.)

6. Select your agenda

As we have mentioned before, there are different tracks you can run on.

If you don't know each other, you will probably want to spend a couple of sessions getting acquainted in Track One — the communication games. Then, once you have "become a group," you may want to switch tracks and get into something deeper.

You will find the actual instructions for the sessions in the middle of each book. A quick glance at the "purpose" at the beginning of the sessions will give you a good idea of what to expect.

7. Keep an empty chair

Three or four people are enough to start a group, and it will grow in number if the group is functioning properly.

As the class grows, you will have to divide into groups of three or four at each session so that everyone is able to participate in the sharing experience.

At all costs, avoid the temptation to think of yourselves as a closed corporation. This can lead to all sorts of problems and will eventually lead to the death of the group.

Newcomers should have no problem coming into the group in the middle of the course, because the nature of the sharing is "personal experience." In fact, newcomers will keep the group fresh.

8. Find a mission

Once you have started to discover the secret of "koinonia," you will want to find ways of sharing your experience with others. If you don't, something is wrong.

The mission you decide upon must grow out of your experience as a group if it is to be your own. Therefore, we have not prescribed the particular form of mission for you, but we have given you some direction in the study assignments.

In the back of the books you will find helpful suggestions and/or accounts of what some people have done as a natural outreach of their community concern. You can decide together what you are going to give yourself to as a group.

Here's how to conduct a practice session

Are you all fired up about starting a small group — but don't know anybody else to join? How about putting on a practice session for all of your friends?

It's simple. Get your friends together and do some of the communication games — and let your friends decide for themselves if they want to continue in a course.

The perfect atmosphere for the get-together is a social. Don't worry about the fancy frills. Just serve them a cup of coffee and ask them to sit down in groups of four — with someone they don't know very well but would like to know. If you happen to have enough card tables, great. Otherwise, arrange the chairs in groups of four.

Then, explain the instructions for the game as though you were the leader. Without realizing it, the guests will find themselves involved in a beautiful experience of sharing with each other.

After the session, explain a little bit about the meaning of small groups and invite anyone who is interested in belonging to an experimental group for six or eight weeks to speak to you afterward. You are going to be amazed at the readiness of your friends to sign up.

"In a poker game, no man discloses the content of his hand to the other players. Instead, he tries to dissemble and bluff . . . (and) in a society which pits man against man, as in a poker game, people do keep a poker face; they wear a mask and let no one know what they are up to . . . .

"We are said to be a society dedicated, among other things, to the pursuit of truth. Yet, disclosure is often penalized. Impossible concepts of how man ought to be—which, sadly enough are often handed down from the pulpit—make man so ashamed of his true being that he feels obliged to seem different . . . . Yet, when a man does not acknowledge to himself who, what, and how he is, he is out of touch with reality, and he will sicken and die; and no one can help him without access to the facts."

Sidney M. Jourard in
The Transparent Self

How to Enable the Best in Each Other

The purpose of a small group is to help each one in it to reach his full potential. This is a game where everyone must win — everyone must come out on top.

And the way this is done is called *enabling*. The word *enable* means to pull forth from, to call forth, to allow to emerge, to realize the potential of. This is what a small group is all about.

Most people realize about 10 percent of their potential. The other 90 percent lies beneath a pile of fears, failures, broken dreams, painful childhood memories and guilt feelings that add up to make us feel that we are not going to make it in anything we do. And with that kind of outlook, we definitely will not.

This is where a small group comes in. In the company of sympathetic, caring, loving people, we are able to open up and talk about our hangups and fears as well as our hopes and dreams for the future. Instead of getting negative feedback from others, we get positive feedback — affirmation. *I affirm you in this venture . . . I affirm this gift . . . I affirm this task in your life . . .* Slowly, the affirmation from those we have come to love and trust overcomes the negative feelings we have fed into our computer over the years . . . and we are able to say, *I am worthwhile . . . I have unique gifts . . . I can accomplish the thing . . . I will try again . . .*

Three levels of sharing

All of us yearn for fellowship where we can feel a oneness and call forth the best in each other. In a word, to minister to one another as the Body of Christ. Before this can happen, however, we must run the risk of being known — and this is scary. We are afraid that if people find out who we are inside they will reject us. So, to cover up the real person inside, we talk about the weather, about football, about the latest joke in town. And all the while, down deep inside, we are crying out for love.

But love is the result of knowledge, and knowledge comes when we are willing to let another person know us as we really are.

One of the best ways to bring a group face to face with their level of commitment to each other is to ask them to evaluate their experiences according to the three levels of sharing: (1) mouth-to-mouth, (2) head-to-head and (3) heart-to-heart. The mouth-to-mouth sharing is simply conversational doodling — the weather, football, etc. The head-to-head sharing

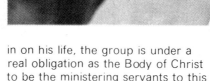

is more serious in that it is exchanging ideas and concepts — but the exchange is strictly as ideas detached from the persons. The heart-to-heart sharing, on the other hand, lets the other person know where *you* stand in relation to ideas and how you *feel* about them on the inside. The heart-to-heart sharing might be referred to as communing . . . and communing is the stuff from which community is born.

A small group can very easily sit and play verbal volleyball with each other, and this is okay. But don't expect real Christian community in this atmosphere. Community happens when one person dares to say, *This is the way I feel . . . In all honesty, this is where I am . . . This is me . . . see me . . . know me . . . I want to be a part of you and I want you to be a part of me . . . I want you to know me . . . I want to know you — deeply.* When this starts to happen in a group, watch out.

Four tips to keep in mind

When one person in a group takes the leap and decides to let the others

in on his life, the group is under a real obligation as the Body of Christ to be the ministering servants to this person.

First, don't interrupt. Keep your mouth shut — and let the person talk. The chances are that he has never had anyone in his life to really listen to him. The greatest thing we can offer is our ears. Many times this is all a person needs — and wants. Remember, the greatest counselors say the least.

This may mean dispensing with the agenda in your small group and giving over the entire session to a person who needs to share how he is really feeling and hurting on the inside. After all, the purpose of the group is to *enable each other*, not to cover the agenda. The leader of the group should be sensitive at this point and be prepared to adjust the schedule. He can ask, *Have you said all that you have to say about this?* or, *Would you like to add anything before we go on?* or, *Are you trying to tell us something?* These questions are enabling questions that let a person go a little deeper in his sharing.

Second, don't probe. There is a thin line between listening and probing, but it is a very important one. To listen is to enable a person to say all that he wants to say. To probe is to make a person share what he does not want to say — and should not reveal at this time. A probing question takes the initiative away from the person who is sharing — and this is bad.

If someone in the group starts to probe, the leader should step in immediately with, *Let's let Bill tell*

it the way he sees it, or, *Why don't we give Bill a chance to finish what he has to say?*

Third, don't give advice. The cheapest thing in the world is advice. Very often, the person with the least information is the most free in his advice — and the results are disastrous. If someone in the group has had a similar experience, he can share his experience — without telling the other person what he ought to do.

If someone in the group starts to give advice, the leader should break in immediately and say, *Why don't you share your experience but let Helen make her own application?* or, *Let's hold off on the advice and stick just to our own experience!*

Fourth, don't judge. If the group is really one, some sensitive areas of disagreement in lifestyle, theology and outlook are going to come up. Here is the place where love is going to be put to the test. When you violently disagree with another person, can you give him the right to his own viewpoint? Can you not only affirm him, but release him to be himself to think as he must? This does not mean giving in or making concessions. This means telling him, *I cannot see it the way you see it . . . but I love you and I accept you just as you are and with what you believe.*

When this kind of listening, caring, loving, accepting thing happens in a group, you will know it . . . and so will everyone else. This is what it is all about.

Remember, "to enable" is to call forth the best in another person, to see the best in him, to affirm the best in him. Are you an enabler?

Crowd Breakers

FOR LARGE GROUPS

To "wake up" a crowd—in the morning, after a heavy lunch or after a long message—how about some simple calisthenics.

Warm-Up Calisthenics

SLAP DOWNS Stretch your left arm straight out and slap it down with your right hand—from the shoulder to the finger tips and back again. Then do the

same with your right arm, using your left hand. Then stand up and with both hands, slap down your left leg. And finally, your right leg.

SHOULDER RUB DOWN Stand, turn to the right and rub down the shoulders of the person in front of you. Then turn in the opposite direction and do the same.

TRIANGLE SLAP DOWN Get together in 3's. One person bends over, letting his hands fall free and keeping his knees straight. The other two stand on either side of him and in perfect rhythm pat his back, starting at the shoulders and moving down to the hips and back up, going faster and faster. Then they gradually diminish the patting until their hands are again gently resting on the back.

    After about 45 seconds, call time and the second person is slapped down, etc.

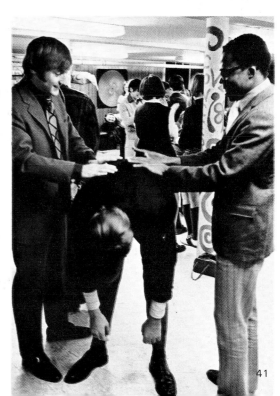

PEOPLE MACHINE Get together in 8's. Each person acts out a mechanical part: a piston that goes up and down (raise and lower hands) or a gear that goes round and round (move arms in circular motion). The challenge is to assume a creative position and original and creative motions that utilize more than one arm or leg.

When everyone has started his own motion and sounds, the challenge is to interlink his part of the machine with the other parts to form a "musical" unit of gears, pistons, wheels, etc.

Tension Breakers

FINGERS UP Pair off in 2's or 4's. Put hands behind backs. On the word *go,* everyone brings his hands out in front of him with any number of fingers up. The first person to call out the correct total number of fingers up (between you and your partners) wins. Repeat three times for the best two-out-of three competition.

MORAH (ITALIAN KARATE) The same as "Fingers Up" except each person puts just *one* hand in front of him with any number of fingers up and calls out a total *before* seeing any fingers! Keep playing until one of the partners gets a right number.

MIRROR *In Twos:* one person puts his hands up, fingers out, and proceeds to hand-dance, moving his hands as against a glass. The partner, with his hands about an inch away, should try to keep up with the movement exactly, as though he were the reflection in a mirror. Then reverse the roles and do it again. *In Fours:* two pair of partners get together, criss-cross each other. Each pair tries to hand-dance as though the other pair were not there. (For added fun, allow body and feet movements as well.)

Fun Songs

Sing some of the childhood songs that can be set to motions, and enjoy the fun.

IF YOU'RE HAPPY AND YOU KNOW IT, CLAP YOUR HANDS
Clap your hands twice after each time it is called for:

*If you're happy and you know it, clap
  your hands,* (clap clap)
*If you're happy and you know it, clap
  your hands,* (clap clap)
*If you're happy and you know it, then
  your life will surely show it!*
*If you're happy and you know it,
  clap your hands.* (clap clap)

Sing again with: "stamp your feet."
A third time: "shout Amen." A fourth
time: "do all three."

HEAD, SHOULDERS, KNEES, TOES
To the tune of *There's a Tavern in the Town,* sing the following and touch the corresponding parts of the body.

*Head and shoulders, knees and toes,
  knees and toes.*
*Head and shoulders, knees and toes,
  knees and toes.*
*Eyes and ears and mouth and nose,
Head and shoulders, knees and toes,
  knees and toes.*

MY HAT IT HAS THREE CORNERS
While you sing, use the fitting actions:
(a) *my*—hand on your heart, (b) *hat*—hand on top of head, (c) *three*—hold up three fingers, (d) *corners*—stick out left elbow, (e) *not*—shake your finger.

*My hat it has three corners;
Three corners has my hat;
And had it not three corners,
It would not be my hat.*

THE NOBLE DUKE OF YORK Use

three positions: (a) *up*...standing, (b) *down*...sitting, (c) *halfway*...halfway up.

Oh, the noble Duke of York,
He had ten thousand men;
Marched them up to the top of the hill
And marched them down again.

And when they were up, they were up,
And when they were down, they were
*   down,*
And when they were only halfway up,
*   they were neither up nor down.*

HOKEY POKEY Act out the motions

of the song.

Put your right hand in.
Put your right hand out.
Put your right hand in and shake it all
*   about.*
You do the hokey pokey.
And turn yourself around.
That's what it's all about.

Then continue with: (a) left hand,
(b) right foot, (c) left foot, (d) your
whole self.

ROW, ROW, ROW YOUR BOAT To

the words, use four motions: (a) rowing,
(b) gently, (c) merrily, (d) dream. Sing
as a round, faster and faster.

Row, row, row your boat,
Gently down the stream.
Merrily, merrily, merrily, merrily,
Life is but a dream.

LOVE ROUND Divide the audience

into 3 groups. Start one group on the
first line. When they begin the second
line, bring the next group in on the
first line. As the first group moves to
the third line, bring in the last group.
Sing through the song twice, cutting
out each group as it concludes.

Love, love, love,
That's what it's all about.
'Cause God loves us, we love each other,
Mother, father, sister, brother,
Everybody sing and shout!
'Cause that's what it's all about!

Nonsense Rhymes

To get the crowd on the edge of their chairs, try doing the same thing at the same time in rhyme and rhythm:

RABBIT Slap your legs, then your hands.
Rabbit in the bean patch
Possum in the pot
Try to stop the fiddler
While the fiddler's hot.

HARRY *Oh* (make O with fingers), *I* (point to eye) *say* (point to mouth) *have you heard* (ear) *about Harry* (hair) *who just* (chest) *got back* (back) *from the front* (stomach) *where he was needed* (knee) *at the foot* (shoe) *of the army* (arm). *Everybody's* (hands up) *heard* (ear) *about Harry* (hair). *Hip* (hip) *Hip* (hip) *Hurray* (hands up).

DUM DUM Slap your knees twice as you say the words: *Dum Dum.* Then grab your nose with your left hand and your left ear with your right hand while you say *Diddy Diddy.* Slap your knees twice again to the words: *Dum Dum.* Now grab your nose with your right hand and your right ear with your left hand while you say: *Da Da.* Go faster and faster. *Dum Dum Diddy Diddy Dum Dum Da Da. Dum Dum Diddy Diddy Dum Dum Da Da,* etc.

Celebration Dances

Allow a large crowd to participate together in a corporate act of celebration by putting some of the simple square dance steps to religious songs. Here are a couple suggestions.

WE ARE ONE IN THE SPIRIT Stand in rows, put your arms over the shoulders of those on either side, step out on your left foot in the left direction—three steps and a kick with your right foot. Then reverse direction—three steps and a kick...like the *Can Can.*

We (step) *are* (step) *one* (step and kick) *in* (step) *the* (step) *spirit* (step and kick).

We are one in the Spirit,
We are one in the Lord,
We are one in the Spirit,
We are one in the Lord,
And we pray that all unity may one day
  be restored:
And they'll know we are Christians by
  our love, by our love,
Yes, they'll know we are Christians by
  our love.

IT'S A SMALL WORLD From Disneyworld, here is an enchanting, childlike song that goes perfectly with the *Bunny Hop.* Have the group turn in rows and form a conga line with their hands on the hips of the person in front of them. Put the steps of the *Bunny Hop* to the beat of the music: right foot—two kicks to the right; left foot—two kicks to the left; one hop forward; one hop backward; three hops forward. Repeat.

It's a world of laughter, a world of tears:
It's a world of hope and a world of fears.
There's so much that we share that it's time we're aware.
It's a small world after all.

  It's a small world after all,
  It's a small world after all.
  It's a small world after all,
  It's a small, small world.

There is just one moon and one golden sun and a smile means friendship to everyone.
Though the mountains divide and the oceans are wide,
It's a small world after all.

  It's a small world after all,
  It's a small world after all.
  It's a small world after all,
  It's a small, small world.

LORD OF THE DANCE Sing with the steps of the *Bunny Hop*— same as *It's a Small World.*

"Dance, then, wherever you may be;
I am the Lord of the dance," said he,
"And I'll lead you on wherever you may be,
And I'll lead you on into the dance,"
  said he.

Fun Group-finders

FIND YOUR SONG MEMBERS Using as many songs as there will be groups, put each title on eight slips of paper. Mix and pass out. Everybody sings his song until his group is formed.

FIND YOUR PUZZLE MEMBERS Using as many pictures as there will be groups, cut each into eight pieces. Mix up and distribute. Each person, being one-eighth of a puzzle, will look for the puzzle pieces corresponding to his to put the picture together again.

SERENDIPITY BINGO Question one person on a point. If he answers "yes," put his name in the square. Let him question you. Then ask someone else a question. Keep going until someone has six "yes" answers in a row, horizontally, vertically or diagonally.

Uses mouthwash regularly.	Can whistle "Dixie."	Lies about age.	Has hole in sock now.	Plays chess regularly.	Watches "Sesame Street."
Likes to go skinny-dipping.	Used an outhouse.	Once danced the Charleston.	Refuses to walk under ladders.	Loves mountain oysters.	Believes in women's lib.
Can touch palms on floor.	Detective story fan.	Listens to soap operas.	Expelled from school.	Wearing Fruit of the Loom.	Uses Hai Karate.
Likes caviar.	Writes poetry.	Weighs under 100.	Loves mustard greens.	Can do back bend.	Reads "Peanuts."
Never changed a diaper.	Owns a motor-cycle.	Stole a watermelon.	Loves Bach.	Has scar 3 inches long.	Played Post Office.
Can touch tongue to nose.	Lived in log cabin.	Can wiggle ears.	Eats natural foods.	Overdrew bank account last month.	Can recite books of Bible.

Communication Exercises

FOR SMALL GROUPS

IMAGINARY BALL Make believe there is an imaginary ball in your group and throw it back and forth. To add excitement, ask everyone to change the shape and weight of the ball before tossing it. When it gets going, holler out, *"It's hot — move it fast!"*

MOTORBOAT Make believe your small group is a motor. See how much speed you can achieve. At the word *go,* the first person turns his head to the right, saying the sound for the specified motor; then the next person turns his head to the right, repeating the sound, etc. The first group to finish the number of laps should clap.

Round One: *Go-carts*...for five laps... and the sound is "putt."

Round Two: *Motorcycles*...for seven laps...and the sound is "rrrrrr."

Round Three: *Racing cars at the Indianapolis Speedway*...for ten laps...and the sound is "zooooommmm."

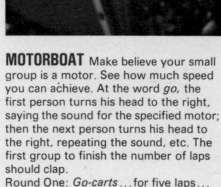

CHARADES Place a name tag (*Lady Godiva, Liberace, Romeo and Juliet, Raquel Welch,* etc.) on the back of one person in each small group. This person stands and turns around so the others in the group can see the tag. Then, in silence, the group members act out this thing or person until the one with the name tag guesses who he is. When he guesses, clap, and another name tag will be placed on someone else's back.

51

CATEGORIES

CATEGORIES Same rhythm as above, except that instead of numbers or actions you use categories: *football players, opera singers, nursery rhymes, etc.,* and a little different procedure.

First, everyone thinks of a category, preferably one that has two words or syllables. Everybody slaps his knees twice, and then the number one person calls out *"Cate"* as he snaps his right fingers, *"gory"* as he snaps his left fingers. Everybody slaps his knees twice, and the next person in the group (going clockwise) responds by calling out a particular category, such as *auto...mobiles.* Again, everyone slaps his knees twice, and the next person must answer by naming something within the category, such as *Chev...rolet,* as he snaps his fingers.

The group slaps their knees and snaps their fingers as each person around the circle calls out the name of a car...until someone cannot think of one. Then the person simply says, *"Cate...gory."* And the next person must call out a new subject.

Repeat the procedure.

RHYTHM

RHYTHM First, count off around your group: *one, two, three, etc.* Then altogether, slap your knees twice, snap your right fingers, and then your left fingers. This is the rhythm to keep repeating. Now, after you have slapped your knees twice, the number one person calls out his number ("*One*") when he snaps his right fingers...and then somebody else's number (such as "*Three*") when he snaps his left fingers.

When your number is called, you respond with your number when you snap your right fingers...and somebody else's number when you snap your left fingers.

NONVERBAL RHYTHM

NONVERBAL RHYTHM Same rhythm as above, except you use signs instead of numbers. First, everyone thinks of a crazy action and demonstrates it to the group. You could *scratch your ear,* another might *rub his stomach,* another *pull his hair, etc.*

Now, after your group has slapped their knees twice, the number one person does his sign (such as pulling his hair)...and somebody else's sign (such as scratching his ear). Then, everybody slaps his knees twice in rhythm and the one whose sign was given shows his sign...and someone else's sign, etc.

If anyone breaks the rhythm or fails to come in when his sign is called, he goes to the end of the line and everyone moves up a seat, *but keeps his own sign.*

SCULPTURING *In Twos:* One person is the modeling clay and one is Michelangelo. Sculpture feelings like fear, joy, tension, despair. *In Fours:* Two people are the clay and two are Michelangelo. Sculpture relational words like distrust, trust, confrontation, affirmation. *In Eights:* Four are clay; four are Michelangelo. Sculpture collective terms like celebration. *In Eights:* Everyone can be clay — or any substance! Sculpture a Rube Goldberg Machine...and then Christian community.

PASS THE BALLOON Throw the balloon to each other as quickly as possible so you are empty handed when the whistle blows. If you are caught, here are the penalties. *First offense:* must stand up and sit down before you pass the balloon. *Second offense:* must stand up, turn around and sit down before you pass the balloon. *Third offense:* must stand up, turn around, go like a hyena and sit down before passing the balloon. *Fourth offense:* must stand up, turn around, go like a hyena, and flap your arms like a bird and sit down.
Pass out a balloon to every tenth person or one balloon to each group.
Toss the balloon back and forth. The leader blows the whistle after 10 seconds and explains the penalty to those caught holding the balloons. Repeat.

ONE FROG Work together on a riddle about a frog: first, one frog; then, two frogs, etc., until you get up to ten frogs. Here is the riddle:

One frog.
Two eyes.
Four legs.
In the pond.
Kerplunk.
Kerplunk.

One person in the group says, *"One frog"*; the next person says, *"Two eyes"*; the next, *"Four legs"*; the next, *"In the pond"*; the next, *"Kerplunk"*; and the next, *"Kerplunk."*

Then the next person says, *"Two frogs"*; the next person, *"Four eyes"*; the next, *"Eight legs"*; the next, *"In the pond"*; the next, *"In the pond"*; the next, *"Kerplunk"*; the next, *"Kerplunk"*; the next, *"Kerplunk"*; and the next, *"Kerplunk."*

Remember, you need one *In the pond* and two *Kerplunks* for every frog. And here's the catch! If you mess up, you have to go back to *one frog*. So, it is a race against skill as well as time.

BUZZ-FIZZ Count up to 50 as fast as you can, but instead of saying, *"five,"* or any multiple of five, call out, *"BUZZ."* Instead of saying, *"seven,"* or any multiple of seven, call out, *"FIZZ."* For example, each person, in turn, around the group will sound off with *"one," "two," "three,"* *"four,"* and the next person will say, *"BUZZ"*; the next, *"six"*; the next, *"FIZZ"*; etc.

If the number is a multiple of five and seven, say, *"BUZZ-FIZZ"!* If you mess up, start over again at *one*. The first group to reach 50 should cheer.

THIS IS A CUP! A WHAT? Pass two objects around your group at the same time in opposite directions. But there's more to it. One person holds a cup; the person on his left holds a saucer. At the word go, the person with the cup turns to the person on his right, passes the cup and says, *"This is a cup!"* The person asks, *"A what?"* And the first person answers, *"A cup!"* Then the second person turns to the one on his right, passes the cup and says, *"This is a cup!"* The third person asks, *"A what?"* Then the second person must turn back to the original person and ask, *"A what?"* And the original person replies, *"A cup!"* and the second person turns again to the third person and says, *"A cup!"*

In other words, each time the cup is passed, the *"A what?"* must be asked all the way back to the original person and the answer, *"A cup!"* must be returned all the way.

At the same time the cup is going to the right, the saucer is being passed to the left. *"This is a saucer!"* *"A what?"* *"A saucer!"* etc.

The first group to finish should cheer.

PASS THE FEETBALL Each group passes a balloon around their circle five times...using only feet and ankles. The first group to finish sits on the balloon and pops it.

Sensory Exercises

TRUST WALK Pair off with someone you don't know very well. One person keeps his eyes closed while the other leads him around the room, in the hall and even outside for 5-10 minutes. Ask questions to stimulate the imagination, such as, "What does this texture make you think of?" "What kind of music comes to your mind now?" "What does this remind you of?" "Do you feel safe?" Reverse roles and go for another trust walk.

Take a couple minutes to fill out the questionnaire. Partners share their answers and explain the reasons behind them.

TRUST WALK QUESTIONNAIRE

1. How would you describe the inner feelings that you had on the trust walk?

2. What was the most significant moment for you during your blind walk?

3. How would you describe your partner if your only experience with him was the trust walk?

4. What did you discover about yourself during this time?

5. What experience out of your past did this blind walk bring to mind?

SENSORY ROCK Have double the number of rocks and pieces of driftwood as there are people. The group divides into 4's. Put an assortment of rocks and driftwood in the center of each group. Choose one and, with eyes closed, feel it with your fingers, in the palm of your hand and against your cheek. Put it back and choose another. Get acquainted with the personality of several pieces taking about 30 seconds for each one. Do not talk.

Select two that portray your personality—the way you are now and the person you want to be.

Go around the group, each one explaining his feelings.

CHOOSE YOUR APPLE Have a selection of apples—one for each person. Sit in circles of 4's or 8's. Everyone examines his group's pile of apples and picks out one particular apple that reminds him of himself—because of certain marks and characteristics. Everyone studies his apple, polishes it and puts it back.

Mix them up. Ask everyone to find his apple and explain to someone why he chose that one. Then each person explains (a) one area of his life where he shines, (b) one area where he needs a little polishing.

Conversation Starters

With strangers, the best group to start with is a group of two. With one other person, you are less self-conscious than with a larger number and are more open to sharing yourself.

SENTENCE COMPLETIONS One of the quickest and easiest ways to get a conversation started among strangers is to give them a list of half-finished sentences to complete and explain — or to let the partners interview each other, turning the sentences into questions.

The best sentences to use are ones that are completely non-threatening and yet give a person a chance to share some interesting facts about himself, such as sentences that begin with "My favorite" or "If."

1. My favorite time in the day is....

2. My favorite room in the house is....

3. My favorite holiday in the year is....

4. My favorite kind of literature is....

5. If I could visit any place in the world, I would like to visit....

6. If I had a million dollars to spend for the benefit of mankind, I would....

7. If I could change my vocation, I would like to be a....

8. If I could ask God one question, I would ask....

9. If I knew I had only one year to live, I would spend the year...

10. The thing that gives me the greatest satisfaction is...

11. The thing that causes me the greatest concern is...

12. The time I feel most alive is...

13. The time I feel most alone is...

MULTIPLE-CHOICE QUESTIONNAIRE

A series of sentences, each with a set of choices, allows a person to get into deeper material without wasting a lot of time.

Indicate your first and last choices for completing the sentences, then each person in the group explains his choices for the first sentence, and why. The *why* is more important than the answer because it allows a person to volunteer a little more about himself.

1. My idea of a good time is:
   a. a quiet evening with a good book
   b. a stroll through the park with someone I like
   c. a shopping spree
   d. watching a pro football game
   e. a long walk in the country by myself
   f. a good bull session
   g. going out to eat with some friends

2. Nothing touches me like:
   a. a full moon on a clear night
   b. a stirring opera by Wagner
   c. the new-fallen snow on the mountains
   d. the smell of a juicy steak cooking
   e. the feel of a little baby
   f. the waves breaking on the seashore
   g. rock-and-roll music

3. Nothing burns me up like:
   a. a slow driver in a fast lane
   b. a lukewarm cup of coffee
   c. a book with a page missing
   d. a car that will not start
   e. a toothpaste tube mashed in the middle
   f. an overdrawn bank account

1. Choose a *color* and explain. (For instance, you might say, "I feel bright orange, because I know God took care of all the details for my getting here — and I'm thankful!")

2. Choose a WEATHER CONDITION and explain. (You might say, "I feel cloudy, because I've got a problem I just can't cope with.")

3. Choose a NUMBER from one to ten. Assume that "one" is the lowest you could possibly feel and that "ten" is the highest. ("I feel like number seven today, because....")

JOHN WESLEY QUESTIONNAIRE

The founder of the Methodist Church, John Wesley, started the sharing at the weekly class meeting with the question: "How is it with your soul?" How would you answer? Try describing your spiritual condition right now in one of the following ways!

BILLFOLD SCAVENGER HUNT

Another "can opener" is to ask everyone to take four items from his billfold and explain them to his partner. (A billfold is likely to contain personal memorabilia which one can draw upon to introduce himself.)

Find and share:

1. The most worthless item.

2. The most priceless item.

3. The most revealing item.

4. The most memorable item.

REMINISCING CHOICES

This is similar to the sentence completions, but you choose only *one* of the four experiences and go on to describe it. Include interesting anecdotes or significant lessons you learned from the experience.

1. The first time I tried to swim....
2. The first time I tried to dance....
3. The first time I tried to smoke....
4. The first time I tried to play hookey....

FOUR QUAKER QUESTIONS

A series of questions develop a particular subject area. They range from the ridiculous to the sublime and can deal with areas such as friendships, games, heroes, expectations, etc. Each person in the group answers the first question and elaborates on it. Then each person answers the second question, etc., until you have gone around on all four questions. See how the following series develops the subject area of "warmth."

1. Where were you living between the ages of seven and twelve... and what were the winters like?

2. How was your home heated during that time?

3. What was the center of warmth in your life when you were a child? (This can be a place in the house, a time of year — or a person.)

4. When did God become a "warm" person to you... and how did it happen?

talker _____ listener

thinker _____ doer

leader _____ follower

rabbit _____ turtle

adventurer _____ nester

pitcher _____ catcher

giver _____ receiver

SPECTRUM LINES On the lines, pinpoint where you see yourself between the two extremes. When you are through, get together in groups of 4's. Let each person share his profile and see if the others agree with his estimate.

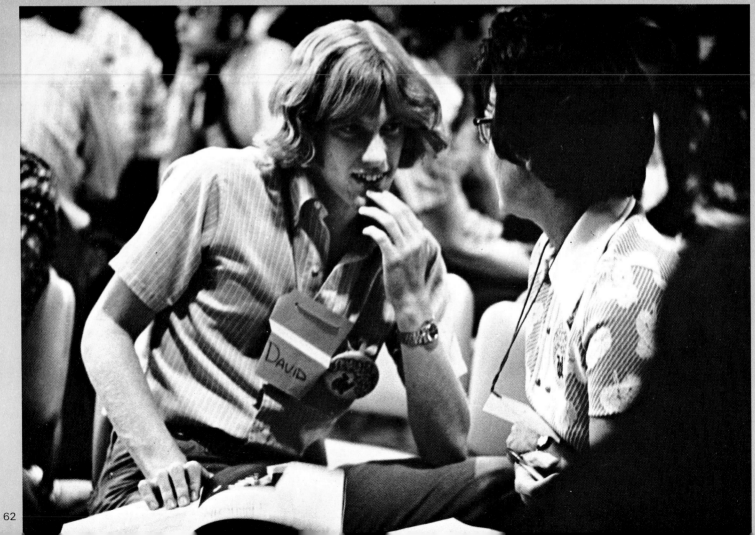

PICTURE ASSOCIATION The old "ink blot" test with a new twist offers the imagination a chance to go wild and come up with all sorts of significant (and hilarious) history-giving. For instance, in the drawing, which child do you identify with or which one best portrays you right now? Why?

Or, turn it into an affirmation exercise by assigning each person in your group to a child in the picture.

FANTASY Similar to the picture association exercise is "plan a vacation" to give your fantasies full flight. Think and dream your perfect vacation.

You can also "dream-a-vacation":

1. Where would you like to go?

2. What transportation would you like to use?

3. Who would you like to visit along the way?

4. What book would you like to re-read while you are gone?

5. What would you like to bring home with you?

SELF-EVALUATION CHART People can see how they've grown through a program, a conference, a retreat. Put a mark on the top lines for the way you feel at the beginning and a mark on the bottom lines for the way you feel at the end.

About myself, I'm feelin'...

kinda blah	whoopee
mixed up	back together
useless and worthless	valuable and important

About my group, I'm feelin'...

really uptight	completely at ease
inferior	confident
I could not tell them anything	I could tell them anything

About God, I'm feelin'...

very cold	very warm
apathy	commitment

About the church, I'm feelin'...

indifference	involvement
despair	hope

Pop Quizzes

To surface information in a hurry that can be used as the basis for a sharing experience, one of the best approaches is the Pop Quiz. It gives the person a chance to collect his thoughts for a few seconds before having to share.

Below are four possible models.

FIRE DRILL Jot down the items you would grab and take with you if your house caught on fire. In your imagination, run through every room and jot down the specific items that you would try to take. (Assume the children and pets are safe.)

After 30 seconds, in groups of four, share the three most important items on your list and explain why.

MY TEN ITEMS:

1.

2.

3.

4.

5.

6.

7.

8.

9.

10.

SUCCESS ANALYSIS Jot down two accomplishments for each of the age periods given. For instance, when you were between 7 and 12 you may have won in a hopscotch contest and placed in a soap box derby.

Then, in groups of four, share your accomplishments and explain how they reveal your changing values.

Age 7-12

Age 13-17

Age 18-30

Right now

FAMILY FUN TIMES
Quickly jot down nine or ten things your family enjoys doing together, such as camping, playing ball, eating popcorn, square dancing, etc. Then, beside each activity, put the symbols that apply.

$ if it requires more than $10.

T if it requires traveling more than 100 miles.

O if it brings your family closer together.

↑ if it brings you closer to God.

✝ if your family has done it in the last three months.

Now, put a circle around your three favorite activities.

MOON TRIP
Close your eyes and imagine yourself packing for a trip to an uncivilized continent to start life over. Think of ten things you would want to take with you.

You might list a stack of books, a microwave oven, your guitar, a text book on organic gardening, a motor-cycle with solar-powered engine, your scrapbook, golf clubs, your dog, etc. You are free to use literary license and put down things that are impractical in a primitive society.

Now the load must be lightened, so you can take only half the number of items. Check the five things most important to you.

MY FAMILY LIKES . . .

___ 1.

___ 2.

___ 3.

___ 4.

___ 5.

___ 6.

___ 7.

___ 8.

___ 9.

___ 10.

TEN THINGS I'D LIKE TO TAKE

1.

2.

3.

4.

5.

6.

7.

8.

9.

10.

GOAL SETTING WITH A PLAN

Here, you can sort through the major concerns in your life and come up with specific goals and tangible, measurable targets towards which to work together as a team. You are to hold one another accountable for the best that is in you.

In the left hand column below, jot down the major concerns in your life, such as deciding where to go to college ...what to major in...finding a summer job ...paying off your debts.... Rank these concerns, 1, 2, 3, etc., in the order of priority.

Then take the number 1 concern and write in the middle column all of the things that you "wish" you could do about this. Don't let lack of time, money, ability or opportunity deter you from jotting something down. For instance, if "building a bridge of communication between the black and white community" is your number 1 concern, you might put

down: (a) I wish I could get some of these people together in my home for a talk, (b) I wish I could convince the newspaper to write up the good things that are going on, (c) I wish I could get on the school board, etc. Now rank these 1, 2, 3, etc., in order of urgency or procedure.

Finally, in the last column, put down the plan you would like to follow in carrying out these priorities. Where appropriate, include quotas, deadlines, dates, etc.

MY MAJOR CONCERNS   **I WISH I COULD**   **MY PLAN OF ACTION**

HERO ANALYSIS Jot down two heroes for each of the age periods given below. For instance, when you were between 7 and 12 years old your heroes may have been Hopalong Cassidy and Robert Louis Stevenson.

Then, in groups of four, share your heroes and explain what they reveal about your changing values.

Age 7-12

Age 13-17

Age 18-30

Right now

PROJECTION EXERCISE Jot down in the space provided what you recall as your major (a) interest, (b) problem, (c) hope or dream when you were in the sixth grade.

Then consider your life right now and fill in the same three categories. Project yourself ten years into the future and jot down what you feel will be true then.

In groups of 4's, share your feelings of those areas when you were in the sixth grade. Go around the group again and each one explain his present feelings, etc.

When I was in the sixth grade

Interest:_____

Problem: _____

Hope:_____

Right now in my life

Interest:_____

Problem: _____

Hope:_____

Ten years from now

Interest:_____

Problem: _____

Hope:_____

Guessing Games

To make the process of getting acquainted exciting, reverse the procedure of describing yourself and have the others guess your answers. This increases the interest and multiplies the group involvement.

BACK TO BACK Get together in groups of two. Once you have been introduced to your partner through one of the games on the preceding pages, sit with your back to his and try to recall or predict how your partner would answer the following. Then face each other and check out your answers.

1. Color of eyes?

2. Weight?

3. Size of shoes?

4. Favorite TV program?

5. Favorite magazine?

6. Favorite hobby?

7. The thing that gives him the greatest fulfillment?

8. The word that characterizes his outlook on life right now?

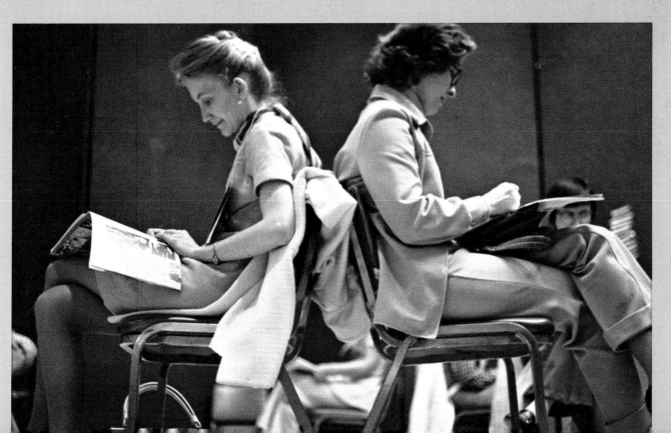

FOUR FACTS/ONE LIE Get together in 4's. Complete the following statements truthfully — except for one. Yet make that one believable! Then one person at a time reads his answers and lets the others guess where he is lying. Finally, he confesses which "fact" was a lie and what would be his honest answer.

1. My favorite game as a child —

2. My hero at age 12 —

3. My favorite music when I was a teenager —

4. My favorite pastime right now —

MYSTERY MAN On a blank sheet of paper, answer the questions below. Fold the slips of paper and place them in a bowl in the center of the group. One person takes out a slip, reads the clues aloud, and everyone tries to guess which group member matches the answers. Finally, the mystery man confesses and explains the last answer.

1. A **COLOR** that reveals your personality.

2. An **ANIMAL** that portrays the way you see yourself.

3. A **SONG** that illustrates your philosophy of life.

4. A **CAR** that symbolizes you in some way.

5. A **COMIC STRIP** or **TV CHARACTER** that you identify with.

TWENTY QUESTIONS

TWENTY QUESTIONS Someone in the group thinks of a person in the circle. Then each group member asks one question — not to find out the age or sex, though — that will give a clue as to who it is. For instance:

1. What movie star does this person remind you of? (*Robert Redford...*)
2. What would this person do between halves at a football game? (*watch the band*)
3. If our group were a zoo, which animal would this person be? (*a tiger*)
4. How would this person dress for a masquerade ball? (*Superman*)
5. What character out of history (or the Bible) does this person remind you of? (*Jonah*)

After everyone has asked a question, go around again, each one trying to guess from the clues who the person is. Then the one who began reveals the name and explains why he sees the person as he does. Repeat the procedure until everyone has been the subject.

SALVADOR DALI Each person creates a verbal picture of someone else in the group by comparing him to the following:

1. **A BODY OF WATER.** *(If the person I am thinking of were a body of water, he would be a deep flowing stream, a rushing river, or...)*

2. An **INSTRUMENT** in a symphony orchestra. *(kettle drum, French horn, piccolo...)*

3. A **FLOWER** in a garden. *(violet, morning glory, bright red rose...)*

4. A **PERFORMER** in a circus. *(lion tamer, clown, tightrope walker...)*

5. A **PLAYER** on a football team. *(If our group were a football team, this person would be quarterback, offensive tackle, coach...)*

Begin by having each person in the group write his name at the top of a slip of paper and put it in the center of the circle. After mixing up the slips, everyone draws one and jots down a comparison for the five categories above. Then one person at a time reads his list aloud, and the others try to guess who the subject is. After the person is identified, the one describing him explains his answers for the first two: BODY OF WATER and INSTRUMENT of the orchestra. You might say, I put down a *deep, flowing stream,* because I see Jim as a deep thinking person.

Nonverbal Statements

There is more than one way to express yourself...and sometimes the best way is not with words. This is especially true when it comes to explaining how you feel about something, how you feel about yourself, how you feel about God.

We have discovered that you can help a person get in touch with his feelings by giving him an inanimate object with which to role-play. By action, without saying a word, he can share what he is feeling on the inside about a given subject.

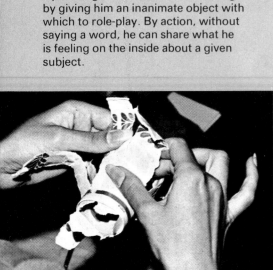

PASS THE CUP Give each group of eight a paper cup. Ask one person in the group to do to the cup what he would like to do to the institutional church (anything from kissing it to ripping it open). Then, without comment, he passes the cup to the next person. The second person considers the state in which he receives the cup (the church) and does what he would like to do. He passes the cup on, etc., until everyone in the group has expressed his feelings. Then break the silence and talk about it.

PASS THE COAT Give each group of eight a heavy coat. Ask one person to take the coat and do to the coat what he would like to see happen to himself during the get-togethers. Then, without comment, he passes the coat to the next person, etc., until everyone has treated the coat according to what he would like to see happen to himself. Then pass the coat around a second time and let each one explain what he did.

PASS THE CHALICE Pass a chalice around the group, having each person do with it as he would like to do with Jesus Christ. Pass the chalice a second time and let everyone explain what he did.

Another possibility is to have a towel, a hard roll and a cup of juice. Each person, in turn, uses the three articles to minister to the others in the group in the way he feels Jesus would minister to them.

Show and Tell

For sheer enjoyment and universal appeal, there is nothing like making something with our hands. It helps us collect our thoughts, surface our feelings and create a piece of primitive art that we can use to explain our feelings to others.

Here are a number of different approaches to self-discovery craft.

MAKE YOUR NAME TAG Instead of having prepared name tags, make your own. Tear a piece of colored construction paper into a shape symbolic of you — a heart, a butterfly, a.... Write your first name on it, punch two holes in it and wear it on a string around your neck like a medallion.

When groups are formed, explain your name tag to your group.

MAGAZINE COLLAGE Leaf through a pictorial magazine or daily newspaper and tear out titles, pictures, words, slogans, want ads, that portray you in some way, such as: (1) the concerns in your life at the moment, (2) the important things in your world, (3) your hopes and dreams for the world, etc. Then paste your tear-outs together on a sheet of newsprint and add color, design or graffiti with poster paints or Magic Markers.

PLAY-DOH With a piece of Play-Doh about the size of a golf ball make an object that symbolizes you in some way, such as a box, an animal, a free-form piece of sculpture. In your group, explain why you see yourself as you do.

WIRE SCULPTURE Using bailing wire (available from farm supply stores) or pipe cleaners make a sculpture that describes your spiritual ups and down... or your spiritual life at the moment.

When you are in your small group, share the meaning behind your sculpture.

TIME LINE/TURNING POINTS

Assuming the line below is your lifetime, divide the line into the major periods of your life, such as childhood, adolescence, college, young adult, and adult. Think back over your life and try to pinpoint on this line the major "turning points." A turning point can be considered

anything that has significantly influenced or altered your life, or shaped your present values. It can be a happy or painful experience, but it is one which is now viewed by you with great meaning. It may be the death of your mother when you were 12, a spiritual commitment you made while in high school, etc.

TIME LINE

THIS IS YOUR LIFE Create a TV special on the places where you have lived. Think of the various moves you have made. What was significant about each place for you? How did they contribute to the person you are today?

Then, make a drawing of each location and feature something that symbolizes your feelings during that period in your life. For instance, for your childhood, you might draw a *simple frame house* with a *tall oak tree* — the oak tree for the strength and stability in the home. For your next home, you might draw a *large brick house* with a swimming pool in the back yard...and also an *oak tree*. However, you might draw the tree *without any leaves* because your family was filled with tension during this time.

CHILDHOOD

ADOLESCENCE

YOUNG ADULT

RIGHT NOW

COLOR SLIDES Be an artist.

Insert a piece of clear acetate into 35mm slide frames and create a series of psychedelic slides. Use special acetate inks (available from Serendipity House) to draw designs that symbolize your feelings, such as loneliness, togetherness, sorrow, happiness...or the four periods of your emotional life, such as (a) your childhood, (b) your adolescence, (c) your present, (d) your hopes for the future. Then, in your group, use the slides as you share your life story.

YOUR SKETCH

DRAW YOUR SPIRITUAL PILGRIMAGE

Everyone thinks over the ups and down in his life from as far back as he can remember to this moment, symbolizing the low and high points with color and design. For instance, early adolescence might be portrayed by a sunburst because everything was sunshine. The high school years might be portrayed by clouds because it was a period of doubt and frustration.

YOUR TREE

YOUR TABLE

DRAW YOUR FAMILY TREE Draw a tree to symbolize the life of your family. Choose: (1) a type of tree that represents your family, such as a *tall elm* or a *scrub oak*, (2) colors for the foliage to represent mood, such as *red and orange* because your childhood was bright and cheerful, or color in no leaves at all because your childhood was painful, (3) roots to represent your spiritual formation, such as *straight and deep* or *shallow and barren*, (4) additions to represent your dominant childhood memories, such as a *bird* because your family sang a lot.

DRAW YOUR CHILDHOOD TABLE

Remember back to the time you were between 7 and 12 years old. Draw the shape of the table where you ate most of your meals. Then for each person who was at the table pick a color that suggests his personality and draw him in where he sat. You might use *blue* for your father because he was serious and draw him at the head of the table; *orange* for your mother, next to your father, etc. Finally, color the center of the table to represent your childhood. The table might be *black and brown* with splashes of *purple* to indicate the somber tone and the times of fun.

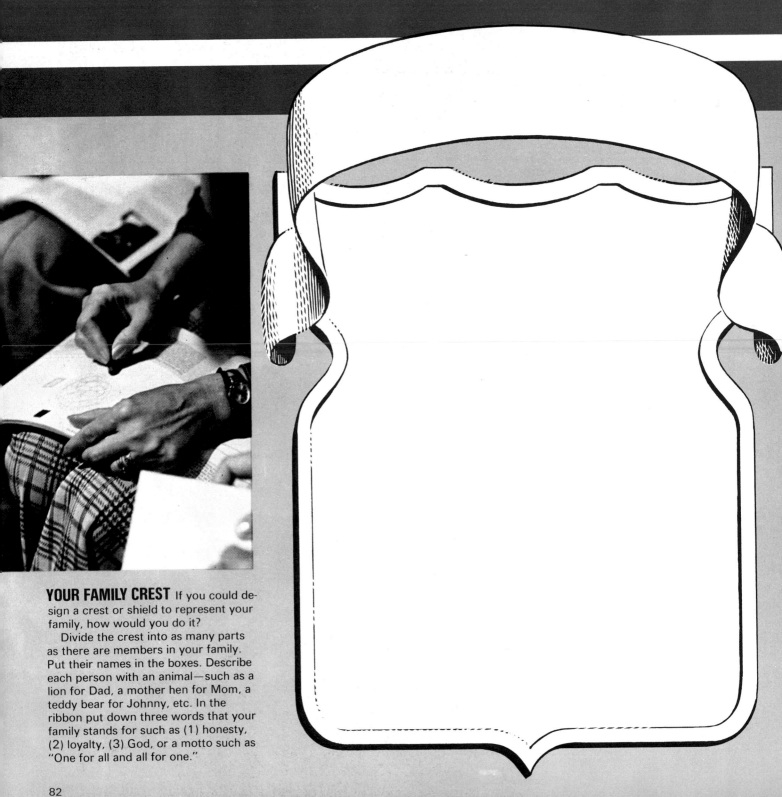

YOUR FAMILY CREST If you could design a crest or shield to represent your family, how would you do it?

Divide the crest into as many parts as there are members in your family. Put their names in the boxes. Describe each person with an animal—such as a lion for Dad, a mother hen for Mom, a teddy bear for Johnny, etc. In the ribbon put down three words that your family stands for such as (1) honesty, (2) loyalty, (3) God, or a motto such as "One for all and all for one."

Group Show and Tell

GROUP BANNERS Each group of eight makes a banner with materials from a paper sack. In the sack are: one balloon, four different colors of tissue paper, a strip of white wrapping paper six feet long, and some masking tape. Your group decides upon a theme that expresses what you are experiencing together. You work out the design with the materials available and hang the banner on the wall.

INSTANT BALLADS Be a composer. Jot down the ten most important words in your life...and use these words as the makings of a free verse poem that expresses what you are feeling at the moment. The easiest way to get started is to write down one word or phrase — a cry or question that summarizes how you are feeling, such as "It's real" or "Stop the world" or "I've got a feeling." This is the first line of your poem. Then rephrase your idea, expand upon it, and you've got a second and a third line. Before long, the thoughts will come faster than you can write them down. Then as a small group, put the poem to sound effects with makeshift instruments and guitars.

COMMUNAL DOODLE Each group of 4 takes a large sheet of paper and a handful of crayons to make a drawing. Select a crayon of the color that best expresses your feelings at the moment and, without talking, draw a symbol or design that describes it. For instance, if you are feeling uptight and are ready to strike out at somebody, you might draw a lightning flash. If you are feeling creative, you might draw a flower.

Now, still without speaking, communicate to the others by relating to their drawings. For instance, if one person draws a brick wall and you are concerned about him, you may draw a rambling rose climbing the wall.

If you find your feelings changing during this time, alter your original drawing. For example, if you have drawn a closed clam shell, you may want to open the shell a little.

After the drawing, each person explains what he felt the others in his group meant by their original designs or symbols and then shares why he related to their drawings as he did.

COMMUNITY CONSTRUCTION In

groups of 4's assume that you can
create a new church and community
for your area. Consider the master
plan for the community as well as the
architectural design for the church.

In brainstorming fashion, decide
what the community should look like—
the roads, the shopping center,
schools, neighborhoods—whatever
should be in an ideal community. Share
resources and come up with ideas to
meet your needs and those of the
people living around you.

Focus on the kind of church you
would want in this community—the
building, with the arrangement of the
sanctuary, educational rooms, etc.
Don't worry about matters of tradition,
negative reactions or cost.

Put everything into the model that
you feel is important; leave everything
out of the building that you feel is
unimportant.

It would be helpful at the beginning
for the leader to show a rough sketch
of what he considers to be an ideal
community and also a half-finished
model of his ideas for a church building.

Affirmation

Affirmation games are designed for the members of a group to share their positive feelings for each other, to recognize the strengths and gifts in each other, and to express their concern and love for each other. Used correctly, they can be profoundly valuable. Used incorrectly, they can be dangerous.

Affirmation games are best used after a group has had time to get to know each other — to listen to each other's past history, present concerns and future hopes.

There are two basic forms: (1) verbal games, such as Colors, Animals, Strength Bombardment — where impressions are described through similes, (2) nonverbal games, such as Affirmation Circles, Circles of Love, etc. — where feelings are expressed through touch.

COLORS One person is silent while the others try to think of a color that would best describe his personality. For example, one person might think of the color *bright orange* to describe Bill, because he is outgoing. Another person might think of the color *deep blue* because he is strong and verile. A third might see Bill as *light green* because he appears so fresh and springlike.

Then, go around and let each person share the color that came to mind and why. Finally the person explains the color he would use to describe himself. Bill might have chosen *light brown* because he sees himself as quiet, timid and conservative.

Repeat for each person in the group.

ANIMALS One person in the group sits in silence while the others try to think of an animal that would best describe his personality. Each one in the group tells the animal he has chosen and explains why. Then the person names the animal he would choose for himself and explains why.

Repeat the procedure for each person.

STRENGTH BOMBARDMENT One person in the group sits in silence while the others think of a particular strength they see in his life. Each of the group then tells the strength he has selected and explains why. For instance one might say, "Jim, I see the quality of *compassion*—because you have a tremendous ability to care.
Another might say, I see in you a quality of *childlikeness*—because you are beautifully honest and transparent."
A third might say, "I have appreciated your *sense of humor*—and *freedom of lifestyle;* they are refreshing."
Then the person finishes the sentence, "The one thing I would like to change about myself is..." Repeat the procedure for each person.

FRUIT INSPECTION Scripture has many lists of gifts, virtues and strengths that could be made into affirmation exercises. One is in Galatians 5:22-23.

Study each fruit carefully and jot down the names of the people in your group next to the particular traits in which you feel they are strongest. For instance, you might jot down Mary next to "peace" because you see Mary as the peace person.

When everyone is through, one person sits quietly while the others share how they identified him and why. Then, he shares two fruits: (a) one where he is strong, (b) one where he is weak.

Repeat the process.

_____ **LOVE** *(the giving person, caring, sensitive to other's needs)*

_____ **JOY** *(exuberance flowing from deep, inner spiritual reservoirs, sunny, cheerful)*

_____ **PEACE** *(quiet, inner serenity — having come to terms with God and yourself)*

_____ **PATIENCE** *(staying power, enduring the most trying situations without getting uptight)*

_____ **KINDNESS** *(warmhearted and gracious, helpful, gives the shirt off his back)*

_____ **GOODNESS** *(unimpeachable, 14 carat integrity)*

_____ **FIDELITY** *(never forgets a friend, always there when needed, true blue)*

_____ **GENTLENESS** *(strength wrapped in understanding, tenderness)*

_____ **SELF-CONTROL** *(keeps his cool, "heat resistant," stable)*

AFFIRMATION HATS

Use an actual assortment of hats or a list of hats. In silence, look for a hat that fits the personality of each member of your group and put his name beside it.

Don't worry about professional role or rank — match the inner person you see. For instance, you might give the *football helmet* to a bank president, because you see him as the All-American boy.

After assigning a hat to everybody in your group, one person sits in silence while the others share the hats they chose for him and explain why. When everyone is finished, the person explains his choice for himself.

_____ Fancy **EASTER HAT**: *pink and pretty — light and frilly, just right for the parade.*

_____ High **TOP HAT**: *grand and stately, proper and elegant, fit for the inaugural ball.*

_____ Shabby, old **FISHING HAT**: *homey and comfortable, showing the marks of lots of use and of good times out in the open.*

_____ Bright red **FOOTBALL HELMET**: *just like the one on the Wheaties boxtop for the perennial All-American boy.*

_____ Ten-gallon **COWBOY HAT**: *designed for the drugstore cowboy to wear when telling about the good ole days when men were men.*

_____ Shiny **MOTORCYCLE HELMET**: *for cool cats and modern-day adventurers whipping along the open road.*

_____ Mexican straw **SOMBRERO**: *for the happy-go-lucky, easy-going romantic who sees life as a song.*

_____ Rugged **COONSKIN CAP**: *for the spirited pioneer who is always looking for new frontiers.*

_____ Birthday party **FUN HAT**: *childlike, playful, delightfully mischievous.*

_____ African **SAFARI HAT**: *rugged, designed for the most daring adventurer, lover of danger and challenge.*

_____ English **BOWLER**, with umbrella: *proper, precise, for the undauntable, in control even if the world falls in.*

_____ Floppy **BEACH HAT**: *for outdoors, sunny, just right for teasing.*

_____ Construction worker's **HARD HAT**: *strong, protective, ready for hazardous missions.*

_____ Bright, checkered **BONNET**: *sweet and untainted, for the hard-worker, holding to what's right.*

_____ **SANTA CLAUS CAP**: *for the happy one who loves to give surprises.*

_____ Wrap-around **TURBAN**: *silent, mysterious, aloof, yet probably wanting to be known.*

_____ Peach-blossom **CHIFFON VEIL**: *provocative, alluring and mischievous, for the open-hearted flirt.*

_____ Hand-knit **STOCKING CAP**: *beautifully childlike, good for long walks in the woods and making snowmen.*

_____ Artist's **BERET**: *sensitive, a bit rakish, just right for lovers of all ages.*

_____ Luminous **SPACE HELMET**: *out-of-this world, just right for the high-flying dreamer.*

_____ **MORTARBOARD**, with tassle: *brainy, sophisticated, worn invisibly to the meetings of the Board.*

_____ White **SAILOR HAT**: *unpretentious, for the one eager to see the world, at home on sea or land or anywhere.*

_____ **STRAW HAT** and cane: *for the showman, gallant and fun-loving.*

_____ Marked-up, well-worn **BEANIE**: *relaxed, light-hearted, for the carefree, some-nonsense, jolly fellow.*

SLOGANS

SLOGANS Write the names of the people in your group next to the slogan you would associate with them. For instance, you might jot down Joan's name beside "You've come a long way, baby..." because you have seen Joan really "come forth" as a person. Then one person in the group sits in silence while the others share the slogan they chose for him and explain why. When everyone has shared, this person names the slogan he would choose for himself and explains why.

_____ I'd rather fight than switch. *(Tarrington)*

_____ ...has a better idea. *(Ford)*

_____ Leave the driving to us. *(Greyhound)*

_____ When you care to send the very best. *(Hallmark)*

_____ ...helps make it happen. *(Westinghouse)*

_____ Everything goes better with... *(Coca Cola)*

_____ Put a tiger in your tank. *(Esso)*

_____ Come to where the flavor is. *(Marlboro)*

_____ The wings of man. *(Eastern Air Lines)*

_____ You've come a long way, baby. *(Virginia Slims)*

_____ Pleasing you more. *(Ozark Air Lines)*

_____ Once you try it, you'll love the difference. *(Dr. Pepper)*

_____ We try harder. *(Avis)*

_____ It's the real thing. *(Coca Cola)*

_____ We're trying to make things better. *(Shell Oil)*

_____ Since we're neighbors, let's be friends. *(Safeway)*

_____ We're specialists. We have to do a better job. *(Midas)*

_____ I'd walk a mile for... *(Camel)*

_____ The quality goes in before the name goes on. *(Zenith)*

_____ When it comes to compromise, we make no contribution. *(Jaguar)*

_____ You're in good hands with... *(Allstate)*

_____ Put the snap, crackle, pop, into your life. *(Kelloggs)*

_____ You only go around once in life, so reach for the best. *(Schlitz)*

_____ Life is too short not to go first class when you can. *(Mercedes-Benz)*

_____ As you travel, ask us. *(Standard Oil)*

_____ Think small. *(Volkswagon)*

_____ Fly the friendly skies... *(United)*

_____ The slowest ketchup in the West. *(Heinz)*

_____ I can't believe I ate the whole thing. *(Alka Seltzer)*

_____ I didn't know that! *(Ford)*

_____ Getting people together. *(Boeing)*

FICTIONAL CHARACTERS In silence look over the given list of characters and jot down the names of the people in your group beside the one you would identify with them. For instance, you might write Mary's name beside *Santa Claus* because you see Mary as the "giving one" in the group. Then one person sits in silence while the others share the characters they associated with him and why. When everyone has finished, this person names the character he would choose for himself and explains why.

_____ Charlie Brown
_____ Don Quixote
_____ Winnie the Pooh
_____ Walter Mitty
_____ Superman
_____ Snoopy
_____ Peter Pan
_____ Huckleberry Finn
_____ Little Lord Fauntleroy
_____ Lucy
_____ Marcus Welby, M.D.
_____ Scarlet O'Hara
_____ The Sundance Kid
_____ Mary Poppins
_____ Scrooge
_____ Tiny Tim
_____ Santa Claus
_____ Smokey the Bear
_____ Jonathan Livingston Seagull

_____ Alfred E. Newman
_____ Little Eva (*Uncle Tom's Cabin*)
_____ Jack Armstrong
_____ The Cowardly Lion (*Wizard of Oz*)
_____ The Ugly Duckling
_____ Cinderella
_____ John Boy (*The Waltons*)
_____ Rip Van Winkle
_____ Tarzan
_____ Pied Piper
_____ Little Orphan Annie
_____ Mr. Magoo
_____ Hamlet
_____ Juliet
_____ Mary Worth
_____ Sherlock Holmes
_____ (other)

RECOGNITION CEREMONY Award time! If you could give an award to each member of your group for his contribution or growth during this session, what would it be? Jot down the name of each group member beside his award.

_____ **GOLDEN HELMET:** *For the Don Quixote who saw in us only beautiful things and called forth "The best in all of us."*

_____ **GLASS SLIPPER:** *For the Cinderella who came to the party and discovered she was a princess.*

_____ **PURPLE HEART:** *For the one who shared our hurts and gave of himself for our healing.*

_____ **ROYAL GIRDLE:** *For the person who drew us together.*

_____ **CROSS OF MONONUCLEOSIS:** *For the frog-kissin' free spirit who touched us all.*

_____ **MEGAPHONE:** *For the person who cheered us on.*

_____ **NOBEL PEACE PRIZE:** *For the one who harmonized our differences of opinion without diminishing anyone.*

_____ **CHAMPION SUPPORTER:** *For the person who undergirded the group with his inner strength and care.*

_____ **SPARK PLUG:** *For the person who ignited the group.*

_____ **DEAR ABBY AWARD:** *For the one who patiently listened, giving the rest of us a chance to unload.*

_____ **KING ARTHUR'S SWORD:** *For the one who found his mission and set out to do it.*

_____ Diamond-studded **SERENDIPITY CROWN:** *For the Miss or Mr. Serendipity of our group who was the surprise of the day!*

FROG TEMPERAMENTS Each is a prince!
Below are four different kinds of temperaments as Hippocrates, the philosopher, analyzed people about 400 B.C. Read over the description of each frog carefully. Then, jot down the names of the people in your group on the frogs, and under each name, write the particular temperament or temperaments you see. For instance, for John, you might jot down: 60% super salesman and 40% super leader, because you see John as an extrovert with a lot of leadership skills.

When everyone has finished, one person sits in silence while the others share how they see him. The person then describes himself.

Repeat the process for each person.

SUPER SALESMAN (sanguine)

This frog is warm, friendly, outgoing, energetic, optimistic and fun to be around. Could sell a refrigerator to an Eskimo. Also makes a good preacher, actor, after-dinner speaker and Dale Carnegie promoter. This frog is the "life of the party," a "now" person, happy-go-lucky — at least on the surface. He usually covers up any feelings of inadequacy or insecurity. Better at short dashes than long distance runs. Voted "most likely to succeed" in high school, but not always does.

To kiss this frog, give him a chance to "take off his mask." To feel accepted for who he is, not for his jokes. To get in touch with his feelings...and his "spiritual resources." Ask him to share his dreams....and don't let him cop-out when the going gets tough.

SUPER LEADER (choleric)

This frog is the strong, self-willed driver that makes the free enterprise system work. He's an organizer, practical, capable — extremely talk-oriented. Comes across as sure, self-confident and determined. This frog has given the world its generals, crusaders and politicians. Can be cruel, sarcastic and intolerant of others or be the selfless, dedicated champion of the down-trodden. Usually successful in what he undertakes — he sometimes wears himself out first.

To kiss this frog, let him know that he is important for his own sake, not for his accomplishments. Help him to discover the secret of "inner peace" in being, not doing. Help him to celebrate the "now" — to love and be loved, to touch and be touched.

SUPER IDEALIST (melancholic)

This frog is imaginative, creative, sensitive and artistic — a real lover of beauty, solitude and perfection. Usually quiet, gentle and withdrawn. Experiences extreme emotional highs and lows; either effervescent and exuberant or moody, touchy and depressed. This frog has given the world most of its artists, composers, writers, thinkers, inventors, theoreticians, saints and sinners. Intensely loyal to friends and deeply hurt when friendships turn sour.

To kiss this frog, help him to affirm his great gifts and strengths. To accept his ups and downs without dwelling on them. To claim the spiritual stability of an ever-constant God. To celebrate his God-given capacity to feel deeply.

SUPER GUY (phlegmatic)

This frog is easy-going, likable, dependable — ever-cautious, conservative and practical. The original "nice" guy. He never gets upset or excited, never rocks the boat, avoids conflict at all costs — even at the expense of his own rights. This frog has promoted diplomats, civil servants, social workers, teachers, spectators and spouses to the strong-willed leaders. Invaluable as a peacemaker. Extremely loyal, goes the "second mile" without complaint. Can be stepped on by others to the extent that his own self-esteem is diminished.

To kiss this frog, encourage him to take a chance, to take a stand on issues and the initiative on things. Give him a lot of positive feedback and reinforcement when he steps out. Call him to face up to his own responsibility for his life and for his spiritual potential as a person.

GIVING GAME In silence, think of your group and ask yourself the question, "If I could give each one of these people a gift, what would I want most to give them?" Take out your billfold and the things in your pockets and try to find a token to symbolize the real gift you would like to give to each person. For instance, you might choose a *watch* for Dan, because of the appreciation you want to give him for all the good times you have had together ...a *blank check* for Mary, to represent the trust you have in her...a *house key* for Jim, to symbolize that your house is always open when he needs to talk to someone. Don't give out the gifts yet. Just put them in front of you — one gift for each person in your group.

When everyone has chosen his gifts (after 2 or 3 minutes) one person sits in silence while the others give him their gifts and explain them. Then move on to the next person and the next, repeating the procedure, until everyone has received his gifts.

Finally, go around a second time, with each person accepting the gifts and sharing in what way they mean something to him.

THIS HOPE CHEST BELONGS TO _____

DRAWING OF HOPES AND EXPECTATIONS

HOPE CHEST This is similar to the Giving Game, but you sketch your hopes and expectations in each other's books so that they can be remembered.

Simply pass your books around the group. Each person adds to the others' "Hope Chests" something based on his own love and concern for them as persons.

When the books have gone all the way around, one person sits in silence while the others explain what they drew and why. For instance, one person might say _I drew a "horn of plenty" with lots of tender, loving care coming out of it, because you need it to go through the very difficult situation you've told us about._ Another person might say, _I drew a deep river of water, because I want you to have the deep strength that comes from trusting God completely._

Nonverbal Affirmation

There is more than one way to say *I love you* — as every lover knows. In fact, the best ways to convey this feeling are *not* verbal.

The same is true when it comes to affirming another person's worth...and to show your feelings for him. This is the reason for the nonverbal approaches. More can be said in the giving of a gift, the touch of the hand, the meeting of the eyes, than could be put in a thousand words. Hence, the importance of affirmation without words.

Warning: These exercises should not be attempted with persons who are unacquainted with each other.

CARING CIRCLES The Trust Walk has a new twist. Stand in a circle. One person steps into the center and closes his eyes. Then someone from the circle goes to him and ministers without words. This can be anything from a warm back rub to a walk around the room, but it should convey your love and concern for the person. Then lead him to another person in the group. Repeat the procedure until everyone has had a chance to minister nonverbally to the one in the center. (Remember, this person keeps his eyes closed all the time.)

When everyone has expressed his feeling to the person in the center, sit down as a group and let him debrief the experience — explaining what it meant to him. Repeat for each one in the group.

THE SILENT HANDSHAKE In silence, stand in circles of 8's. Put your hand in front of you — palm up. Then one person at a time steps into the middle and goes around, expressing his feelings for each of the others. For instance, you might shake hands with Bill and pat him on the back, you might squeeze Mary's shoulder, you might take Dan's hand and just hold it for a while, looking into his eyes.

Take your time to think about each person and let your action demonstrate what you are feeling inside.

When you are all through, sit down as a group and talk about your feelings for each other.

Notes

Bible Study

CREATIVE TECHNIQUES

Purpose: To relate Scripture to life today — *your* life, to excite and arouse your interest in Scripture, to apply new psychological testing techniques to its study and to do all this through the group process.

If the goal of Bible study is "changed behavior" as well as Bible information, then we ought to approach the Scripture in ways that expose our own feelings, motives, values and relationships to the truth of Scripture. We can facilitate this process by using simple psychological testing instruments to measure our responses to the Scriptures as we are reading them. Not only is this approach exciting and meaningful, but it also provides a framework for a depth sharing experience as we discuss the results of the test in a small group.

Recollection Technique

To remember a particular episode in your life may help you to understand the emotional, psychological or physiological background for something in Scripture. For instance, if you have ever come close to drowning, you may be able to understand the panic of the disciples when they felt they were about to drown in the "storm" passage.

The idea is to go back into your own life and recall how you felt, thought or acted during a time or experience related to the Bible portion being studied. Then you transfer your feelings into the Scripture passage as a basis for understanding it.

The exercise here is based upon this approach.

CHILDLIKENESS
AND YOU Read over the Scripture. Then, go back to your own childhood and jot down the first thing that comes to mind for the four items below. Finally, in the box entitled "Qualities of Childlikeness," jot down three or four characteristics that you feel Jesus might have been referring to...such as *simple trust, freedom to let it all hang out,* etc.

At that time the disciples came to Jesus and asked, 'Who is the greatest in the kingdom of Heaven?' He (Jesus) called a child, set him in front of them, and said, 'I tell you this: unless you turn round and become like children, you will never enter the kingdom of Heaven. Let a man humble himself till he is like this child, and he will be the greatest in the kingdom of Heaven....'
MATTHEW 18:1-4 NEB

MY FAVORITE CHILDHOOD GAME	MY FAVORITE CHILDHOOD PET	QUALITIES OF CHILDLIKENESS
MY FAVORITE CHILDHOOD HIDING PLACE	MY FAVORITE CHILDHOOD PERSON	

Projection Technique

To project yourself into the shoes of a person in Scripture and live through the experience with him and then to respond to the questions on the worksheet as though you are he, gives you a new view into the reality of Scripture.

PETER'S EMOTIONAL PILGRIMAGE

Below are 10 episodes taken from the life of Peter. Read each Scripture passage and indicate on the scale how you feel Peter would have felt after each one. Assume that 1 on the scale is severe depression and 10 on the scale is supreme ecstasy. For instance, after the first episode (A. Jesus' Call to Peter), you might put a mark at number 8 to indicate that you think Peter was probably excited and elated at the thought of being with Jesus.

After you have read all the episodes and put a mark to indicate the feeling response to each, connect the marks with a line to show the ups and downs of Peter's emotional pilgrimage.

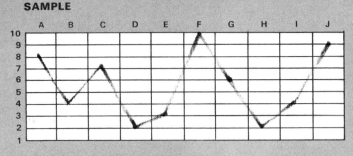

SAMPLE

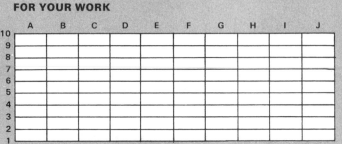

FOR YOUR WORK

A. JESUS' CALL TO PETER. "Jesus was walking by the shore of the Sea of Galilee when he saw Simon and his brother Andrew on the lake....'Come with me, and I will make you fishers of men.' And ...they left their nets and followed him" (Mark 1:16-18).

B. JESUS HEALS PETER'S MOTHER-IN-LAW. "He came forward, took her by the hand, and helped her to her feet. The fever left her..." (Mark 1:31).

C. JESUS' UNEXPECTED COMEBACK. "'Who do you say I am?' Peter replied: 'You are the Messiah.' He began to teach them that the Son of Man had to undergo great sufferings....At this Peter took him by the arm and began to rebuke him. But Jesus turned round and...rebuked Peter. 'Away with you, Satan; you think as men think, not as God thinks'" (Mark 8:29-33).

D. JESUS' TRANSFIGURATION BEFORE PETER. "...and in their presence he was transfigured; his face shone like the sun, and his clothes became white as the light..." (Matthew 17:1-2).

E. JESUS' TRIUMPHAL ENTRY ON PALM SUNDAY. "...approaching Jerusalem... (many) spread their cloaks...while others spread brushwood...(and) shouted, Hosanna! Blessings on him who comes in the name of the Lord!" (Mark 11:1-9).

F. GETHSEMANE. "He took Peter and James and John with him. Horror and dismay came over him, and he said to them, 'My heart is ready to break with grief; stop here, and stay awake'" (Mark 14:33, 34).

G. PETER'S DENIAL OF JESUS. "Peter followed...at a distance....In the courtyard...another girl, seeing him, said, 'This fellow was with Jesus of Nazareth.' ...At this he broke into curses and declared with an oath, 'I do not know the man.' At that moment the cock crew.... He went outside, and wept bitterly" (Matthew 26:58-75).

THE EMPTY TOMB. "Then Simon Peter came up...and he went into the tomb. He saw the linen wrappings lying, and the napkin...rolled together in a place by itself" (John 20:6, 7).

I. JESUS APPEARS TO PETER AFTER PETER HAS GONE BACK TO FISHING. "'Simon... do you love me more than all else?...Then tend my sheep'" (John 21:15, 16).

J. JESUS ASCENDS UP TO HEAVEN. "...as they watched, he was lifted up, and a cloud removed him from their sight" (Acts 1:9).

Analytical Technique

To stand outside the experience in the Scripture passage and analyze the episode from the viewpoint of a newspaper reporter, psychiatrist, militant, skeptic, can provide you with a kaleidoscope of views — and insight.

PSYCHIATRIC REPORT ON PAUL

Assume for a moment that you are a psychiatrist and that a new patient came to your office and proceeded to share the information about himself contained in the Bible portion. How would you analyze this person's personality? Read over the Scripture slowly, pausing along the way to jot down your "first impressions" in the margin every two or three lines, such as "mixed up"..."guilty about something"...etc. Then, when you are through, take your notes and write out a psychiatric report about this person in the space provided, beginning with the words, "This man is...."

"I know that in me (that is, in my flesh,) dwelleth no good thing: for to will is present with me: but how to perform that which is good I find not. For the good that I would I do not: but the evil which I would not, that I do. Now if I do that I would not, it is no more I that do it, but sin that dwelleth in me....

For I delight in the law of God after the inward man: But I see another law in my members, warring against the law of my mind, and bringing me into captivity to the law of sin which is in my members. O wretched man that I am! who shall deliver me from the body of this death?"

ROMANS 7:18-24, KJV

FOR YOUR PSYCHIATRIC REPORT

Allegorical Technique

Symbolic

Literal

Expressionistic

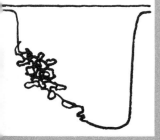

To look at an event in Scripture as an allegory of your own life and "stop the camera" at the point in the story where you find yourself at this moment makes Bible truth relevant to you. If there are two or three people in the story, the first step is to select the person with whom you most *identify*. Then on a second reading, "stop the camera" at the point in the story where it *touches* your life right now.

THE PRODIGAL AND YOU

Read over the Scripture passage and try to relive the experience of the Prodigal Son. See if you can divide his experience into three or four parts. Then, try to illustrate each part with a drawing that portrays the inner feelings of the Prodigal at that time. For instance, in the second part, you might draw a wine glass with bright hot reds and yellows to symbolize his "eat, drink and be merry" lifestyle. (Note the various styles of art you can use.)

When you have made the drawings, go back and select the one that best portrays your own life now. For instance, you might identify with the Prodigal where he came to an end of himself.

If you have time left over, try to portray your own spiritual pilgrimage in a drawing — using colors and symbols to explain the high and low times.

There was once a man who had two sons; and the younger said to his father, "Father, give me my share of the property." So he divided his estate between them. A few days later the younger son turned the whole of his share into cash and left home for a distant country, where he squandered it in reckless living. He had spent it all, when a severe famine fell upon that country and he began to feel the pinch. So he went and attached himself to one of the local landowners, who sent him on to his farm to mind the pigs. He would have been glad to fill his belly with the pods that the pigs were eating; and no one gave him anything. Then he came to his senses and said, "How many of my father's paid servants have more food than they can eat, and here am I, starving to death! I will set off and go to my father, and say to him, 'Father, I have sinned, against God and against you; I am no longer fit to be called your son; treat me as one of your paid servants.'" So he set out for his father's house. But while he was still a long way off his father saw him, and his heart went out to him. He ran to meet him, flung his arms round him, and kissed him. The son said, "Father, I have sinned, against God and against you; I am no longer fit to be called your son." But the father said to his servants, "Quick! fetch a robe, my best one, and put it on him; put a ring on his finger and shoes on his feet. Bring the fatted calf and kill it, and let us have a feast to celebrate the day. For this son of mine was dead and has come back to life; he was lost and is found." And the festivities began.

LUKE 15:11-24 NEB

AT THE BEGINNING	LIVING IT UP	THE LOW MOMENT	ON THE WAY BACK

Sensory Awareness Technique

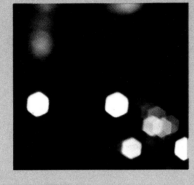

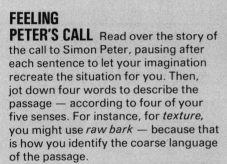

To describe the mood of an event in Scripture with your five senses (sight, sound, touch, taste and smell) involves you in the emotional feelings of the passage. For instance, to say that a portion comes across to you as *hot orange* is another way of saying that it probably is exciting and warm.

The exercise below is based on this approach.

FEELING PETER'S CALL

Read over the story of the call to Simon Peter, pausing after each sentence to let your imagination recreate the situation for you. Then, jot down four words to describe the passage — according to four of your five senses. For instance, for *texture*, you might use *raw bark* — because that is how you identify the coarse language of the passage.

Finally, go back and pinpoint where you are in the story — that is, where you would "stop the camera" to explain where you are in your relationship with Jesus Christ.

A COLOR (SIGHT)

A NOISE (SOUND)

A TEXTURE (TOUCH)

A SMELL

WHERE YOU ARE / STOP THE CAMERA

One day as he [Jesus] stood by the Lake of Gennesaret, and the people crowded upon him to listen to the word of God, he noticed two boats lying at the water's edge; the fishermen had come ashore and were washing their nets. He got into one of the boats, which belonged to Simon, and asked him to put out a little way from the shore; then he went on teaching the crowds from his seat in the boat.

When he had finished speaking, he said to Simon, "Put out into deep water and let down your nets for a catch." Simon answered, "Master, we were hard at work all night and caught nothing at all; but if you say so, I will let down the nets."

They did so and made a big haul of fish; and their nets began to split. So they signaled to their partners in the other boat to come and help them. This they did, and loaded both boats to the point of sinking.

When Simon saw what had happened he fell at Jesus' knees and said, "Go, Lord, leave me, sinner that I am!" For he and all his companions were amazed at the catch they had made; so too were his partners James and John, Zebedee's sons. "Do not be afraid," said Jesus to Simon; "from now on you will be catching men." As soon as they had brought the boats to land, they left everything and followed him.

LUKE 5:1-11, NEB

Multi-media Interpretation Technique

YOUR DRAWING OF PENTECOST

PENTECOST IN SOUND AND LIGHT

Read over the Scripture passage three times. Concentrate upon (1) the sense of hearing, (2) the sense of seeing, (3) the sense of feeling. With various colors of crayons, doodle the overall feeling of the passage. Your doodle can be a sketch, a design or a patch-work quilt, but it should somehow communicate the feeling of the passage *as though you were there*.

If you have time, translate your doodle into a folk ballad by writing a poem, using the word or question that leaps out to you from the passage. Then try reading your poem while improvising sound effects with bongo drums, guitar strings or the strings inside the piano—with your foot on the loud pedal.

If you want to express yourself even more, try putting your color doodles onto 35 mm slides with acetate inks (available from Serendipity House). Here is the possibility of making the Scripture reading into a full sound and light show for your next worship service.

While the day of Pentecost was running its course they were all together in one place, when suddenly there came from the sky a noise like that of a strong driving wind, which filled the whole house where they were sitting.

And there appeared to them tongues like flames of fire, dispersed among them and resting on each one. And they were all filled with the Holy Spirit and began to talk in other tongues, as the Spirit gave them power of utterance.

ACTS 2:1-4

Creative Writing Technique

Close to the Multi-media Interpretation Technique is one of creative writing, in which you seek to interrelate your impression of the Scripture with your own creative expression.

CREATION OF MAN AND YOU

Read over the Scripture passage, pausing after each sentence to think about its meaning. Then in the space provided jot down a series of short definitions of man. Begin each sentence with *I am*. For instance, *I am... a creature of God...a person of unique worth because I have been made in the image of God.*

If there is time, compose a free verse poem or ballad based on what you have discovered. Start with one of your definitions as the first line and add whatever thought comes to mind. Use a little literary license and let your imagination take flight. For instance:

> *I am a creation of God —*
> *conceived in his mind*
> *shaped by his hand*
> *to share his love*
> *his life*
> *and his universe.*
> *I am a person of unique worth —*
> *possessing the mark of God's own*
> *image...*
> *his mind*
> *his thoughts*
> *his dream for his creation.*
> *I am free —*
> *free to be me*
> *to laugh*
> *to sing*
> *to live life to the fullest!!*

Another way to compose your free verse poem is to again take one of your definitions as your first line, but then in the second line react according to your real feelings at the moment. For example:

WHO ARE YOU?
"I am..."

> *I am the creation of God —*
> *but I feel like a slob.*
> *I am a child of God —*
> *but I feel like a stranger*
> *in a foreign land*
> *alone*
> *and forsaken.*
> *I am somebody worthwhile —*
> *but I am nobody.*
> *I am free —*
> *but I am a slave.*
> *I am here for a reason —*
> *but I don't know where*
> *I'm going.*

Then God said, "Let us make man in our image and likeness to rule the fish in the sea, the birds of heaven, the cattle, all wild animals on earth, and all reptiles that crawl upon the earth." So God created man in his own image; in the image of God he created him; male and female he created them. God blessed them and said to them, "Be fruitful and increase, fill the earth and subdue it, rule over the fish in the sea, the birds of heaven, and every living thing that moves upon the earth."

God also said, "I give you all plants that bear seed everywhere on earth, and every tree bearing fruit which yields seed: they shall be yours for food. All green plants I give for food to the wild animals, to all the birds of heaven, and to all reptiles on earth, every living creature." So it was; and God saw all that he had made, and it was very good. ***GENESIS 1:26-30 NEB***

Paraphrase Technique

DISCOVERING YOUR NEW LIFE

Read over the Scripture, pausing after each verse to jot in the margin one of the following symbols:

△ If you understand the verse clearly
? If you have a question about the meaning
↑ If you get special inspiration from the verse
↓ If you really get convicted about something in your life

Read the verse again, and starting with the first part, rewrite it in your own words. (Note the sample.)

Try to include in your paraphrase what the verse really means in the situation where you live.

○
△ *17. When anyone is united to Christ, there is a new world; the old order has gone, and a new order has already begun.*

? *18. From first to last this has been the work of God. He has reconciled us men to himself through Christ, and he has enlisted us in this service of reconciliation.*

↓ *19. What I mean is, that God was in Christ reconciling the world to himself, no longer holding men's misdeeds against them, and that he has entrusted us with the message of reconciliation.*

2 CORINTHIANS 5:17-19 NEB

(17) The moment I got hitched up to Christ, a whole new administration took over in my life. The old administration was kicked out — and a new deal started.

(18) This was not my doing. It was God's! He chose me for His team by making me a friend — and gave me the challenge to sign up others. Whoopee!

FOR YOUR APPLICATION

1. If your spiritual life could be compared to a house, which room needs a little cleaning — the living room, the library, the attic, the basement, the game room?

The library — my thought life

2. At what time or period in your life were you most aware of the presence of God in your life? Why?

My high school years — because of daily time with God.

3. Where do you need to grow the most — in solitude or in relationships?

In solitude

The purpose of a sharing group is to build deep, warm, supportive relationships.

Therefore, the four exercises in track one are designed to provide a basis for the group members to get to know one another on a deep level. Each exercise has three parts: (a) Warm-up—to break the ice, (b) Going Deeper—to go beneath the surface, (c) Overtime Challenge—to go for broke if you have extra time.

Also, the size of the sharing groups are designed to encourage the building of confidence. For the Warm-up, the groups are to be two people each; for the Going Deeper, two groups are put together for a group of four; for the Overtime Challenge, two four-somes are put together to form a group of eight. This permits maximum participation in a minimum of time and encourages the quiet, timid person to share.

The material is purposefully designed to encourage easy, non-threatening sharing. The Warm-ups are simple, mischievous ideas to help two people talk about themselves and each other in a fun way; Going Deeper is open-ended questions with multiple-choice options to help lead each person in his sharing; and the Overtime Challenge is a creative exercise that encourages everyone to do some deeper thinking and sharing when the group is ready.

The approaches in these exercises are designed for total strangers and for groups who have been acquainted for years but haven't really known each other deeply.

Group Building

STRUCTURED SESSIONS

Objective: To start the process of building support groups.

PROCEDURE:

The instructions are given in the words you can use in leading the group.

Silent Preparation / 5 min.

Turn to page 12 in your player's book and fill out the questionnaire.

Warm-up / 2's / 10 min.

Get together in 2's (find the person you know least) and share your answers to the Warm-up— and explain. (*Share how you would answer the Warm-up and Going Deeper, setting an example for openness and honesty by the way you explain your answers. Then ask the group to pair off in 2's and do the same. After 10 minutes, call time and move on.*)

Going Deeper/4's/15 min.

With your partner join another

WARM-UP

I prefer (*circle your choice in each category*):

1. drive-in . . . . fancy restaurant
2. going steady . . . . . playing the field
3. staying up late . . . getting up early
4. to be a big frog   to be a little frog
   in a little pond . . . . . . in a big pond
5. a blind date . . . . . . a second choice
6. getting a B in   getting an A in
   a tough course . . . . an easy course
7. playing touch . . . . . . watching pro
   football . . . . football
8. total honesty . . . . . insincere praise
9. to be second-   to be first-string
   string varsity . . . . . . junior varsity
10. playing it safe . . . .   going for broke

GOING DEEPER

1. For me, the toughest thing about school is (*circle two*):
   a. getting up in the morning
   b. studying
   c. monotony
   d. homework
   e. getting along with teachers
   f. staying awake in class
   g. grades
   h. tests
   i. English
   j. making friends
   k. hassles from parents
   l. becoming popular
   m. feeling lonely

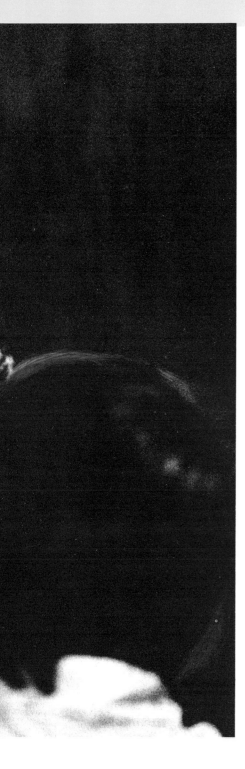

2. **After a tough day at school, I like to relax by** *(circle two):*
   a. napping
   b. watching TV
   c. goofing off
   d. snacking
   e. changing my clothes
   f. playing ball
   g. talking on the phone
   h. reading
   i. taking a walk
   j. going somewhere with a friend

3. **Before a big test, I** *(circle three):*
   a. am nervous and shaky
   b. talk a lot
   c. get very quiet
   d. munch constantly
   e. forget about it   i. can't sleep
   f. do crazy things   j. get worried
   g. cram   k. pray a lot
   h. get a headache   l. can't eat

4. **I look upon school as** *(choose three and rank 1, 2, 3):*
   _____prison
   _____good times
   _____getting me ready for life
   _____wasted time
   _____a chance to make friends
   _____a refuge from home
   _____mind-building
   _____a chance to prove myself
   _____part of growing up
   _____unnecessary
   _____something I have to do
   _____the best days of my life

OVERTIME CHALLENGE

(Choose the five goals that are most important to you and rank them 1, 2, 3, etc.)
During this program I want to:
   _____have a ball
   _____discipline myself
   _____learn more about the Bible
   _____meet some new friends
   _____discover myself
   _____get my feet on the ground
   _____improve my personal habits
   _____learn to love
   _____belong to a group of people who are really serious about God
   _____develop some deep friendships
   _____learn about God's will for my life
   _____settle down in school
   _____deal with my boredom

twosome (people you know the least) and make a foursome. Then share your answers to the first question in Going Deeper, explaining the whys. Then go around a second time with the second question, etc. (*Share your answer to the first question and set the pace for openness and honesty. Call time after 15 minutes and move on.*)

Overtime Challenge / 4's or 8's / 15 min.

(You will have to decide if there is time to share the Overtime Challenge and, if so, whether to use groups of 4 or 8. If you are limited for time, stay with the 4's. If you have plenty of time, ask the groups of 4 to double up to make groups of 8.)

Go around your group and let each person share his first, second and third choice and why. (*Share your own top three choices and set the pace for openness and honesty.*)

Close-out

Stack your hands together in the center of your group *(Now offer a brief prayer, saying something like: "Thank you, God, for each other. Amen." Before dismissing the group, ask everyone to write his name on his book. Then collect the books so they are available for the next session.)*

CONVOY

Objective: To start the process of building support groups.

PROCEDURE

The instructions are given in the words you can use in leading the group.

Silent Preparation / 5 min.

Turn to page 12 in your player's book and fill out the questionnaire.

Warm-up / 2's / 10 min.

Get together in twos (find the person you know least) and give your answers to the Warm-up in the questionnaire—and explain. *(Share how you would answer the first couple of things and set an example for openness and honesty by the way you explain your answers. After 10 minutes call time and move on.)*

Going Deeper / 4's / 15 min.

With your partner join another twosome (people you know least) to make a foursome. Share your answers to the first question in Going Deeper in the questionnaire and why. Then go around on the

WARM-UP

I am more like a...than a...*(circle one in each category)*:

1. trapeze artist.........circus clown
2. sprinter..........distance runner
3. television...............CB radio
4. magnifying glass........telescope
5. first and 10.............goal to go
6. Johnny Cash.......Johnny Carson
7. picture...................puzzle
8. candle..................light bulb
9. amusement park..........library
10. quarterback........blocking back
11. dill pickle.............sugar plum
12. dictionary..........encyclopedia
13. in the game...........on the side
14. golf ball................mush ball
15. hotel..................hospital
16. bear.....................tiger
17. spark plug..............battery
18. New York City..........Arkansas
19. bridge...................tower
20. oak tree...............evergreen
21. ballet dancer.........two left feet

GOING DEEPER

1. Around people I don't know, I am usually *(circle two)*:
   a. Mr. Super Cool
   b. nervous g. clumsy
   c. quiet h. a little uptight
   d. out-going i. the liberated woman
   e. goosey j. the life of the party
   f. confident k. all thumbs
   l.

3. The qualities I look for in a friend are *(choose three and rank 1, 2, 3)*:

   ___ honesty ___ easygoingness
   ___ openness ___ brown eyes
   ___ understanding ___ spiritual depth
   ___ loyalty ___ good looks
   ___ warmth ___ compatibility
   ___ compassion ___ sharp dresser
   ___ fun ___ moral guts
   ___ muscles ___ social prestige
   ___ personality ___ popularity

OVERTIME

If your friends were to describe you with some of the modern-day advertising slogans, which ones would they pick for you? *(choose 3 and rank 1, 2, 3, on the left. On the right rank the top three to describe your group—if there is time.)*

YOURSELF **YOUR GROUP**

___ I'd rather fight than switch
(*Tarreyton*) . . . . ___
___ ...has a better idea (*Ford*) . . . . ___
___ It's the real thing (*Coke*) . . . . . . ___
___ When you care enough to send
the very best (*Hallmark*) . . . . . . ___
___ Put a tiger in your tank (*Esso*) . ___
___ Find someone and share it
(*Canada Dry*) . . . . ___
___ I'd walk a mile for...(*Camels*) . . . ___
___ We try harder (*Avis*) . . . . ___
___ You've come a long way, baby
(*Virginia Slims*) . . . . ___
___ Once you try it, you'll love the
difference (*Dr. Pepper*) . . . . ___

___ Since we're neighbors, let's be
friends (*Safeway*) . . . . ___
___ Put the snap, crackle, pop, into
your life (*Kelloggs*) . . . . ___
___ The slowest ketchup in the
West (*Heinz*) . . . . ___
___ You only go around once in life,
so reach for the gusto
(*Schlitz*) . . . . ___
___ I can't believe I ate the whole
thing (*Alka Seltzer*) . . . . ___
___ ...are looking for a few good
men (*U.S. Marines*) . . . . ___
___ Fly now, pay later
(*Travel agencies*) . . . . ___
___ The quality goes in before the
name goes on (*Zenith*) . . . . ___
___ Life is too short not to go first
class when you can
(*Mercedes-Benz*) . . . . ___
___ Getting people together
(*Boeing*) . . . . ___

second question, etc. *(Explain your answer to the first question with the whole group and set the pace for openness and honesty. Call time after 15 minutes and move on.)*

Overtime Challenge / 4's or 8's / 15 min.

(You will have to decide if there is time to share the Overtime Challenge and, if so, whether to use groups of 4 or 8. If time is limited, stay with the 4's. If there is plenty of time, ask two groups of 4 to get together to make groups of 8.)

Go around your group and let each person share the top three slogans his friends would choose for him and explain why. If there is time, go around a second time and let everyone explain the top three slogans he chose for his group. *(Share your top three choices for yourself and set the pace for honesty.)*

Close-out

In each group, stack your hands together in the center. *(While everyone's hands are stacked, say something like: "Thank you, God, for each other. Amen." Ask every-one to write his name on his book. Then collect the books to have them available for the next session.)*

Objective: To start the process of building support groups.

PROCEDURE:

The instructions are given in the words you can use in leading the group.

Silent Preparation / 5 min.

Turn to page 12 in your player's book and fill out the questionnaire.

Warm-up / 2's / 10 min.

Get together in twos (find the person you know least) and share your answers to the Warm-up in the questionnaire—and explain

WARM-UP

I am someone who would *(circle Y for yes, N for no, M for maybe)*:

Y N M 1. holler at the umpire

Y N M 2. kiss on the first date

Y N M 3. gamble on fourth down

Y N M 4. rather walk than ride

Y N M 5. blush at the mention of sex

Y N M 6. stand up for the underdog

Y N M 7. go to the bathroom when the movie got scary

Y N M 8. leave if the game got dull

GETTING IN THE SWING

Y N M 9. slurp for the last drop

Y N M 10. go on a blind date

Y N M 11. rather play ball than eat

Y N M 12. tell a friend he has bad breath

Y N M 13. stay in shape year around

Y N M 14. get to a game early to watch the practice

GOING DEEPER

1. The most exciting thing that is happening in my life at the moment is *(circle one)*:
   a. being in love
   b. getting to know God personally
   c. discovering who I am
   d. belonging to a real Christian fellowship
   e. being on the team at school
   f. making it with my family
   g. discovering my independence
   h. starting a new venture
   i. studying the Bible for myself
   j. running around with friends

2. **In new situations, I usually feel** *(circle two)*:
   a. frightened
   b. comfortable
   c. funny/awkward
   d. outgoing
   e. painfully shy
   f. relaxed—easy going
   g. uptight
   h. tongue-tied

3. **The way I feel about this group is** *(circle two)*:
   a. OK, but...
   b. warm   e. serene
   c. uneasy   f. excited
   d. a little   g. mixed
      threatened h. huh?

OVERTIME CHALLENGE

A variety of things are necessary for a healthy, balanced life. Rank the following from 1 to 10, where you need to improve. For instance, you might rank number one "regular physical exercise" because you are getting flabby.

_____ regular physical exercise
_____ healthy self-image
_____ consistent devotional habits
_____ well-organized study/work habits
_____ clearly defined life goals
_____ good family relationships
_____ strong personal convictions/values
_____ peace of mind about being in God's will
_____ steady growth in assuming responsibility
_____ good, solid friendships

them. *(Share how you would answer a couple of items and set an example for openness and honesty. Then ask the group to pair off and do the same. After 10 minutes call time and move on.)*

Going Deeper / 4's / 15 min.

With your partner join another twosome (a pair you know the least). Share your choices in the first part of Going Deeper and explain why. Then go around on the second question, etc. *(Explain your answer to the first question and set the pace for openness and honesty. Call time after 15 minutes and move on.)*

Overtime Challenge / 4's or 8's / 15 min.

(You will have to decide if there is time to share the Overtime Challenge and, if so, whether to use groups of 4 or 8. If the time is limited, stay with the 4's. If there is plenty of time, ask two 4's to get together to make groups of 8.)

Go around your group and let each person share the things he ranked 1, 2 and 3 on the list and why. *(Share your own top three and set the pace for openness and honesty.)*

Close-out

Stack your hands together in the center of your group. *(While hands are stacked, say something like: "Thank you, God, for each other. Amen." Ask everyone to write his name on his book. Then collect the books so they are available for the next session.)*

DOWN MEMORY LANE

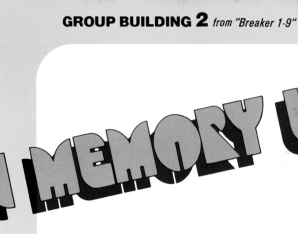

Objective: To continue the process of building the *same* groups that were started in the previous session/s.

PROCEDURE

The instructions are given in the words you can use in leading the group.

Silent Preparation / 5 min.

Turn to page 14 in your player's book and fill out the questionnaire.

Warm-up / 2's / 10 min.

Get together with someone from your group of 8 in the last session and explain your answers to the questionnaire Warm-up. (*If you have new people at the meeting, it would be better to start a new group—unless one of the old groups is short. When everyone is paired off, share how you would answer the first two items on the list, setting an example for openness and honesty by the way you explain your answers. After 10 minutes, call time and move on.*)

Going Deeper/4's/15 min.

With your partner join another twosome (from your group of 8 in the last session). Then share your

WARM-UP

(Circle the words that best describe the way you see yourself.) I see myself more like a _____ than a _____.

1. quiet lake . . . . rushing stream
2. newsstand . . . . library
3. cultured pearl . . . diamond in rough
4. glossy photo . . . . . . original painting
5. sunrise . . . . sunset
6. clinging vine . . . . touch-me-not
7. country road . . . . . . super highway
8. short story . . . . heavy novel
9. mountain . . . . seashore
10. yesterday . . . . tomorrow
11. morning . . . . evening
12. 100-yd. dash . . . cross-country run
13. Cadillac . . . . jalopy
14. Burt Reynolds . . . . John Wayne
15. rock music . . . . . . country western

GOING DEEPER

1. When I was a youngster, I really looked forward to (*circle two*):
   a. summer vacations
   b. family picnics
   c. Little League
   d. Christmastime
   e. state fairs
   f. visits from my grandparents
   g. the day school was out
   h. getting my braces off

2. When school was out, my favorite thing in the summer was (*circle two*):
   a. camping out   e. going to camp
   b. staying up late   f. playing ball
   c. sleeping over   g. hanging around
   d. goofing off   h. reading a lot

3. The best adult friend I ever had outside my family was my (*circle one*):
   a. boss
   b. next door neighbor
   c. scoutmaster
   d. church youth leader
   e. coach
   f. teacher
   g. friend's parents
   h. Sunday School teacher
   i. uncle/aunt

4. The best way for my parents to bring out the best in me is to (*choose three and rank 1, 2, 3*):
   _____ trust me
   _____ leave me alone
   _____ lay it on me
   _____ encourage me
   _____ ask my opinion about something
   _____ let me know I'm important
   _____ try to understand me
   _____ love me
   _____ work out expectations with me
   _____ tell me they are proud of me

OVERTIME CHALLENGE

How would you describe yourself with a recognition plaque? (*Fill in the open areas according to your own self-understanding. Start at the bottom and work up.*)

My Creed. I want my life to stand for *(list three qualities):*

MY RECOGNITION PLAQUE

Two things I am good at
(like singing and swimming):

Two things that turn me on
(like a sunset and country music):

Two words that describe
how I see myself
(like timid and caring):

Two words that describe
how I think my friends see me
(like friendly and fun-loving):

answers to the first question in Going Deeper and explain why. Then go around a second time on the second question, etc. *(Share your own answer to the first question to help everyone get started. After 15 minutes call time and move on.)*

Overtime Challenge / 4's or 8's / 15 min.

(You will have to decide if there is time to share the Overtime Challenge and, if so, whether to use groups of 4 or 8. If you are limited for time, stay with the 4's. If you have plenty of time, use the groups of 8 from the last session.)

Go around the group, each person sharing what he put down in the upper left box: *Two things I am good at.* Then go around with: *Two things that turn me on.* Cover all four areas, going around four times. Finally, go around for the fifth time with the three things you put across the top. *(Share what you put down in a couple boxes and set the pace for openness and honesty.)*

Close-out

Stack your hands together in the center of your group. *(Now give a few words of prayer, saying something like: "Thank you, God, for giving us life. Amen." Be sure everyone has written his name on his book. Then collect the books so they are available for the next session.)*

Over Your Shoulder

Objective: To continue the process of building the same teams or support groups that were started in the previous session/s.

PROCEDURE

The instructions are given in the words you can use in leading the group.

Silent Preparation / 5 min.

Turn to page 14 in your player's book and fill out the questionnaire.

Warm-up / 2's / 10 min.

Get together in twos (with someone from your group of 8 in the last session) and share your answers to the Warm-up in the questionnaire —and why. *(If you have new people at the meeting, start a new group—unless one of the old groups is short. When everyone is paired off, share how you would answer the first three or four things in the Warm-up. Be candid. Be honest. Your explanation will set the pace for sharing. After 10 minutes call time and move on.)*

WARM-UP

Down deep inside I am a...*(put a dot on each line someplace between the two words to indicate where you are):*

1. listener _____ talker
2. spender _____ saver
3. driver _____ rider
4. optimist _____ pessimist
5. loner _____ grouper
6. leader _____ follower
7. doer _____ thinker
8. pitcher _____ catcher
9. rabbit _____ turtle
10. fighter _____ peacemaker
11. giver _____ receiver
12. player _____ spectator
13. pioneer _____ settler
14. right now _____ later
15. easy going _____ hyper

GOING DEEPER

1. When I was a kid, the high point of my summer vacation was *(circle one)*:
   a. playing ball
   b. family trips
   c. reading lots of books
   d. camp
   e. goofing off
   f. visiting my grandparents
   g. biking
   h. swimming
   i. going fishing
   j.

2. The event I remember most in my childhood was *(circle one)*:
   a. the assassination of John F. Kennedy
   b. the death of my pet
   c. winning the _____
   d. my first holy communion

   e. the first time I played hooky
   f. my own brush with death
   g. my biggest licking
   h.

3. Outside my parents, the people who had the greatest influence upon my life were my *(rank top three 1, 2, 3)*:
   ___ teachers   ___ uncle/aunt
   ___ grandparents   ___ youth leader
   ___ pastor   ___ brother/sister
   ___ scoutmaster   ___ sports heroes
   ___ coach   ___ friends

MY CHILDHOOD SCRAPBOOK

At age 6, my favorite TV show

At age 10, my favorite sport
(like soccer or horseback riding)

At age 12, the hero in my life
(like O.J. Simpson or Robert Redford)

The biggest disappointment I ever had

OVERTIME CHALLENGE

If you were to compile a scrapbook of what you liked best as a child, what pictures would you collect? *(For each photo jot down a word or sketch.)*

At age 8, my favorite pet
(like my pony or turtle)

The time in my life when God became more than a name to me *(like at summer camp or first communion)*

Going Deeper / 4's / 15 min.

With your partner join another twosome (from your group of 8 in the last session) to make a foursome. Take the first question and let everyone give his answer and explain why. Then go around on the second question, etc. *(Share your own answer to the first question. Be honest. Call time after 15 minutes and move on.)*

Overtime Challenge / 4's or 8's / 15 min.

(You will have to decide if there is time to share the Overtime Challenge and, if so, whether to use groups of 4 or 8. If time is limited, stay with the 4's. If there is plenty of time, use the groups of 8 from the last session.)

Go around your group and let each person share what he put in the top left box. Then go around on another box, etc.

Close-out

In each group stack your hands together in the center. *(While everyone's hands are stacked, say something like: "Thank you, God, for this time together. Amen." Ask newcomers to write their names in their books. Then collect all of the books.)*

Objective: To continue the process of building the same teams or groups that were started in the previous session/s.

PROCEDURE

The instructions are given in the words you can use in leading the group.

Silent Preparation / 5 min.

Turn to page 14 in your player's book and fill out the questionnaire.

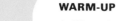

CALLING 'EM THE WAY YOU SEE 'EM

WARM-UP

1. When it comes to making a tough decision, I generally *(circle one)*:
   a. struggle for days
   b. make a snap decision
   c. wait to see what someone else will do
   d. ask for advice
   e. never ask for advice
   f. hope it will go away
   h. take myself on a long walk

2. The hardest decisions for me are usually when *(rank top three)*:
   ____ money is involved
   ____ friendship is involved
   ____ my reputation is on the line
   ____ my popularity is at stake
   ____ my moral values are involved

3. The biggest fear I have to deal with in standing up for what I believe is *(circle one)*:
   a. being laughed at
   b. standing alone
   c. getting someone else in trouble
   d. being wrong
   e. losing my friends
   f.

4. In my home, my parents stressed that morality is *(circle one)*:
   a. a very individual thing
   b. a matter of black and white
   c. the mark of a gentleman/lady
   d. relative
   e. dependent upon the circumstances
   f.

Warm-Up / 2's / 10 min.

Get together in twos (find someone from your previous group of 8) and explain your answers to the Warm-up in the questionnaire. *(Take a moment and explain your answer for the first question. Set the pace for good-natured fun. After 10 minutes call time and move on.)*

Going Deeper / 4's / 15 min.

With your partner join another pair (from your previous group of 8). Share your answers to the first question in Going Deeper and explain why. Then go around on the second question, etc. *(Share your own answer to the first question and set the pace for*

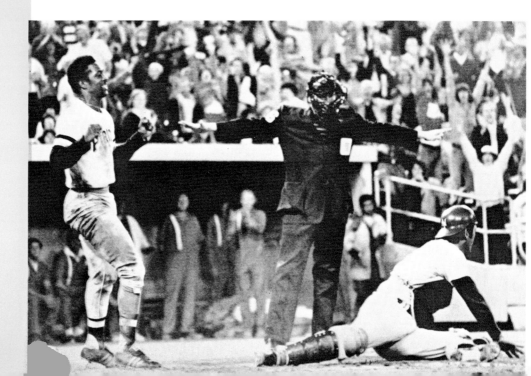

GOING DEEPER

There are many touchy situations in life that call for decisions. You may take one of a variety of actions or do nothing. (Choose one for each situation below.)

1. You don't agree with the behavior of a friend. What do you do?
   a. ignore it
   b. confront him about it
   c. stop running around with him
   d. talk to someone else about it

2. You are the friend of someone who has been deliberately omitted from a party. What do you do?
   a. ignore the affront and go
   b. refuse to go
   c. call and ask why

3. Your friends are going out for a beer bust and you're invited. What do you do?
   a. tell them you don't drink
   b. make some excuse
   c. go along but don't drink
   d. join the party
   e. tell their parents

4. Your best friend never studies. It's exam time and he wants to cheat off your paper. He'll flunk if you don't let him. What do you do?
   a. let him copy
   b. tell the teacher
   c. cover your paper
   d. quietly explain your feelings about cheating
   e. refuse him but offer to help him study for the next exam

OVERTIME CHALLENGE

When it comes to making the major decisions in your life, whom are the people you consult—or unconsciously listen to? (Write the names in the proper categories around the table. You may use two names for one position or the same name twice if the person serves in both capacities. Then go back and write the appropriate symbols next to the names.)

1. *Head Coach:* makes the final decision, the overall strategy, the game plan.
2. *Assistant Coach:* back-up person; carries out coach's instructions; go-between for coach with players.
3. *Offensive Coach:* mainly works on forward movement for players.
4. *Defensive Coach:* mainly works on holding the line, neutralizing the opposition.
5. *Trainer:* helps with conditioning; soothes players after workouts.

✗ if you would like to remove the person from your staff

↑ if the person gives you a lot of encouragement and uplift

↓ if the person tends to drag you down or exert negative influence

✓ if the person were freely chosen by you to serve on your staff

☆ if the person is likely to remain on your staff a long time

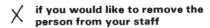

Head Coach

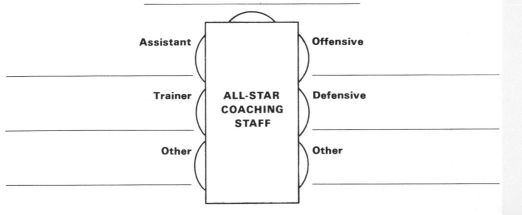

honesty. Call time after 15 minutes and move on.)

Overtime Challenge / 4's or 8's / 15 min.

(You will have to decide if there is time to share the Overtime Challenge and, if so, whether to use groups of 4 or 8. If you are limited for time, stay with the 4's. If you have plenty of time, have the groups of 8 from the last session get together.)

Go around your group and let each person explain his All-Star Coaching Staff. In particular, tell why you chose the person you did as Head Coach. (Explain whom you put down for your Coaching Staff and set the pace for openness and honesty with your explanation.)

For instance:
Head Coach—my group of friends
Assistant Coach—myself
Offensive Coach—my teacher
Defensive Coach—my father
Trainer—my mother
Other—my coach
Other—my girlfriend/boyfriend

Close-out

Stack your hands together in the center of the group. (While everyone's hands are stacked, say something like: "Thank you, God, for giving us life. Amen." Be sure everyone has his name on his book. Then collect the books so they are available for the next session.)

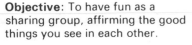

Objective: To have fun as a sharing group, affirming the good things you see in each other.

PROCEDURE

The instructions are given in the words you can use in leading the group.

Silent Preparation / 5 min.

(Ask the groups of 8 who have been together up to now in the program to sit together so they can see each other while filling out the questionnaire. If you have newcomers, ask them to join the group where they know most of the people.)

Turn to page 16 in your player's book and fill out the questionnaire.

Warm-up / 8's / 10 min.

In your group of 8, ask one person to sit in silence while the others explain the handles they picked to describe him and why. When everyone has finished, let this person explain the handle he picked for himself.

Then ask the next person to stay quiet while the others explain

WARM-UP

If you had to describe the others in your group with a "handle" (the C.B. term for signal) what would you choose? *(Below are a series of possible choices. Jot the name of each person next to the handle you would pick for him. Then, choose a handle for yourself.)*

_____ Sly Fox
_____ Sunshine
_____ Teddy Bear
_____ Phantom
_____ Beaver-watcher
_____ Red Baron
_____ Blue Bird
_____ Easy Rider
_____ Easter Bunny
_____ Little Red Hen
_____ Hot Potato
_____ Holy Smoke
_____ Saint Bernard
_____ Frog-kisser

_____ Playful Kitten
_____ Yogi Bear
_____ Blue Daisy
_____ Silver Pussycat
_____ Hai Karate
_____ Jack Rabbit
_____ White Lightning
_____ Deputy Dog

GOING DEEPER

If you were asked to give an award to each person in your group, based on the contribution each has made to your life and the life of the group, what would you give them? *(Jot the name of each person next to the award you feel he deserves.)*

_____ **SPARK PLUG:** for the person who ignited the group experience.
_____ **MEGAPHONE:** for the

person who came to the party and showed the rest of us how exciting the Christian lifestyle really is.

——————— KING ARTHUR'S SWORD: for the one who found a new mission in life and caused the rest of us to stop and think.

——————— SERENDIPITY CROWN: for the person who as far as I am concerned has shown the greatest growth during this program.

OVERTIME CHALLENGE

To describe how you feel about the crazy group of guys and gals in this program, how about comparing your involvement to a football stadium! *(Put three marks on the diagram to symbolize your feelings. For instance you might put the 0 in the grandstand because you felt like a spectator at the beginning of the program. And you might put the X on the bench because right now you are on the team but not really in the game.)*

○ where you were at the beginning of this program

✕ where you are right now

☆ where you would like to be soon

```
┌─────────────────────────────┐
│      GRANDSTAND             │
│    (for spectators)         │
└─────────────────────────────┘

        ┌──────────────┐
        │ BENCH (team) │
        └──────────────┘

┌─────────────────────┐   ┌─────┐
│                     │   │ T S │
│   PLAYING FIELD     │   │ H H │
│  (where the action  │   │ E O │
│      is)            │   │   W │
│                     │   │   E │
│                     │   │   R │
│                     │   │   S │
└─────────────────────┘   └─────┘
```

Also:
1. What is the score right now in the game?
2. Is your team ahead or behind?

3. What is the next play you would call?

person who cheered us on with his encouragement.

——————— DEAR ABBY AWARD: for the person who cared enough to listen whenever someone had a problem to unload.

——————— ROYAL GIRDLE: for the person who drew us together into a real team.

——————— WATER BALLOON: for the person who came through at the right moment with a little humor to keep us laughing.

——————— ROCK OF GIBRALTER: for the person who stood strong in the tough times when we needed a rock.

——————— RHINESTONE COWBOY: for the person who went out of his way to accept me and make me feel good.

——————— GLASS SLIPPER: for the

their choices of handles for him, etc., until everyone has been covered. *(Pick somebody in a group near you and explain the handle you would pick for him. Set the pace for good-natured fun with your explanation. Give the groups 10 minutes, then call time and move on.)*

Going Deeper/8's/15 min.

Stay with your group and move on to Going Deeper. Ask one individual to sit in silence while the others explain the awards they picked for him and why. Then, move on to the next person and go around again, etc., until everyone has been the subject. *(Pick out one person and explain the award you would give him and why. By your example set the pace for genuine, sincere affirmation.)*

Overtime Challenge / 8's / 15 min.

Go around in your group and let each person show where he put the three marks on his stadium diagram and explain why. *(Describe your feelings by explaining to the group where you put your marks.)*

Close-out

Stack your hands together in the center of your group. *(Offer a brief prayer, saying something like: "Thank you, God, for giving us one another. Amen." Ask newcomers to write their names in their books. Then pick up all the books.)*

Objective: To have fun affirming the good things you see in each other as a support group.

PROCEDURE

The instructions are given in the words you can use in leading the group.

Silent Preparation / 5 min.

(Ask the groups of 8 who have been together up to now in the program to sit together so that they can see each other while filling out the questionnaire. If you have newcomers, ask them to join a group in which they know most of the people.)

Turn to page 16 in your player's book and fill out the questionnaire.

Warm-up / 8's / 10 min.

In your group of 8, ask one person to sit in silence while everyone else explains the car he picked for this person and why. When everyone has finished, let this person name the car he would pick for himself and explain why.

Then move on to the next person. Ask him to remain quiet while the others explain the cars they have chosen for him and why, etc., until everyone has been covered. *(Name someone in a group near you and explain which*

WARM-UP

If you were to choose cars for the members of your group, what kinds would you get? *(Jot the name of each group member next to the car you feel best fits him.)*

_____ fire-red Corvett with telephone (used)

_____ Dune Buggy with a roll bar

_____ rebuilt 62 Chevy convertible with lots of class

_____ pink T-Bird with fur steering wheel and leopard skin interior

_____ customized van with hand painted exterior and built-in hi-fi

_____ Volkswagen with Rolls Royce front

_____ 4-wheel-drive Jeep—built for wilderness driving

_____ 1929 Model T Ford with rumble seat

_____ pick-up truck with high-jacks for all the girls

_____ Lincoln Continental, with built-in "refreshment" bar

_____ good used car with low mileage, dependable transportation

GOING DEEPER

If you were to compare the various members in your group to essential car parts, based on the contributions they have made to the group, what would you choose for each one? *(Jot each person's name next to the part you feel fits him.)*

_____ tire—carries weight of group, takes bumps, keeps us going

_____ accelerator—sets the pace for the group

_____ headlights—gives us a clear view of where we're going

_____ springs/shocks—willing to cushion the hard knocks

_____ radio: music—keeps us inspired all along the way

_____ air conditioner—helps us to keep our cool

_____ transmission—good at shifting into deeper things

_____ steering wheel—outspoken decision maker

_____ roll bar—comes through in times of crisis

_____ road map—keeps us heading in the right direction

_____ spark plug—gets things started with lots of energy

_____ brakes—avoids the collisions that hurt

OVERTIME CHALLENGE

Explain how you feel about this program and the group you are in by comparing your feelings to a basketball game! Here is a basketball court with the various positions where you might be. *(Put three marks on the diagram. For instance, you might put an O in the bleachers because you felt like a spectator at the beginning of the program. And you might put an X on the player's bench because you are on the team now but not yet really in the game.)*

○ where you were at the beginning of the program

✕ where you are right now

☆ where you want to be

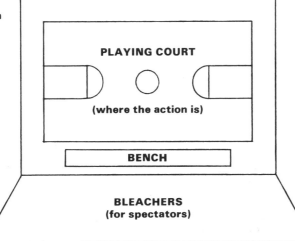

SHOWERS

PLAYING COURT

(where the action is)

BENCH

BLEACHERS
(for spectators)

Also:

What is the score right now?

What is the game plan for the next quarter?

---

car you would choose for him and why. Set the pace for good-natured fun and honest affirmation. After 10 minutes call time and move on.)

Going Deeper / 8's / 15 min.

Stay with your group but move on to Going Deeper in the questionnaire. Ask one person to remain silent while the others explain why they chose the particular car parts they did for him. Move on to the next person and go around again, etc., until everyone has been covered. *(Pick out one person and explain the parts you would choose for him. Set the pace for genuine, honest affirmation.)*

Overtime Challenge / 8's / 15 min.

Go around in your group and let each person explain where he put the marks in his basketball diagram and why. *(Start this off with your own explanation.)*

Close-out

In each group, stack your hands together in the center of your group. *(While everyone's hands are stacked, say something like: "Thank you, God, for what we have experienced together as a support team. Amen." Ask newcomers to write their names in their books. Collect all the books.)*

CHOOSE YOUR TEAM

Objective: To have fun affirming the good things you see in each other as a support group.

PROCEDURE

The instructions are given in the words you can use in leading the group.

Silent Preparation / 5 min.

(Ask the groups of 8 who have been together up to now in this program to sit together so they can see each other while filling out the questionnaire. If there are newcomers, ask them to join the groups in which they know the most people.)

Turn to page 16 in your player's book and fill out the questionnaire.

Warm-up / 8's / 10 min.

In your group of 8, ask one person to sit in silence while the others explain which special jeans they picked for him and why.

When everyone has finished, let the person explain which ones he picked for himself. Then move on to the next person. He remains quiet while the others explain their choices of jeans.

WARM-UP

If you had to get a pair of jeans for everybody in your group, what kind would you get to fit each one's personality? *(Jot down the names of the people in your group beside the jeans you feel they would be most comfortable in.)*

_____ green jeans
_____ new jeans
_____ cut-offs
_____ overalls
_____ holey jeans
_____ patched jeans
_____ jeans with style
_____ lots of pockets
_____ hip huggers
_____ fringed jeans
_____ embroidered jeans
_____ straight-legged
_____ faded
_____ tie-dyed
_____ tight
_____ flares
_____ boot-cut

GOING DEEPER

If you had to pick one person from your sharing group for each of the following situations, who would you pick? *(Write one name beside each situation.)*

_____ you are in trouble and need someone to talk to at 3a.m.
_____ you need someone to be the godparent of your child
_____ you need a best man or maid of honor for your wedding
_____ you need someone to accompany you around the world
_____ you need someone in charge of your estate after you die
_____ you need a business partner
_____ you need someone to go shopping with
_____ you need someone to entrust your kids to in the event of your death
_____ you need someone to go backpacking with you in the wilderness for seven days
_____ you need someone from whom you can get a quick loan
_____ you need someone to stand by you when the whole world is against you—no matter what the consequences are

OVERTIME CHALLENGE

If you had to describe how you felt about your support group by comparing your involvement to a baseball game, how would you do it? *(Put three marks someplace on the diagram. For instance, you might put an O in the grandstand because you felt like a spectator at the beginning of the program; you might put an X on the player's bench because now you feel that you are really on the team but not yet in the game.)*

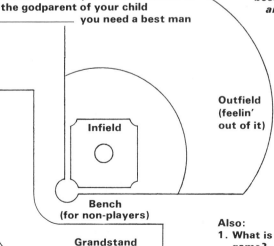

O where you were at the beginning of this program

X where you are right now

☆ where you would like to be soon

Also:

1. What is the score right now in the game? _____
2. What strategy would you suggest for the next inning? _____

until everyone has been covered. *(Choose someone in a group near you and explain the product you would pick for him. Set the pace for good-natured fun with your explanation. After 10 minutes call time and move on.)*

Going Deeper / 8's / 15 min.

Stay with your group and move on to Going Deeper in the questionnaire. Ask one person to sit silently while the others explain the occasion they picked for him and why. Then move on to the next person and go around again, etc., until everyone has been covered. *(Choose a person and explain the occasion you would like to share with him and why. Set the pace for genuine, sincere affirmation by what you say.)*

Overtime Challenge / 8's / 15 min.

Go around in your group and let each person explain where he put the three marks on the baseball diagram and why. *(Model this by explaining to the group where you see yourself.)*

Close-out

In each group, stack your hands together in the center of your group. *(While everyone's hands are stacked, say something like: "Thank you, God, for giving us one another. Amen." Ask newcomers to write their names in their books. Then pick up all the books.)*

WHAT'S YOUR GAME PLAN?

Objective: To evaluate the program up to this point.

PROCEDURE

The instructions are given in the words you can use in leading the group.

Silent Preparation / 5 min.

Turn to page 18 in your player's book and fill out the questionnaire.

Warm-up / 4's / 10 min.

Get together with 3 other people from your group of 8 and share your answers to the Warm-up in the questionnaire—one question at

WARM-UP

1. The time I do my best thinking is *(circle one)*:
   a. in the shower
   b. late at night
   c. when I'm alone
   d. at camp
   e. listening to music
   f. at church
   g. when I'm challenged

2. The thing that causes me to stop and think about my life is *(circle two)*:
   a. sickness
   b. death in the family
   c. loss of a close friend
   d. failure
   e. a big disappointment
   f. being alone
   g. coming to a crossroads

3. When I die, I would like it to be said of me *(circle one)*:
   a. I followed the quest
   b. I had a ball
   c. I gave it all I had
   d. I was true to my convictions
   e. I lived life to the fullest
   f. I was a loyal friend
   g. _____

4. If I could give three things to my children, I would want them to have *(rank your top three choices 1, 2, 3)*:
   ____ good health
   ____ happy marriage
   ____ secure job
   ____ a lot of money
   ____ an opportunity to make something of themselves
   ____ moral courage
   ____ success in their fields
   ____ leaders in the community

GOING DEEPER

1. The thing I appreciate most about this program is *(circle one)*:
   a. the good time together
   b. the deep friendships
   c. the time away from home
   d. the chance to talk about our problems
   e. our spiritual growth

2. The two greatest things I have learned during our times together are *(circle two)*:
   a. it's not "sissy" to be a Christian
   b. it's OK to have problems
   c. I have some great gifts
   d. I need to work on my spiritual priorities
   e. living a Christian life isn't easy
   f. I am an important member of God's team

3. If I had the chance to do this program again, I think I would *(circle one)*:
   a. get more involved at the beginning
   b. open up more
   c. get others involved
   d. take it more seriously
   e. have to think about it
   f. not join the next time

OVERTIME CHALLENGE

The three playing fields represent three areas of your life. Where do you see yourself? *(Place three marks on each field.)*

○ where you were at the beginning of this program

✕ where you are right now

☆ where you want to be a year from now

A. IN MY RELATIONSHIP WITH MYSELF: believing in myself—that I am important, that I have unique ability, that I am a valuable person.

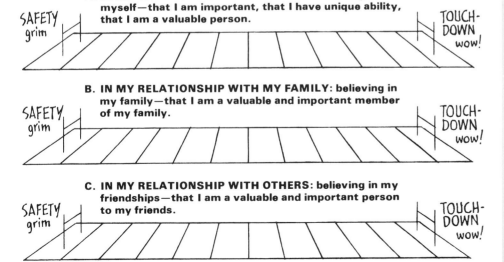

SAFETY grim ———— TOUCH-DOWN wow!

B. IN MY RELATIONSHIP WITH MY FAMILY: believing in my family—that I am a valuable and important member of my family.

SAFETY grim ———— TOUCH-DOWN wow!

C. IN MY RELATIONSHIP WITH OTHERS: believing in my friendships—that I am a valuable and important person to my friends.

SAFETY grim ———— TOUCH-DOWN wow!

a time. Go around on the first question; then go around a second time on the second question, etc. *(Share your answer to the first question and set the pace for openness and honesty. Give the group 10 minutes, then call time and move on.)*

Going Deeper/8's/15 min.
Regather your group of 8 and give everyone a chance to share his answers to Going Deeper— one question at a time. *(Share your answer first and set the pace for honesty.)*

Overtime Challenge / 2's / 15 min.
Pair off with someone from your group of 8 and give each other a chance to describe the three relationships in your life and how you marked yourself. Explain in detail the reasons for marking yourself as you did. *(Set the pace here for openness and honesty by taking one of the three areas and explaining how and why you marked yourself as you did.)*

Close-out
Stack your hands together in the center of your group. *(Offer a few words of prayer, saying something like: "Thank you, God, for the chance to be together and to discover what you want in our lives. Amen." Collect the books.)*

Objective: To evaluate the program up to this point and make plans for the days ahead.

PROCEDURE

The instructions are given in the words you can use in leading the group.

WARM-UP

1. The place I retreat to when I need to "get myself together" is *(circle one)*:
   a. the park
   b. a lake
   c. fishing spot
   d. the bathtub
   e. TV
   f. the woods
   g. a quiet chapel
   h. a ball game
   k. the movies
   l. the beach
   m. the mountains
   n. an easy chair
   o. my room
   p. out of the house
   q. anywhere

2. The person I admire most is *(choose three and rank 1, 2, 3)*:
   ____ Ralph Nader
   ____ Billy Graham
   ____ Mother Theresa
   ____ John Denver
   ____ Chris Evert
   ____ Olivia Newton John
   ____ Aleksandr Solzhenitsyn
   ____ Helen Keller
   ____ Martin Luther King, Jr.
   ____ Albert Einstein
   ____ Pope John
   ____ Albert Schweitzer
   ____ Edmund Hillary
   ____ Marie Curie
   ____ Vince Lombardi
   ____ Cesar Chavez

3. My philosophy of life might be summarized by the phrase *(circle first and last choice)*:
   a. if it feels good, do it
   b. what the "heck"
   c. grab all the "gusto" you can
   d. love and be happy
   e. do unto others as you want them to do unto you
   f. look out for number one
   g. roll with the punches
   h. I don't want to grow up
   i. if you want something bad enough you'll get it

4. If I had a million dollars, I would *(circle one)*:
   a. quit school / work right now
   b. buy a yacht
   c. start my own business
   d. run for president
   e. take my friends around the world
   f. feed everybody
   g. invest it all
   h. get my parents to retire and enjoy life
   i. give it all away and stay as I am
   j. have one great, big, continuous party

GOING DEEPER

1. As I think back, the reason why I started coming to this group was (circle one):
   a. someone made me
   b. everyone else was coming
   c. someone special invited me
   d. I wanted to find out what this was all about
   e. I didn't have anything else to do
   f. I was searching for something and I thought this might help
   g. don't know

2. The experience of opening up and sharing my ideas and problems with this support group has been (circle two):
   a. scary
   b. invaluable
   c. very difficult
   d. OK, but
   e. exciting
   f. just what I needed
   g. a life-changing experience
   h. a beautiful breakthrough

3. The high point for me in this program has been the (circle two):
   a. fun
   b. times of prayer
   c. feeling of belonging to others who really care
   d. being with people who are committed to Christ

   (continued)

   e. knowing you are not alone in your problems
   f. finding myself again
   g. Bible study
   h. learning to deal with my hangups

OVERTIME CHALLENGE

How about a strategy program for helping you to think through your personal goals?

a. *First column. (Jot down three concerns in your life right now, such as: to increase my grades, to work on my relationships at home, to save some money for college.)*

b. *Second column. (Take the most important concern and jot down three "wishes" you would like to make about that area of concern. For instance if working on your relationships at home was number 1, then your wishes might be: I wish I could talk to my dad alone, I wish I could explain to him how I feel, etc.)*

c. *Third column. (With your wishes in mind, list three specific projects for this next week—to start solving your most important concern. For instance: I will write my dad a note telling him how I feel and asking him to give me an hour next week, I will invite him out for a hamburger where we can talk alone, etc.)*

MY MAJOR CONCERNS	I WISH I COULD	I WILL

Silent Preparation / 5 min.
Turn to page 18 in your player's book and fill out the questionnaire.

Warm-up / 4's / 10 min.
Get together with four people from your group of 8 and share your answers to the Warm-up— one question at a time. That is, go around on the first question; then go around on the second question, etc. *(Share your answer to the first question and set the pace for openness and honesty. After 10 minutes call time and move on.)*

Going Deeper / 8's / 15 min.
Regather your group of 8 and give everyone a chance to share his answers to Going Deeper in the questionnaire—one question at a time. *(Share your answer to the first question and set the pace for honesty.)*

Overtime Challenge / 2's / 15 min.
Pair off with one other person from your group of 8 and give each other a chance to explain his goal-setting exercise. Go into detail on the second and third columns —"I wish I could" and "I will." Nail down the plan of action you intend to take in the next seven days. *(Set the pace here for openness and honesty by explaining your own wishes and your plan of action.)*

Close-out
In each group, stack your hands together in the center. *(While everyone's hands are stacked, say something like: "Thank you, God, for this chance to think through the next steps in our lives. Amen." Collect the books.*

Objective: To evaluate the program up to this point.

PROCEDURE

Instructions are given in the words you can use in leading the group.

Silent Preparation / 5 min. .

Turn to page 18 in your player's book and fill out the questionnaire.

Warm-up / 4's / 10 min.

Get together with four people from your group of 8 and share your answers to the Warm-up—one question at a time. That is, go around on the first question; then go around on the second question, etc. *(Share your answer to the first question and set the pace for openness and honesty. After 10 minutes call time and move on.)*

WARM-UP

1. I put the most effort into doing a good job when *(circle two):*
   a. I get near my goal
   b. others are watching me
   c. I am challenged
   d. everything is new
   e. there is a lot of competition
   f. someone needs my help
   g. the pressure is intense
   h. everything is great at home
   i. there is no one else to do it
   j. no one thinks I can do it
   k. everyone thinks I can do it
   l. the pay is right

2. When I lose out on something I want, I usually *(circle two):*
   a. get down on myself
   b. blame somebody else
   c. hide from people
   d. throw a tantrum
   e. stay calm and cool
   f. shake it off easily
   g. am deeply hurt
   h. take it out on someone at home
   i. expected the worst
   j. am terribly angry
   k. cry and get over it

GOING DEEPER

1. Since being in this ~~support~~ youth group, I feel that I have made real progress in *(rank top three 1, 2, 3):*
   ____ sorting out my priorities
   ____ settling down at school or at work
   ____ developing my self-confidence
   ____ developing my spiritual life
   ____ letting others know me
   ____ dealing with my family hassles
   ____ dealing with my relationships at school/on the job

2. I still have a long way to go in *(rank top three):*
   ____ working on my temper
   ____ cleaning up my thought-life
   ____ risking deeper relationships
   ____ my spiritual consistency
   ____ my quality of work
   ____ my self-confidence

3. If I am going to go any further, I will need a little more *(circle one):*
   a. guts
   b. group support
   c. spiritual commitment
   d. help from God
   e. determination
   f. time alone
   g. self-confidence

OVERTIME CHALLENGE

Below are three baseball diamonds to represent three relationships of your life. *(On each baseball diamond, put two marks.)*

O where you were at the beginning of this program

X where you are right now

A. MY RELATIONSHIP WITH MYSELF:
I am feeling good about myself; believing I have real abilities, a lot of things going for me; able to love myself.

B. MY RELATIONSHIP WITH OTHERS:
I am feeling good about sharing myself with others without fear of being put down or laughed at. I am able to reach out, care about others, share my deep feelings—even some of my needs and problems.

C. MY RELATIONSHIP WITH GOD: *I am feeling good about knowing God personally through Jesus Christ. I am getting my spiritual life together, putting God first in my life.*

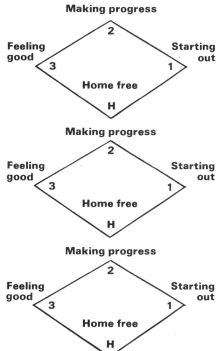

Making progress

2

Feeling good   3   1   Starting out

Home free

H

Making progress

2

Feeling good   3   1   Starting out

Home free

H

Making progress

2

Feeling good   3   1   Starting out

Home free

H

Going Deeper / 8's / 15 min.

Regather your group of 8 and give everyone a chance to share answers to Going Deeper—one question around at a time. *(Share your answer to the first question and set the pace for honesty.)*

Overtime Challenge / 2's / 15 min.

Pair off with one other person from your group of 8 and explain to each other why you marked the three relationships in your life as you did. Go into detail. *(Set the pace here for real honesty by taking one of the areas and explaining how and why you marked yourself as you did.)*

Close-out

In each group, stack your hands together in the center of your group. *(While everyone's hands are stacked, say something like: "Thank you, God, for the chance to be together this way, supporting one another. Amen." Collect the books.)*

Notes

The secret to Values Clarification is a series of self-inventory exercises or strategies that are designed to force a person to think for himself and come up with his own values—or to clarify the values he has. In this program we have gone one step further and linked each exercise with one of the New Testament parables that Jesus used to get at the same issue. Thus, the Values exercises are used to run interference for the parables, and the parables, in turn, are used to reinforce the application of the exercises.

In this approach, there is no right or wrong answer, no attempt to moralize or judge a particular act as good or bad. A person is free to evaluate, choose, and act in whatever way he wishes. Please don't misunderstand me. We are not saying that there is no right or wrong or good or bad. Rather, it is the responsibility of the student to sort through all of the conflicting opinions, pressures and judgments that are laid on him by society and to come up with his own set of values and beliefs. This is what track two is all about. (Note: Tracks three and four, also based on the teachings of Scripture, go further in providing specific guidelines for developing moral and spiritual values.)

The group becomes a sounding-board. Each person explains his choices (values), thereby aiding the process of group-building by further history-giving and understanding.

In the leader's column alongside the exercise, you will find suggestions for dividing the support groups into 2's, 4's and 8's at various times to increase the participation and depth sharing.

Keep the same groups that were formed in the group-building exercises of track one. This is important for developing a spirit of loyalty and confidence in each other.

Values Clarification

STRUCTURED SESSIONS

Objective

Objective: To examine your possessions in the light of the parables of the Hidden Treasure and the Pearl of Great Price, and to use your results as the basis for a sharing experience.

PROCEDURE

The instructions are given in the words you can use in leading the group.

Silent Preparation / 5 to 10 min.

Turn to page 22 in your player's book and fill out the questionnaire.

Warm-up / 4's / 5 min.

Get together with 3 other people from your group of 8 and share the items you would grab in the event of fire. *(Take a moment and share your list with the entire group. Set the pace for honesty and openness. Then ask each group of 4 to proceed. After 5 minutes call time and move on.)*

Going Deeper / 4's / 15 min.

Stay in your group of 4 and, starting with the first symbol, let everyone explain where he placed

2-MINUTE FIRE DRILL

THE PARABLE OF THE HIDDEN TREASURE

Jesus said, "The Kingdom of heaven is like a treasure hidden in a field. man happens to find it, so he covers it up again. He is so happy that he goes and sells everything he has, and then goes back and buys the fiel

THE PARABLE OF THE PEARL

"Also, the Kingdom of heaven is like a buyer looking for fine pearls. W he finds one that is unusually fine, he goes and sells everything he has and buys the pearl."

MATTHEW 13:44-46

WARM-UP

Assume for a moment that your house is on fire. The people and pets in the house are safe. You have two minutes to run through the house and snatch the the most important possessions in your life. In your imagination run through every room, including the garage. *(Jot down the specific items that you would grab—because of their personal value to you. For instance: letter jacket, hi-fi, checkbook, Honda, etc. Don't put down just "clothes"; put down which clothes. The more specific the better! And consider size and weight no problem!)*

_____

_____

_____

_____

_____

_____

_____

_____

_____

GOING DEEPER

Read over the Scripture passage and consider the "treasures" you just listed. How would you describe them? *(Place the following symbols beside the appro-priate items. You may use a symbol twice and you may apply two or three symbols to the same item.)*

○ has just recently become of value to me

↓ will likely go down in value *to me* in five years

↑ will likely go up in value *to me* in five years

△ to get this item I would risk returning to the house while it's in flames

✗ its loss would seriously affect my life and lifestyle

☆ would come the closest to being the "pearl of great price" in my life right now

P would probably be on my parents' list too

F would probably be on my friends' list too

OVERTIME CHALLENGE

1. From this exercise, it seems to me that my values, as far as my possessions are concerned, are *(circle one in each category)*:
   a. really changing . . fairly constant
   b. fuzzy . . . . clear
   c. centered around centered around
      people . . . . things
   d. closer to my   closer to my
      parents'. . . . . friends'
   e. close to the   far from the
      meaning of the   meaning of the
      Pearl of Great   Pearl of Great
      Price . . . . Price

2. Right now, the "pearl of great price" in my life is probably *(circle two)*:
   a. girls
   b. sports   h. Christ
   c. fun   i. me
   d. grades   j. don't know
   e. popularity   k. money
   f. a college degree l. success
   g. kicks   m. the church

3. In comparison to the things on my list, I value the Kingdom of heaven *(circle one)*:
   a. to the same degree
   b. the same, but
   c. but...but...
   d. ouch
   e. more all the time

it and why. Then go around on the next symbol, etc., until you have covered all of them. *(Take a moment and tell where you placed the circle and explain why. Be honest. Your example will set the pace for the groups. After 15 minutes call time and move on.)*

Overtime Challenge / 2's or 8's / 15 min.

Decide if there is time to share the Overtime Challenge and, if so, whether to use groups of 2 or 8. If you are limited for time, have the groups divide into 2's. If there is plenty of time, ask that the previous groups of 8 get together again—or the groups of 4's to double up.)

Take the first question and go around your group, letting each person explain his choices. Then go around on the second question, etc. *(Take a moment and share your choices on the first question. Be painfully honest!!! Your example will set the pace for the groups to follow.)*

Close-out

In each group, stand together in a close circle—with your arms over each other's shoulders. *(Pray briefly, saying something like: "Thank you, God, for giving us something of great value to live for. Amen." Ask everyone to write his name in his book. Collect the books.)*

DIAL·A·SAMARITAN

Objective: To examine your friendships in the light of the parable of the Good Samaritan, and to use your results as the basis for a sharing experience.

PROCEDURE

The instructions are given in the words you can use in leading the group.

Silent Preparation / 5 to 10 min.
Turn to page 22 in your player's book and fill out the questionnaire.

Warm-up / 4's / 5 min.
Get together with 3 other people from your group of 8 in the previous session and explain the phone numbers you use most often. *(Take a moment and explain your list to the entire group. Set the pace for openness and honesty. Then ask each group of 4 to proceed. After 5 minutes call time and move on.)*

Going Deeper / 4's / 15 min.
Stay with your group of 4 and explain to each other where and why you placed the symbols as you did. Start with the first symbol

WARM-UP

What phone numbers do you use the most right now? (*List the numbers you call most frequently. If you cannot remember a number, jot down the person or location. Include your home and church phone numbers.*)

THE PARABLE OF THE GOOD SAMARITAN

Jesus answered, "There was a man who was going down from Jerusalem to Jericho, when robbers attacked him, stripped him, and beat him up, leaving him half dead. It so happened that a priest was going down that road; when he saw the man he walked on by, on the other side. In the same way a Levite also came there, went over and looked at the man, and then walked on by, on the other side.

"But a certain Samaritan who was traveling that way came upon him, and when he saw the man his heart was filled with pity. He went over to him, poured oil and wine on his wounds and bandaged them; then he put the man on his own animal and took him to an inn, where he took care of him.

"The next day he took out two silver coins and gave them to the innkeeper. 'Take care of him,' he told the innkeeper, 'and when I come back this way I will pay you back whatever you spend on him.'"

And Jesus concluded, "In your opinion, which one of these three acted like a fellow-man toward the man attacked by the robbers?"

The teacher of the Law answered, "The one who was kind to him."

Jesus replied, "You go, then, and do the same."

LUKE 10:30-37 GNFMM

GOING DEEPER

Who would you call when? *(Read the Scripture passage and then think about the phone numbers you listed. Place the following symbols next to the numbers you would call for the various situations. You may use a symbol more than once and more than one symbol next to a number if it is appropriate.)*

$ if you needed money but could not explain why

⚡ if you were at a crossroads in your life and needed some good counsel

P if you had a serious personal problem and needed someone to talk to—one who would keep his mouth shut

† if you had a spiritual problem and needed someone to listen and understand

☺ if you were really down and needed a good laugh and a good time

S if you received a "Dear John" letter and needed a shoulder to cry on

OVERTIME CHALLENGE

1. **When it comes to friends, I tend to** *(circle one in each category):*
   a. make friends quickly . . . . slowly
   b. change friends constantly . . . . never
   c. break off friendships easily . with great pain
   e. when I'm in trouble call on my friends . keep to myself

2. **In times of trouble, I tend to rely on** *(rank top three):*
   —— my partner
   —— my friends
   —— my family
   —— my teachers/coach
   —— myself alone
   —— one friend
   —— God

3. **When one of my friends is in trouble, I am best at** *(circle two):*
   a. listening
   b. going to bat for him
   c. praying
   d. cheering him up
   e. sticking by him
   f. bringing him home
   g. getting others to help
   h. keeping my mouth shut
   i. sharing my struggles with him

and let everyone explain where he placed this symbol and why. Then go around on the next symbol, etc., until you have gone through all of the symbols. *(Take a moment and explain where you placed the first symbol and why. Be honest. Your example will set the pace for the groups. After 15 minutes call time and move on.)*

Overtime Challenge / 2's or 8's / 15 min.

(You will have to decide if there is time to share the Overtime Challenge and, if so, whether to use groups of 2 or 8. If time is limited, use 2's. If there is plenty of time, ask the 4's to double up to make the same groups of 8 as in previous sessions.)

Take the first question and go around your group, letting each person explain his choices. Then go around in your group on the second question, etc. *(Take a moment and share your choices on the first question. Be painfully honest! Your example will set the pace for the others.)*

Close-out

In each group, gather together in a football huddle—with your arms around each other's shoulders. *(While everyone is in a huddle, say something like: "Thank you, God, for giving us friends who love and support us in times of trouble. Amen." Ask everyone to write his name in his book. Then collect all of the books.)*

FIGHTING ISSUES

Objective: To examine your own major concerns in the light of the parables of Salt and Light, and to use your results as the basis for a sharing experience.

PROCEDURE

The instructions are given in the words you can use in leading the group.

Silent Preparation / 5 to 10 min.

Turn to page 22 in your player's book and fill out the questionnaire.

Warm-up / 4's / 15 min.

Get together with 3 other people from your group of 8 in the previous session and share what you put down in the Warm-up phase in the questionnaire—the top five issues in which you would get involved. *(Take a moment and share what you listed as the top five issues. Be honest. Then turn the groups of 4 loose. After 15 minutes call time and move on.)*

WARM-UP

In what current issues are you willing to be involved? *(Here is a list of issues or concerns that are demanding attention today, needing action by those who are interested in a better world tomorrow. Choose five of the following situations and rank 1 to 5 according to your own desire to do something about it.)*

____ ***Ecology:*** **your neighborhood is being polluted by smoke stacks from an industry that employs many townspeople. To close the plants would throw them out of work.**

____ ***Abortion:*** **you know that a clinic in your community is performing illegal abortions.**

____ ***Motorcycle helmets and seat belts:*** **you are forced to take safety measures for your own protection—you feel it is an infringement on**

SALT AND LIGHT

"You are like salt for all mankind. But if salt loses its taste, there is no way to make it salty again. It has become worthless, so it is thrown away and people walk on it.

"You are like light for the whole world. A city built on a hill cannot be hid. No one lights a lamp to put it under a bowl; instead he puts it on the lampstand, where it gives light for everyone in the house. In the same way your light must shine before people, so that they will see the good things you do and give praise to your Father in heaven."

MATTHEW 5:13-16 GNFMM

your own personal freedom.

_____ *Firearms:* in your community the deaths caused from gun wounds have doubled in the last five years because of the unrestricted sale of firearms.

_____ *Smoking:* many public places are crowded with people smoking. The Surgeon General has claimed that smoke inhaled through any means is harmful to a person's health.

_____ *Equality:* a firm in your community has a history of not hiring blacks. You are asked to join a picket line protesting their discriminatory tactics.

_____ *Women's lib:* you have been turned down by an employer in your community because you are a woman.

_____ *Pornography:* the local drive-in is showing hard-core pornography and you have learned that minors are being admitted—illegally.

_____ *Hospital aids:* the local hospital has appealed for volunteers to "empty bedpans" and "serve in the recovery room."

_____ *Conservation:* you have learned that ranchers in your state have killed some eagles by placing poison in sheep carcasses.

_____ *Evangelism:* Billy Graham is holding a crusade in your town and you have the chance to take your friends.

_____ *World hunger:* the Council of Churches is sponsoring a 25-mile walk for UNICEF and you are asked to participate—and get your neighbors to sponsor you.

_____ *Public prayers:* you are asked to say the opening prayer at the Thanksgiving Day football game in front of the whole community.

GOING DEEPER

How would you describe today's issues? *(Read the Scripture passage. Then go back to the list of issues and jot the following symbols beside the appropriate items.)*

↑ issues that have become more important to you since joining this program

↓ issues that have become less important to you since joining this program

⊕ issues that primarily effect your own health, freedom and welfare

♂ issues that primarily effect others' health, freedom and welfare

✗ issues in which you feel a Christian should not get involved

℘ issues in which you feel your parents would get involved

OVERTIME CHALLENGE

1. The issues that seem to get me stirred up are ones that *(circle one in each category):*
   a. threaten my   threaten the lives
      own life or   or interests of
      interests . . . . others
   b. involve physical   involve spiritual
      health and   health and
      well-being . . . . well-being
   c. my friends are   my family is
      concerned about . concerned about

2. I am more likely to get involved in an issue if *(circle two):*
   a. everybody is
   b. it doesn't hurt my popularity
   c. there is a personal principle involved
   d. there is one close friend to support me
   e. I feel I can personally make a difference
   f. I feel this is what Christ would do
   g.

3. As far as being the "salt for all mankind" and "the light for the whole world" that Jesus talked about, I feel I am right now *(circle one):*
   a. still suiting up
   b. waiting for the game to start
   c. playing defense only
   d. in the game, but
   e. needing someone to run interference for me
   f. giving it everything I've got

Going Deeper / 4's / 15 min.
Stay with your group of 4 and share Going Deeper in the questionnaire. Start with the first symbol and let everyone explain where he placed this symbol and why. Then go around on the next symbol, etc. *(Take a moment and explain where you placed the first symbol and why. Set the pace for openness and honesty.)*

Overtime Challenge / 2's or 8's / 15 min.

(You will have to decide if there is time to share the Overtime Challenge and, if so, whether to use groups of 2 or 8. If time is limited, use 2's. If there is plenty of time, have the foursomes double up— to make the same groups of 8 as in previous sessions.)

Take the first question and go around your group, letting each person explain his choice. Then go around on the second question, etc. *(Take a moment and share your choices on the first question. Be painfully honest! Your example will set the pace.)*

Close-out

In each group, gather together in a football huddle—with your arms over each other's shoulders. *(While everyone is in a huddle, say something like: "Thank you, God, for giving us your light, and for the challenge of passing this light to our world. Amen." Ask everyone to write his name in his book. Then collect the books.)*

YOUR TURNING POINTS

Objective: To examine the major turning points in your life in the light of the parable of the Prodigal Son, and to use your results as the basis for a sharing experience.

PROCEDURE

The instructions are given in the words you can use in leading the group.

Silent Preparation / 5 to 10 min.

Turn to page 24 in your player's book and fill out the questionnaire.

Warm-up / 2's / 10 min.

Get together with one other person from your group of 8 and explain the three turning points in your life. *(Show your book to the entire group and explain the three turning points in your life. Go into detail about the reason why you selected one particular experience. Your example will set the pace for everyone. Ask the groups to proceed. After 10 minutes call time and move on.)*

THE PARABLE OF THE PRODIGAL SON

Jesus went on to say, "There was a man who had two sons. The younger one said to him, 'Father, give me now my share of the property.' So the man divided the property between his two sons. After a few days the younger son sold his part of the property and left home with the money.

He went to a country far away, where he wasted his money in reckless living. He spent everything he had. Then a severe famine spread over that country, and he was left without a thing. So he went to work for one of the citizens of that country, who sent him out to his farm to take care of the pigs. He wished he could fill himself with the bean pods the pigs ate, but no one gave him anything to eat.

At last he came to his senses and said, 'All my father's hired workers have more than they can eat, and here I am, about to starve! I will get up and go to my father and say, "Father, I have sinned against God and against you. I am no longer fit to be called your son; treat me as one of your hired workers."' So he got up and started back to his father.

"He was still a long way from home when his father saw him; his heart was filled with pity and he ran, threw his arms around his son, and kissed

him. 'Father,' the son said, 'I have sinned against God and against you. I am no longer fit to be called your son.'

But the father called his servants: 'Hurry!' he said. 'Bring the best robe and put it on him. Put a ring on his finger and shoes on his feet. Then go get the prize calf and kill it, and let us celebrate with a feast! Because this son of mine was dead, but now he is alive; he was lost, but now he has been found.' And so the feasting began."

LUKE 15:11-24 GNFMM

WARM-UP

Thinking over your life, what three times did an event or experience cause a major change in your life, lifestyle or values? *(Assume for a moment that the line below represents your life—from birth to now. Working backward from Right Now, put three dots on the line to represent the three major turning points in your life. Jot a word or two above each dot to describe the experience. For instance: (1) at age 16, divorce of my parents; (2) at age 13, my confirmation; (3) at age 11, death of my little brother. A turning point can be anything that radically affected your life and/or values—for good or bad.)*

BIRTH   RIGHT NOW

GOING DEEPER

Read over the Scripture passage and consider the turning points in the younger son's life. *(Put three symbols on the line below to indicate three kinds of changes in the life of the Prodigal Son.)*

V for the time or times when his values changed

E for the time or times when his emotions (inner feelings) changed

R for the time or times when his relations with his father changed

AT HOME	IN FAR COUNTRY			BACK HOME	
Asks father for his inheritance.	Wastes his money in reckless living.	Broke, lives with pigs.	Starving, decides to go home.	Father runs to meet him.	Party for son.

OVERTIME CHALLENGE

1. If I could compare my life to the parable of the Prodigal Son, I would be *(circle one in each category):*
   a. rebelling against the values of my home . . . .
   living in harmony with the values of my home
   b. wasting the inheritance of my family . . . . . .
   appreciating the inheritance of my family
   c. living with low values . . . .
   living up to the highest values I know
   d. in relationship with my parents . . . .
   out of relationship with my parents
   e. mostly in a far country spiritually . . . . . .
   mostly back at home spiritually
   f. feeling that I've blown it . . . .
   feeling that I've found it

2. Up to this point, my life has been *(circle two):*
   a. purposeful
   b. goofing off
   c. like a yo-yo
   d. steady
   e. meaningless
   f. disappointing
   g. waiting for the game to start
   h. beautiful
   i. OK, but...

Going Deeper / 4's / 10 min.

With your partner get together with two others from your group of 8 and explain where you put the V's, E's and R's for the Prodigal Son. *(Explain to everyone where you placed the V's. Be specific about your reasons. Call time after 10 minutes and move on.)*

Overtime Challenge / 4's or 8's / 15 min.

(Decide if there is time to share the Overtime Challenge and, if so, whether to use groups of 4 or 8. If the time is limited, use the same 4's. If there is plenty of time, use the groups of 8 that have been together before.)

Take the first question and go around your group, letting each person explain his choices. Then go around on the second question. *(Take a moment and share your choices on the first question. Be painfully honest. Your example will set the pace for the groups to follow.)*

Close-out

In each group, stand together in a close circle—with your arms over each other's shoulders. *(Pray briefly, saying something like: "Thank you, God, for the Prodigal Son and for the hope he gives to every one of us when we blow it. Amen." Be sure everyone has his name on his book. Collect all the books.)*

TOUGH CALLS

Objective: To examine your responses in conflict situations in the light of the parable of the Unforgiving Servant, and to use your results as the basis for a sharing experience.

PROCEDURE

The instructions are given in the words you can use in leading the group.

Silent Preparation / 5 to 10 min.

Turn to page 24 in your player's book and fill out the questionnaire.

Warm-up / 2's / 10 min.

Get together with one other person from your group of 8 and share the Warm-up—one situation at a time. *(Explain your choice for the first situation and set the pace for candor and honesty. Remember, your example will set the tone for the whole session. After 10 minutes call time and move on.)*

WARM-UP

Here are a series of true-to-life situations that ask for a moral decision on your part. *(Read over each situation and indicate what you would do.)*

1. The guy next to you in class never studies. It's exam time and he wants to cheat off your paper. He'll flunk if you don't let him. What do you do?
   a. let him copy
   b. tell the teacher
   c. cover your paper
   d. quietly tell him your feelings about cheating
   e. refuse him but offer to help him study for the next exam

2. You want to break up with the person you have been going with for

THE PARABLE OF THE UNFORGIVING SERVANT

Then Peter came to Jesus and asked, "Lord, how many times can my brother sin against me and I have to forgive him? Seven times?"

"No, not seven times," answered Jesus, "but seventy times seven. Because the Kingdom of heaven is like a king who decided to check on his servants' accounts. He had just begun to do so when one of them was brought in who owed him millions of dollars. The servant did not have enough to pay his debt, so his master ordered him to be sold as a slave, with his wife and his children and all that he had, in order to pay the debt.

"The servant fell on his knees before his master. 'Be patient with me,' he begged, 'and I will pay you everything!' The master felt sorry for him, so he forgave him the debt and let him go.

"The man went out and met one of his fellow servants who owed him a few dollars. He grabbed him and started choking him. 'Pay back what you owe me!' he said. His fellow servant fell down and begged him, 'Be patient with me and I will pay you back!' But he would not; instead, he had him thrown into jail until he should pay the debt. ...The master was very angry, and he sent the servant to jail to be punished until he should pay back the whole amount."

And Jesus concluded, "That is how my Father in heaven will treat you if you do not forgive your brother, every one of you, from your heart."

MATTHEW 18:21-35 GNFMM

two years. What would you do?
a. write a letter
b. call the person on the phone
c. speak to the person face to face
d. put off doing anything
e. wait for the person to ask what's wrong

3. Your black friend is conspicuously omitted from a social given by the popular crowd you want to get in with. What would you do?
a. call and ask why
b. refuse to go and explain why
c. refuse but make some other excuse
d. ignore the problem and go
e. call your friend and ask advice
f. crash the party with your friend

4. You are the coach of a team that is tied for the championship. Before the final and deciding game, you learn that one of the "stars" has broken training rules. What would you do?
a. suspend the kid immediately
b. wait until after the game and suspend the kid
c. make an exception for the sake of the team
d. play as though you never heard about it
e. ask the team to decide for you
f. ask the kid to set his own punishment

5. You are the parents of a daughter who was just expelled from school for cutting class. What would you do?
a. give her a stern lecture
b. persuade the principal to accept her back in school
c. complain to the school board that the rules are too strict
d. threaten her with juvenile court
e. find out why she was cutting class
f. get her away from friends who influence her
g. offer her some incentive for attending class
h. don't do anything for her; let her work it out
i. try to deepen your relationship with her and hope for the best

6. While your parents are each drinking a stiff highball, they tell you to stay away from drugs. What do you do?
a. tell them to practice what they preach
b. remain silent but angry
c. refuse to let it bother you
d. figure it is legal for them to drink and illegal for you to take drugs
e. discuss the situation rationally
f. blow up and leave the room
g. laugh at them
h. accept the fact that there are many contradictions in life
i. listen with respect, but say nothing either way

GOING DEEPER

Who or what strongly influenced your decisions in the Warm-up? *(Read over the Scripture passage and then go back to the choices that you marked and add a symbol to indicate who or what influenced you.)*

✝ my commitment to Jesus Christ
⌂ my training at home
F my outside friends
O my participation in this support group

OVERTIME CHALLENGE

1. I find it easier to *(circle one in each category)*:
a. forgive . . . . ask for forgiveness
b. forgive my   forgive my
   friends . . . . family
c. forgive   forgive
   myself . . . . someone else

2. In making moral decisions I tend to *(put a dot someplace between the words)*:
a. follow   rely on my
   the crowd _____ own judgment
b. listen to   listen to
   my parents _____ my friends
c. stick to my   waver back
   convictions _____ and forth

3. Since being in this program my moral principles have changed *(circle one)*:
a. a lot   c. very little
b. some   d. not at all

4. In making moral decisions my commitment to Jesus Christ seems to have *(circle one)*:
a. a great deal of influence
b. some influence
c. very little influence
d. not as much as I would like

Going Deeper/4's/10 min.

With your partner get together with two others from your group of 8 and explain where you put the symbols indicating who or what influenced your choices. *(Take the first symbol and explain where you placed it and why. Be painfully honest! Call time after 10 minutes and move on.)*

Overtime Challenge / 4's or 8's / 15 min.

(You will have to decide if there is time to share the Overtime Challenge and, if so, whether to use groups of 4 or 8. If time is limited, use the same 4's. If there is plenty of time, ask the groups of 8 that have been together before to regather.)

Take the first question and go around your group, letting each person explain his choices. Then go around on the second question, etc. *(Take a moment and share your choices for the first question.)*

Close-out

In each group, gather together in a football huddle—with your arms over each other's shoulders. *(While in the huddles, say something like: "Thank you, God, for the chance to be on your team. Amen." Collect the books.)*

TIME OUT FOR CHECKING STRATEGY

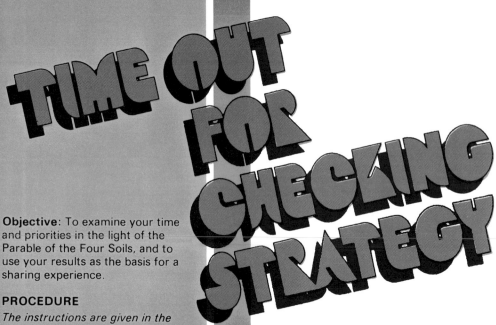

Objective: To examine your time and priorities in the light of the Parable of the Four Soils, and to use your results as the basis for a sharing experience.

PROCEDURE

The instructions are given in the words you can use in leading the group.

Silent Preparation / 5 to 10 min.
Turn to page 24 in your player's book and fill out the questionnaire.

Warm-up / 2's / 5 min.
Get together with one other person from your group of 8 and share the Warm-up—how you spend your spare time. *(Explain how your spare time is spent. Be painfully honest. Your example will set the pace for the others. After 5 minutes call time and move on.)*

Going Deeper / 4's / 15 min.
With your partner get together with 2 others to form a group of 4. Explain the Going Deeper part of the questionnaire—your life at the beginning of the program and your life now. *(Explain the soils in your*

WARM-UP

How much of your spare time is spent in the following areas? *(Jot down a percentage for each item on the list below, making a total of 100%. For instance, reading for pleasure 5%; TV 34%; dating 20%, etc.)*

MY SPARE TIME

_____ reading for pleasure
_____ TV
_____ dating/social life
_____ physical conditioning/sports
_____ family
_____ goofing off with friends
_____ spiritual development
_____ studying/homework
_____ service/helping others
100%

THE PARABLE OF THE SOWER

"Listen! There was a man who went out to sow. As he scattered the seed in the field, some of it fell along the path, and the birds came and ate it up. Some of it fell on rocky ground, where there was little soil. The seeds soon sprouted, because the soil wasn't deep. Then when the sun came up it burned the young plants, and because the roots had not grown deep enough the plants soon dried up. Some of the seed fell among thorns, which grew up and choked the plants, and they didn't bear grain. But some seeds fell in good soil, and the plants sprouted, grew, and bore grain: some had thirty grains, others sixty, and others one hundred."

MARK 4:3-8 GNFMM

FOUR CHARACTERS AND THEIR LIFESTYLES

"On-the-go Goofus" *(seed along the path).* His lifestyle: hectic, always running; into everything; everybody's friend; travels with the "in" crowd on the popular, crowded asphalt paths where nothing has time to take root and grow. *Result:* the good seed is quickly destroyed.

0% ——————————— 100%

"Shallow Sam" *(seed on rocky ground).* His lifestyle: on and off, up and down like a yo-yo; great promise; on everybody's pre-season list but loses interest when the going gets tough; Mr. Good Intentions who never lives up to expectations. *Result:* the good seed withers as the heat increases.

0% ——————————— 100%

"Choke Charlie" *(seed among thorns).* His lifestyle: overcrowded, caught in a thicket of conflicting priorities that sap the time and energy; no time to weed out the unimportant. *Result:* the weeds overtake the good seed and strangle the life out of the plant.

0% ——————————— 100%

"Clutch Clarence" *(seed in good soil).* His lifestyle: purposeful; uncluttered; he knows what he wants to do and makes time for it; the unimportant is weeded out of the schedule. *Result:* the good seed has time to take root and mature and bear fruit to the fullest.

0% ——————————— 100%

GOING DEEPER

1. To represent the kinds of people who are given the "seed," here are four types: (1) On-the-go Goofus, (2) Shallow Sam, (3) Choke Charlie and (4) Clutch Clarence. *(Read the Scripture and the descriptions of the four lifestyles. Under each character, put two marks on the percentage line to indicate how much of your time you are like him. For instance, for On-the-go Goofus, you might put an X in the middle to represent 50% of your time when you started this program; and an O nearer 0% to represent 30% of your time right now.)*

X you at the beginning of this program
O you right now

OVERTIME CHALLENGE

What percentage of time do you spend each day doing things that are the following? *(Fill in the percentages.)*
____ % unnecessary (wasted)
____ % necessary but unexciting (boring)
____ % exciting but not lasting (unproductive)
____ % exciting and productive (lasting)

life before and now. Again, be honest. Be honest. Then turn the groups of 4 loose. After 10 minutes call time and move on.)

Overtime Challenge / 4's or 8's / 15 min.

(You will have to decide if there is time to share the Overtime Challenge and, if so, whether to use groups of 4 or 8. If time is limited, use groups of 4. If there is plenty of time, ask the groups of 4 to double up to make the same groups of 8 that have been together before.)

Go around and let everyone explain the Overtime Challenge—how he would describe the largest percentage of his time—and how he feels about it. If there is time, go around again and share one thing this exercise has taught you about your time and your life. *(Take a moment and explain what you have discovered in this exercise about yourself—and what you plan to do about it.)*

Close-out

In each group, gather together in a football huddle—with your arms over each other's shoulders. *(While everyone is in a huddle, say something like: "Thank you, God, for the challenge to live every day to the fullest—for your glory. Amen." Collect the books.)*

Objective: To examine your growth areas in the light of the parable of the Mustard Seed, and to use your results as a basis for a sharing experience.

PROCEDURE
The instructions are given in the words you can use in leading the group.

Silent Preparation / 5 to 10 min.
(Ask the groups of 8 who have been together up to now in the program to sit together in silence while filling out the questionnaire. This will help them when they start working on the Overtime Challenge.)
   Turn to page 26 in your player's book and fill out the questionnaire.

Warm-up / 2's / 5 min.
Get together with one other person from your group of 8 and share how you feel about the various areas of your life. *(Explain to the group the mark you put on the first line concerning your*

WARM-UP

How do you feel about the various areas of your life? Here are a series of lines to represent your feelings. *(Put two marks on each line. For instance, on the first line you might put the O close to "kinda blah" because you were really feeling down when you joined this* group. And you might put the X in the middle because right now you are sort of in between "blah" and "great.")*

◯ **where you were at the beginning of this program.**

✗ **where you are right now.**

ABOUT MYSELF, I'M FEELING
kinda blah _____ great

ABOUT MY FUTURE
scared _____ excited

ABOUT MY SCHOOL OR WORK
bummer _____ super

ABOUT MY CHURCH
indifference _____ involvement

ABOUT MY GROUP
I could tell _____ I could tell
them nothing   them anything

THE PARABLE OF THE MUSTARD SEED

"What shall we say the Kingdom of God is like?" asked Jesus. "What parable shall we use to explain it? It is like a mustard seed, the smallest seed in the world. A man takes it and plants it in the ground; after a while it grows up and becomes the biggest of all plants. It puts out such large branches that the birds come and make their nests in its shade."

MARK 4:30-32 GNFMM

GOING DEEPER

Read over the Scripture passage and consider how you would describe your spiritual growth. *(On the line put an O* to indicate where you were at the beginning of this program, an X to indicate where you are right now.)*

IN MY RELATIONSHIP WITH JESUS CHRIST

very cold _____ very warm

IN MY UNDERSTANDING OF GOD'S WILL FOR MY LIFE

huh? _____ right on

IN MY PRIVATE STUDY OF SCRIPTURE AND PRAYER

ouch _____ whoopee

IN DEALING WITH MY HANGUPS

woe is me _____ oh, yes!

OVERTIME CHALLENGE

What improvement or growth have you noticed in the members of your group? The series of circles are to represent them. *(Jot a name in each circle. Beside each name write down one thing or area in which you have recognized changes for the positive. For instance, beside Tom's name you might jot down "patience," because he has had more patience getting out the school paper than ever before. For Debbie you might put "consistency," because she has shown a lot of improvement in matching her actions to her words.)*

feelings about yourself. Be honest. Your example will set the pace for their sharing. Then turn them loose for 5 minutes.)*

Going Deeper / 4's / 10 min.

With your partner get together with two others from your group of 8, making a group of 4. Then give everyone a chance to explain the Going Deeper part of the questtionnaire. *(Be the first to share and let your openness and honesty be an example for everyone to follow.)*

Overtime Challenge

Regather your group of 8. Ask one person to remain silent while the others, one at a time, explain the areas where they have observed the greatest growth or improvement in this person. Go around the group until everyone has been covered. *(Pick out someone in a group near you and explain an area in his life where you have observed real growth. It may be in an attitude, a skill or a change in behavior. Be genuine in your affirmation. Your example will set the pace for the group.)*

Close-out

In each group, stand together in a close circle—with your arms over each other's shoulders. *(Pray something like: "Thank you, God, for the growth we have experienced in each of our lives and together as a group. Amen." Collect all the books.)*

GETTING WHAT THEY DESERVE

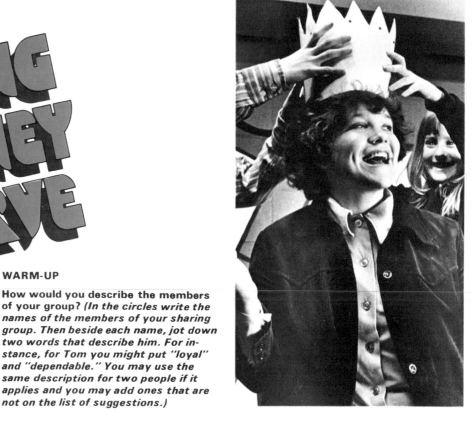

Objective: To affirm the qualities you have observed in one another in the light of the parable of the Final Judgment, and to use your results as a basis for a beautiful affirmation experience.

PROCEDURE

The instructions are given in the words you can use in leading the group.

Silent Preparation / 5 to 10 min.

(Ask the groups of 8 who have been together up to now in the program to sit together while filling out the questionnaire.)

Turn to page 26 in your player's book and fill out the questionnaire.

Warm-up / 8's / 10 min.

Ask one person in your group of 8 to remain quiet while the others

WARM-UP

How would you describe the members of your group? *(In the circles write the names of the members of your sharing group. Then beside each name, jot down two words that describe him. For instance, for Tom you might put "loyal" and "dependable." You may use the same description for two people if it applies and you may add ones that are not on the list of suggestions.)*

THE FINAL JUDGMENT OF SHEEP AND GOATS

"When the Son of Man comes as King, and all the angels with him, he will sit on his royal throne, and all the earth's people will be gathered before him. Then he will divide them into two groups, just as a shepherd separates the sheep from the goats: he will put the sheep at his right and the goats at his left.

"Then the King will say to the people on his right, 'You that are blessed by my Father: come! Come and receive the kingdom which has been prepared for you ever since the creation of the world. I was hungry and you fed me, thirsty and you gave me drink; I was a stranger and you received me in your homes, naked and you clothed me; I was sick and you took care of me, in prison and you visited me.'

"The righteous will then answer him, 'When, Lord, did we ever see you hungry and feed you, or thirsty and give you drink? When did we ever see you a stranger and welcome you in our homes, or naked and clothe you? When did we ever see you sick or in prison, and visit you?'

"The King will answer back, 'I tell you, indeed, whenever you did this for one of the least important of these brothers of mine, you did it for me!'"

MATTHEW 25:31-40 GNFMM

150

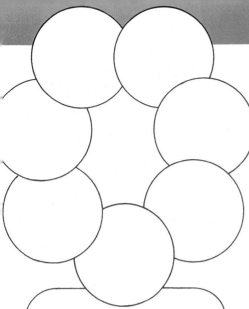

loyal (sticks up for friends)
open-minded (open to new ideas)
enterprising (adventurous)
decisive (initiates action)
conscientious (industrious)
cheerful (happy and contented)
sensitive (aware of others)
gentle (tender and kind)
self-confident (self-assured)
self-controlled (stable)
persevering (strong)
caring (warm)
friendly (smiles easily)
forgiving (no grudges)
well-organized (plans sufficiently)
disciplined (consistent)
imaginative (visionary)
patient (serene)
fun-loving (sense of humor)

GOING DEEPER

How have the members of the group contributed to your life in these sessions? *(Read the Scripture passage. Then read the following "caring" list and jot down the names of each one in your sharing group next to the particular item he has contributed to your life. For instance, you might put Cindy's name next to: "I was a stranger and you received me," because it was Cindy who went out of her way to make you feel welcome in this group.)*

_____ I WAS HUNGRY AND YOU FED ME: Your sharing of yourself in this group has caused me to grow.

_____ I WAS THIRSTY AND YOU GAVE ME DRINK: Your spiritual life and devotion to God has helped me find spiritual refreshment.

_____ I WAS A STRANGER AND YOU RECEIVED ME: Your welcome when I came made me feel at home.

_____ I WAS NAKED AND YOU CLOTHED ME: Your own caring when I felt naked and alone made me feel that somebody understands me.

_____ I WAS SICK AND YOU TOOK CARE OF ME: Your reaching out to me when I was really down caused me to feel better and whole again.

_____ I WAS IN PRISON AND YOU VISITED ME: Your ministry to me when I shared some of my hangups released me from the bondage.

OVERTIME CHALLENGE

1. It is harder for me to *(circle one in each category)*:
   a. give a compliment . . . . receive a compliment
   b. see the good in others . . . . see the good in myself
   c. believe I am OK . . . . believe you are OK

2. When I get a compliment, I *(circle two)*:
   a. don't know what to do
   b. wonder what is coming next
   c. try to pass it off
   d. blush
   e. am deeply touched
   f. try harder than ever
   g. feel awkward and embarrassed
   h. believe in myself more
   i. accept it with no problem

3. My support group in this program has helped me to: *(choose three and rank 1, 2, 3)*:
   _____ believe in myself more
   _____ feel it is OK to have problems
   _____ accept God's love and forgiveness
   _____ show my feelings
   _____ respond when someone else has a need
   _____ say I'm sorry
   _____ compliment others more
   _____ discover what love is all about

go around and explain the two qualities they have observed in his life. Then ask another person to sit in silence while the others explain the qualities they chose for this person, etc., until you have covered everyone in your group. *(Name one person and explain two special qualities you have observed in his life. Be genuine in your praise. Your example will set the pace for the groups to follow. Then turn the groups loose. After 10 to 15 minutes call time and move on.)*

Going Deeper/8's/10 min.

Stay with your group of 8 and repeat the same procedure with the Going Deeper part of the questionnaire. Ask one person to sit in silence while the others explain the "caring" he has given them. Then go on to another person and repeat the process, until everyone in your group has been covered. *(Choose one person and explain the phrase you would use to explain his contribution to your life and group.)*

Overtime Challenge / 2's / 15 min.

(You will have to decide if there is time to cover the Overtime Challenge.)

Divide into pairs and go over the Overtime Challenge with your partner—one question at a time. *(Explain how you would answer the first question.)*

Close-out

Regather your group of 8 and form a football huddle. *(While everyone is in a huddle, say something like: "Thank you, God, for the wonderful presence of your love. Amen." Pick up all of the books.)*

SCOUTING REPORT

Objective: To affirm the strengths you see in each other, and to let each person explain two areas that need work, based on the parable of the Tree and its Fruit.

PROCEDURE

The instructions are given in the words you can use in leading the group.

Silent Preparation / 5 to 10 min.

(Ask each group of 8 who has been together up to now in the program to sit together while filling out the questionnaire.)

Turn to page 26 in your player's book and fill out the questionnaire.

Warm-up / 2's / 5 min.

Get together with one other person from your group of 8 and share the Warm-up part of your questionnaire—two qualities in which you feel you excel from each category. *(Share the two qualities you checked. Be honest. Your*

WARM-UP

Here is a list of qualities or strengths. There are three categories. *(In each category check your two best points.)*

MENTAL *(check two)*
- intelligence
- creativity
- sense of humor
- discernment
- reasonableness
- good memory
- alertness
- understanding
- perceptivity
- comprehension

EMOTIONAL *(check two)*
- warmth
- self-confidence
- stick-ability
- consistency
- endurance
- inspiration
- stability
- dependability
- sensitivity
- cheerfulness
- patience
- enthusiasm
- supportive
- coolness

SPIRITUAL *(check two)*
- dedication
- discipline
- leadership
- purity
- humility
- compassion
- openness
- honesty
- hopefulness
- Bible info
- self-control
- hope

GOING DEEPER

In what qualities do you feel the members of your group are particularly strong? *(Read the Scripture passage. Then write in the circles the names of the other members of your group. Beside each name write three qualities —one from each category—in which you feel this person excels. You may use the same quality for more than one person if it fits.)*

A TREE AND ITS FRUIT

"A healthy tree does not bear bad fruit, nor does a poor tree bear good fruit. Every tree is known by the fruit it bears; you do not pick figs from thorn bushes, or gather grapes from bramble bushes. A good man brings good out of the treasure of good things in his heart; a bad man brings bad out of his treasure of bad things. For a man's mouth speaks what his heart is full of."

LUKE 6:43-45 GNFMM

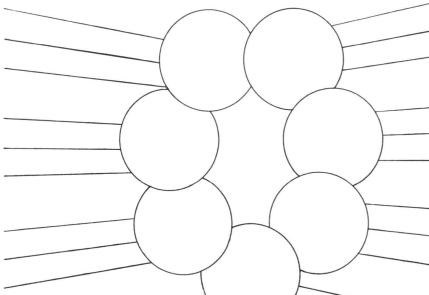

OVERTIME CHALLENGE

Where is the fruit "bad" in your life?
(Check two areas that need to change for the good.)
___ bad temper
___ bad habits
___ bad sportsmanship
___ bad attitude at home

___ bad self-image
___ bad language
___ bad thoughts
___ bad study habits
___ bad training habits
___ bad attitude on the job
___ bad attitude at school

example will set the pace for sharing. After 5 minutes call time and move on.)

Going Deeper / 8's / 15 min.

Get together with your group of 8 and share the Going Deeper part of your questionnaire. Ask one person in your group to remain quiet while the others go around and explain the three qualities they selected for him. Then ask another person to sit in silence while the other seven explain their qualities for him, etc., until you have covered everyone. *(Choose one person and explain the three qualities you would select for this person. Be genuine as well as honest. Then have the groups proceed. After 15 minutes call time and move on.)*

Overtime Challenge / 4's / 15 min.

Divide into groups of 4 and give everyone a chance to explain the two areas in his life where he needs to change. *(Explain your two areas. Again, set the pace for honesty.)*

Close-out

Get together and form a football huddle. *(While everyone is in a huddle, say something like: "Thank you, God, for the help you give us through each other—to live your kind of life. Amen." Collect the books.)*

PLAY TO WIN

Objective: To examine your philosophy of life in the light of the parable of the Talents, and to use your results as a basis for a sharing experience.

PROCEDURE

The instructions are given in the words you can use in leading the group.

Silent Preparation / 5 to 10 min.
Turn to page 28 in your player's book and fill out the questionnaire.

154

WARM-UP

Think back in your life to the all-day Monopoly games and see what your strategy for winning at Monopoly will tell you about your lifestyle.
1. **When I play Monopoly, I usually (circle two):**
   a. get in a fight
   b. give up before the game is over
   c. forget all about being kind and generous
   d. feel sorry for the ones who are losing and help them out
   e. hang in until the bitter end
   f. cheat
   g. get bored and quit

2. **My advice for anyone who wants to win at Monopoly is (choose one):**
   a. Go for broke! Buy everything you land on. Mortgage and swap and sacrifice to get a monopoly. Then risk everything on that monopoly and hang on for the long-run payoff.
   b. Hang loose! Buy the best properties you land on, but hedge your bets with a little caution. Hold back until you see which way the game is going. Then make your move.
   c. Play it safe! Buy only the quick return properties like the utilities and railroads. Put the rest into savings for a rainy day. You don't want to get caught without enough money to pay your obligations.

3. **If I could compare my own philosophy of life to Monopoly, I would say a successful player is one who (circle one):**
   a. wins the game, period!
   b. plays to win, whether he wins or not
   c. has a good time whether he wins or not
   d. learns how to adapt to losing

GOING DEEPER

Read over the Scripture passage and complete the following questions.

1. **If the man who was given one bag of gold were playing soccer, he would probably (circle one):**
   a. immediately charge the man with the ball
   b. wait for the right chance, then charge the man with the ball
   c. wait for the man with the ball to come to him

2. **I feel the man with one bag of gold dug a hole in the ground and hid the money because (circle one):**
   a. he lacked ambition
   b. he was afraid of making a mistake
   c. he was hurt because he was not given as much as the others
   d. he felt insecure and inadequate
   e. he had a defeatist attitude

3. **For the man with one bag of gold, I feel a little (circle one):**
   a. pity   d. identity
   b. sympathy   e. patience
   c. regret   f. remorse

OVERTIME CHALLENGE

How do you deal with the various twists and turns of your life? *(Put a dot on each line somewhere between the two extremes.)*

IN TAKING RISKS, I
never take a risk _____ try anything once

IN LEADING INTO UNCHARTED WATERS, I
am the last to volunteer _____ jump at the chance

IN TOUGH SITUATIONS, I
collapse under pressure _____ hang in all the way

IN LONG-RANGE ENDURANCE, I
tire easily _____ rise to the occasion

THE PARABLE OF THE THREE TALENTS

"It will be like a man who was about to leave home on a trip; he called his servants and put them in charge of his property. He gave to each one according to his ability: to one he gave five thousand dollars, to the other two thousand dollars, and to the other one thousand dollars. Then he left on his trip.

"The servant who had received five thousand dollars went at once and invested his money and earned another five thousand dollars. In the same way the servant who received two thousand dollars earned another two thousand dollars. But the servant who received one thousand dollars went off, dug a hole in the ground, and hid his master's money.

"After a long time the master of those servants came back and settled accounts with them. The servant who had received five thousand dollars came in and handed over the other five thousand dollars...

"Then the servant who had been given two thousand dollars came in and said, 'You gave me two thousand dollars, sir. Look! Here are another two thousand dollars that I have earned.'...

"Then the servant who had received one thousand dollars came in and said. 'Sir, I know you are a hard man; you reap harvests where you did not plant, and gather crops where you did not scatter seed. I was afraid, so I went off and hid your money in the ground. Look! Here is what belongs to you.'

"'You bad and lazy servant!' his master said. 'You knew, did you, that I reap harvests where I did not plant, and gather crops where I did not scatter seed? Well, then, you should have deposited my money in the bank, and I would have received it all back with interest when I returned. Now, take the money away from him and give it to the one who has ten thousand dollars. For to everyone who has, even more will be given, and he will have more than enough; but the one who has nothing, even the little he has will be taken away from him. As for this useless servant—throw him outside in the darkness; there he will cry and gnash his teeth.'"

MATTHEW 25:14-30 GNFMM

Warm-up / 4's / 10 min.
Get together with three others from your group of 8 to form a group of 4. Share your answers to the Monopoly exercise—one point at a time around your group. *(Explain your two choices for the first point. Set the tone for good-natured fun. Then turn the group loose. After 10 minutes call time and move on.)*

Going Deeper / 4's / 10 min.
Stay with your group of 4 and share your answers to Going Deeper in the questionnaire—one point at a time around your group. *(Explain to everyone how you would complete the first sentence.)*

Overtime Challenge / 2's or 8's / 15 min.
(If time is limited, have the groups divide into twos so all can have an opportunity to participate and share. If there is plenty of time, have the groups of 8 regather.) Share your answers to the Overtime Challenge with one another. *(Show where you would put a dot on the first line—and explain why. Then turn them loose.)*

Close-out
In each group, stand together in a close circle—with your arms over each other's shoulders *(Pray briefly, including something like: "Thank you, God, for giving us life and the chance to go all the way with you. Amen." Collect the books.)*

Objective: To examine your life goals in light of the parable of the Rich Fool.

PROCEDURE

The instructions are given in the words you can use in leading the group.

Silent Preparation / 5 to 10 min.
Turn to page 28 in your player's book and fill out the questionnaire.

Warm-up / 4's / 10 min.
Get together with 3 others from your group of 8 and form a group of 4. Share your Warm-up in the questionnaire—the goals you have accomplished and the future goals for your life. *(Take a moment and explain your number 1 accomplishment up to now and several things on your list of future goals. Be painfully honest. Your example will set the pace for the groups to follow.)*

WARM-UP

1. What are your life goals? Here is a line to show your life span. *(At the left end, jot down the year of your*

BIRTH

birth. On the right end write down the year and age you will be at the end of your life. Then put an X for now, along with today's date and your age.

2. Thinking about the time represented by my lifeline up to this point in my life, I feel I have already accomplished the following *(rank top three 1, 2, 3):*
   - ____ a lot of friends
   - ____ good grades
   - ____ good mental attitude
   - ____ settled down in life
   - ____ a lot of fun
   - ____ thought through my values
   - ____ developed my physical body
   - ____ developed my spiritual life
   - ____ made some money
   - ____ practically nothing

3. As I think about my future, my most important priorities are *(rank 1 to 14):*
   - ____ pleasure/fun
   - ____ contentment/inner peace
   - ____ recognition/achievement
   - ____ freedom/opportunity
   - ____ sexual fulfillment
   - ____ self-respect/integrity
   - ____ excitement/adventure
   - ____ happiness/feeling good
   - ____ spiritual fulfillment
   - ____ personal satisfaction
   - ____ money/all the comforts of life
   - ____ deep relationships
   - ____ good health
   - ____ security/guaranteed income

◯ (DEATH)

GOING DEEPER

How would you describe your goals for the future? *(Read over the Scripture passage. Then go back to your list of future goals and put symbols in the margin where they apply.)*

P   probably number 1 on my parent's list

F   probably number 1 on most of my friends' lists

†   was number 1 on my list five years ago

↓   has gone down in value to me most recently

↑   has gone up in value to me most recently

C   is the thing I would like to be number 1 on my children's lists

OVERTIME CHALLENGE

1. When it comes to my life goals, I am *(circle one in each category)*:
   a. pretty definite . . . . pretty confused
   b. closer to my friends' goals . . . . closer to my parents'
   c. rather content . . . . rather disturbed

2. Since I joined this support group, my life goals have *(circle one)*:
   a. come into focus
   b. changed
   c. blurred
   d. stayed about the same

3. My commitment to Jesus Christ has influenced my life goals *(circle one)*:
   a. a lot
   b. a little
   c. not as much as I would like
   d. not at all

THE PARABLE OF THE RICH FOOL

A man in the crowd said to him, "Teacher, tell my brother to divide with me the property our father left us."

Jesus answered him, "Man, who gave me the right to judge, or to divide the property between you two?" And he went on to say to them all, "Watch out, and guard yourselves from all kinds of greed; because a man's true life is not made up of the things he owns, no matter how rich he may be."

Then Jesus told them this parable, "A rich man had land which bore good crops. He began to think to himself, 'I don't have a place to keep all my crops. What can I do? This is what I will do,' he told himself; 'I will tear my barns down and build bigger ones, where I will store the grain and all my other goods. Then I will say to myself: Lucky man! You have all the good things you need for many years. Take life easy, eat, drink, and enjoy yourself!'

"But God said to him, 'You fool! This very night you will have to give up your life; then who will get all these things you have kept for yourself?'"

And Jesus concluded, "This is how it is with those who pile up riches for themselves but are not rich in God's sight."

LUKE 12:13-21 GNFMM

Going Deeper/4's/10 min.

Stay with your group of 4 and share your answers to Going Deeper. Take the first symbol and let everyone explain where he put the P on his list. Then go around a second time on the F, etc., until you have covered all the symbols. *(Explain to everyone where you put the P on your list. Set the pace for fairness and honesty.)*

Overtime Challenge / 2's or 8's / 15 min.

(If time is limited, divide the foursomes so the participation can be greater and the sharing deeper. If there is plenty of time, have the foursomes double up—into the same groups of 8 as in previous sessions.)

Share your answers to the Overtime Challenge with one another. *(Explain your answers to the first question. Then turn them loose.)*

Close-out

Regather your group of 8 and form a football huddle—with your arms over the shoulders of each other. *(While the groups are in huddles, say something like: "Thank you, God, for the chance to build our lives around you. Amen." Pick up the books.)*

Objective: To examine the ultimate values in your life in light of the Parable of Two House Builders, and to use the results as the basis for sharing.

PROCEDURE

The instructions are given in the words you can use in leading the group.

Silent Preparation / 5 to 10 min.
Turn to page 28 in your player's book and fill out the questionnaire.

Warm-up / 4's / 10 min.
Get together with 3 others from your group of 8. Share the Warm-up in the questionnaire—the three things that would be the easiest for you to give up and the three that would be the hardest, and why. *(Take a moment and share how you would rank your losses. Be painfully honest. Your example will set the tone for sharing.)*

WARM-UP

If a situation beyond your control came upon your life causing losses, what could you give up and still continue as a person? (Rank the following 1 to 10, starting with the easiest to give up.)
____ **my health** *(physical stamina)*
____ **my savings** *(my money, stocks and bonds)*
____ **my home** *(my house, clothes, material possessions)*
____ **my country** *(my homeland, political freedom)*
____ **my religious freedom** *(the right to worship God as I please)*
____ **my career** *(my job and the future job opportunities in my field)*
____ **my reputation** *(outside recognition, popularity)*
____ **my friends** *(close relationships)*
____ **my family** *(parents, brothers, sisters)*
____ **my self-esteem** *(sense of worth, importance)*
____ **my faith in God** *(my trust in an all-powerful, all-knowing, personal God who knows me)*

THE TWO HOUSE BUILDERS

"So then, everyone who hears these words of mine and obeys them will be like a wise man who built his house on the rock. The rain poured down, the rivers flooded over, and the winds blew hard against that house. But it did not fall, because it had been built on the rock.

"But everyone who hears these words of mine and does not obey them will be like a foolish man who built his house on the sand. The rain poured down, the rivers flooded over, the winds blew hard against that house, and it fell. What a terrible fall that was!"

MATTHEW 7:24-27 GNFMM

158

LIVING ROOM: I have my life in order; I know what I want to do; my values are well-defined; my moral principles are clear; I am feeling good about myself and my lifestyle right now.

1 2 3 4 5 6 7 8 9 10

RECREATION ROOM: I have a healthy balance in my schedule for leisure; I use my spare time purposefully—to restore my mind and spirit as well as my body. I am feeling good about my priorities and the way I use my time.

1 2 3 4 5 6 7 8 9 10

FAMILY ROOM: I have a good relationship with my family. We have learned to talk about our differences; we deal with our conflicts; we "build up" one another when "outside weather" is a problem; I am feeling good about my family and enjoy being with them.

1 2 3 4 5 6 7 8 9 10

LIBRARY ROOM: I have a balanced diet in my reading habits—for mental and spiritual stimulation as well as pleasure. I try to think for myself, to make my own decisions based on definite values and moral principles, and don't just "cave in" to the pressure of my friends.

1 2 3 4 5 6 7 8 9 10

PHYSICAL FITNESS ROOM: I try to keep in shape; to deal with flabbiness. I feel good about my manhood/womanhood and sexuality, but I do not let my sexual desires get the best of me. I can sleep nights and weather the "storms" without getting fatigued and depressed.

1 2 3 4 5 6 7 8 9 10

GUEST ROOM: I have a good relationship with my friends and schoolmates. I enjoy being with people without feeling dependent upon them. I can belong to the crowd without accepting or bowing to their values. I can stand against social pressure to conform, yet am sensitive to open the door when someone needs a little warmth.

1 2 3 4 5 6 7 8 9 10

GOING DEEPER

How would you describe the above areas of your life? Read the Scripture passage. *Then go back to your "losses" and put the following symbols next to them.)*

↑   has increased in value since joining this sharing group

↓   has decreased in value since joining this sharing group

M   will probably mean more to me in 10 years

F   I would fight to keep this at all cost

C   what I want most for my children

OVERTIME CHALLENGE

Are you ready for bad weather? Imagine that the house in the parable is *your life* and that this house has many rooms. *(Read over the list of rooms and give yourself a building inspector's rating on each room—1 being very shakey and 10 being very strong.)*

Going Deeper / 4's / 10 min.

Stay with your group of 4 and share your answers to Going Deeper. Take the first symbol and let everyone explain where he put an up arrow on your list. Then go around with the down arrow, etc., until you have covered all the symbols. *(Explain to everyone where you put the down arrow on your list and why. Set the pace for fairness and honesty.)*

Overtime Challenge / 2's or 8's / 15 min.

(If time is limited, split into groups of 2, so everyone can share. If there is plenty of time, move back into the original groups of 8.)

Go around your group and let each person explain where he marked himself on the Living Room and why. Then go around on the Recreation Room and why, etc., until the list is covered. *(Explain your markings on the first two and set the pace for sharing.)*

Close-out

Gather together in a football huddle—with your arms over each other's shoulders. *(While everyone is in a huddle, say something like: "Thank you, God, for the strength of belonging to a team of guys who are committed to your things in the world. Amen." Collect the books to have them ready for the next session.)*

Notes

Scripture Happening is another term for relational Bible study. This approach is especially useful in studying the Gospels: Matthew, Mark, Luke and John.

The exercises begin with a reading of a Scripture passage. Then the questionnaire permits the student to relate the passage to his life on three levels: (a) Warm-up —how I would have responded if I had been there (the past), (b) Going Deeper—how I respond in similar situations today (the present), and (c) Overtime Challenge—what I need to do about it (the future).

In sharing the results, the size of the support group is modified for each part of the questionnaire to encourage greater involvement and participation. Groups of two people each work best when time is short or the sharing is rather personal. Groups of four work best when shared ideas need to be discussed. Groups of eight work best for wrap-up times or affirmation exercises.

The questionnaires have been mischievously designed to grab the student at the point of his interest and walk him through the Scripture into his own life—from the past into the present. The "gut" questions are reserved for the Overtime Challenge when the groups have been together long enough to build a "trust level." Also, the questionnaires become progressively deeper.

In writing these exercises, we especially tried to help the student to examine his life and lifestyle in the light of Scripture. No attempt is made to force a person into a particular category or point of view. But every attempt is made to help the student evaluate his life and come up with his own plan of action—with the help of the support group.

Scripture Happenings

STRUCTURED SESSIONS

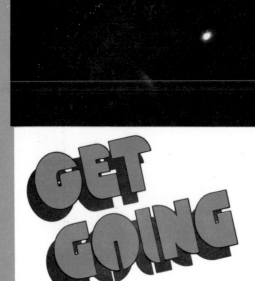

Objective: To discover how your spiritual pilgrimage and the pilgrimage of Simon Peter have points in common, and to use your insights as the basis for a sharing experience with your support group.

PROCEDURE

The instructions are given in the words you can use in leading the group.

Silent Preparation / 5 to 10 min.

Turn to page 32 in your player's book and fill out the questionnaire.

Warm-up / 2's / 5 min.

Get together with someone from your group of 8 and share what you put down in your Warm-up—one question at a time. *(Take a moment and share your answer to the first question. Then ask each twosome to share their answers to the first question with each other, etc...until they have finished all three questions or run out of time. Call time after 5 minutes and move on.)*

Going Deeper / 4's / 15 min.

With your partner get together with 2 others from your group of 8 to form a group of 4. Share your answers to Going Deeper in the questionnaire—one question at a time around your group. Take this

GET GOING

WARM-UP

1. I think Jesus told Simon Peter, *"Push the boat out further to the deep water and...let your nets down for a catch,"* in order to *(circle one):*
   a. get away from the crowd
   b. get to know Peter personally
   c. get his hook into Peter
   d. help Peter in his work in return for Peter's help
   e. demonstrate a larger principle about risk-taking
   f. show that he knew a little about fishing
   g. embarrass Peter

2. If I had been Peter, I would have responded by *(circle one):*
   a. humoring Jesus, but that's all
   b. suggesting that we try it the next morning
   c. telling Jesus how much I knew about fishing
   d. thinking to myself, "who does he think he is to tell me how to fish?"
   e. taking him up on the invitation

3. When Peter said, *"Go away from me, Lord, for I am a sinful man!"* he was really saying *(circle one):*
   a. "Stop bugging me"
   b. "I feel guilty being with you"
   c. "You embarrass me because you know more about fishing than I do"
   d. "I know you are more than a teacher but I am not ready to risk the consequences of following you"
   e. "I don't know how to say 'yes' and 'no' at the same time, but this is how I feel"
   f. "Why do you waste your time helping me?"

JESUS CALLS THE FIRST DISCIPLES

One time Jesus was standing on the shore of Lake Gennesaret while the people pushed their way up to him to listen to the word of God. He saw two boats pulled up on the beach; the fishermen had left them and were washing the nets. Jesus got into one of the boats—it belonged to Simon—and asked him to push off a little from the shore. Jesus sat in the boat and taught the crowd.

When he finished speaking, he said to Simon, "Push the boat out further to the deep water, and you and your partners let your nets down for a catch."

"Master," Simon answered, "we worked hard all night long and caught nothing. But if you say so, I will let down the nets." They let the nets down and caught such a large number of fish that the nets were about to break. So they motioned to their partners in the other boat to come and help them. They came and filled both boats so full of fish that they were about to sink. When Simon Peter saw what had happened, he fell on his knees before Jesus and said, "Go away from me, Lord! I am a sinful man!"

He and the others with him were all amazed at the large number of fish they had caught. The same was true of Simon's partners, James and John, the sons of Zebedee. Jesus said to Simon, "Don't be afraid; from now on you will be catching men."

They pulled the boats on the beach, left everything, and followed Jesus.

LUKE 5:1-11 GNFMM

GOING DEEPER

1. In comparison to Simon Peter's experience, my own "meetings" with God have been (circle one):
   a. tame
   b. more intellectual
   c. just as confusing
   d. about the same
   e. even more crazy
   f. huh
   g. fuzzy
   h. scary
   i. sporadic
   j. mystical
   k. right on

2. The first time I can recall feeling God's call on my life was when I was (circle one):
   a. a child
   b. in trouble— a crisis
   c. away on retreat
   d. all alone
   e. facing death
   f. just recently
   g. all my life
   h. never

3. My relationship with Christ right now might be described by the words (circle two):
   a. grim
   b. confused
   c. blah
   d. growing
   e. struggling
   f. slipping
   g. great
   h. up and down
   i. a new beginning
   j. exciting
   k. don't know

OVERTIME CHALLENGE

1. The idea of "pushing out into the deeper water" with Jesus sounds (circle two):
   a. risky
   b. crazy
   c. exciting
   d. OK, but
   e. corny
   f. difficult
   g. fine, if someone will join me
   h. just the challenge I've been looking for

2. The whole idea of belonging to a group that is committed to helping each other grow spiritually sounds (circle one):
   a. ridiculous
   b. frightening
   c. valuable
   d. just what I need
   e. wonderful
   f. childish
   g. demanding
   h. OK, if everybody else is willing
   i. threatening

3. Before I can honestly join in this venture, I need to (circle one):
   a. get myself together
   b. think it over
   c. consider what this is going to cost
   d. straighten out a few things
   e. get some help
   f. get my relationship with Christ squared away
   g. forget my fear of failure
   h. clean up my life

opportunity to really explain your own spiritual pilgrimage—from the earliest beginnings to this moment. *(Explain something of your own early spiritual "meetings." Set the pace for real openness. After 15 minutes call time and move on.)*

Overtime Challenge / 4's or 8's / 15 min.

(You will have to decide if there is time to share the Overtime Challenge and if so, whether to use groups of 4 or 8. If time is limited, stay with the 4's. If there is plenty of time, use groups of 8 —the same 8's that have been together before.)

Take the first question and go around your group, letting each person explain his answer and why. Then go around on the second question, etc. *(Explain your answer to the first question and set the pace for honesty.)*

Close-out

Stand together in a close circle—with your arms over each other's shoulders. If anyone in your group wants to say a short prayer—a word of thanks or a request for help about something in his life—he can do so while we pause. Then I will close with prayer. *(Wait about 60 seconds then break in with a few words of prayer. Pick up the books so they are available for the next session.)*

Objective: To discover the people who have contributed most to your spiritual life, and to use your insights as the basis for a sharing experience.

PROCEDURE

The instructions are given in the words you can use in leading the group.

Silent Preparation / 5 to 10 min.
Turn to page 32 in your player's book and fill out the questionnaire.

Warm-up / 2's / 5 min.
Get together with someone from your group of 8 and share what you put down in the Warm-up—one question at a time. *(Take a moment and explain your answer to the first question. Call time after 5 minutes and move on.)*

WARM-UP

1. This story about four men removing the roof to get their friend to Jesus sounds *(circle one):*
   a. incredible
   b. beautiful
   c. wild
   d. phony
   e. thrilling

2. If I had been in the room when those four people started to tear away the roof, I probably would have

(circle one):
   a. joined in
   b. objected
   c. suspected something
   d. tried to ignore it
   e. cleared out
   f. hung around to see what would happen

3. If something like this ever happened today in my church, I would be *(circle one):*

JESUS HEALS A PARALYZED MAN

A few days later Jesus came back to Capernaum, and the news spread that he was at home. So many people came together that there wasn't any room left, not even out in front of the door. Jesus was preaching the message to them, when a paralyzed man, carried by four men, was brought to him.

Because of the crowd, however, they could not get the man to Jesus. So they made a hole in the roof right above the place where Jesus was. When they had made an opening, they let the man down, lying on his mat. Jesus saw how much faith they had, and said to the paralyzed man, "My son, your sins are forgiven."

Some teachers of the Law who were sitting there thought to themselves,

GOING DEEPER

1. **The people in my life who have cared enough to bring me to Christ are my** *(rank top three 1, 2, 3):*
   - _____ parents
   - _____ friends
   - _____ relatives
   - _____ Sunday School teachers
   - _____ neighbors
   - _____ pastors
   - _____ support group

2. **The time in my life when I felt closest to God was** *(circle one):*
   a. in my childhood
   b. in my teens
   c. recently
   d. right now
   e. always
   f. never have

OVERTIME CHALLENGE

1. **If I am going to move on in my spiritual life, I need a little more** *(circle two):*

   a. commitment   e. discipline
   b. support   f. understanding
   c. love   g. self-confidence
   d. guts   h. courage

2. **My support group can help me best by** *(circle two):*
   a. holding me to my commitment
   b. listening
   c. being open about their struggles
   d. praying for me
   e. really being my friends
   f. joining me in this commitment
   g. giving me a good kick in the pants when I need it
   h. doing exactly what they're doing

a. overjoyed
b. furious
c. curious
d. concerned about the cost
e. happy to see anything happen

4. **The thing that impresses me about the four friends is their** *(circle one):*
   a. faith   e. total dedication
   b. friendship   f. concern about
   c. ingenuity   their friend's life
   d. determination/persistence

"How does he dare talk against God like this? No man can forgive sins; only God can!"

At once Jesus knew their secret thoughts, so he said to them, "Why do you think such things? Is it easier to say to this paralyzed man, 'Your sins are forgiven,' or to say, 'Get up, pick up your mat, and walk'? I will prove to you, then, that the Son of Man has authority on earth to forgive sins." So he said to the paralyzed man, "I tell you, get up, pick up your mat, and go home!"

While they all watched, the man got up, picked up his mat, and hurried away. They were all completely amazed and praised God, saying, "We have never seen anything like this!"

MARK 2:1-12 GNFMM

Going Deeper/4's/15 min.

With your partner get together with two others from your group. Share your answers to Going Deeper, going around the group. *(Describe how you ranked your spiritual enablers and why. Set the pace for real openness. After 15 minutes call time and move on.)*

Overtime Challenge / 4's or 8's/ 15 min.

(You will have to decide if there is time to share the Overtime Challenge and, if so, whether to use groups of 4 or 8. If you are limited for time, stay with the 4's. If you have plenty of time, have the groups double up to form the same 8's as before.)

Take the first question and go around your group, letting each person explain his answer and the why. Then go around on the second question, etc. *(Explain your answer to the first question and set the pace for honesty.)*

Close-out

In each group, gather together in a football huddle—with your arms over each other's shoulders. If anyone wants to say a short prayer—a word of thanks or a request for help about something in his life—he can do so while we pause. Then I will close with a final prayer. *(Wait about 60 seconds for the groups to pray among themselves. Then break in with a prayer and Amen for all the groups. Pick up the books.)*

BUCKING THE PRESSURE

Objective: To discover where the storms are in your life at the moment and what you can do about them.

PROCEDURE

The instructions are given in the words you can use in leading the group.

Silent Preparation / 5 to 10 min.
Turn to page 32 in your player's book and fill out the questionnaire.

Warm-up / 2's / 5 min.
Get together with someone from your group of 8 and share what you put down in the Warm-up—one question at a time. *(Take a moment and explain your answer to the first question. Call time after 5 minutes and move on.)*

Going Deeper / 4's / 15 min.
With your partner get together with two others from your group. Share your answers to Going Deeper, going around the group.

WARM-UP

1. If I had been one of the disciples when the boat was about to sink in the storm, I probably would have: *(circle one):*
   a. jumped overboard
   b. screamed for help
   c. frozen
   d. started bailing water
   e. taken command of the whole situation
   f. drop out and come back fighting
   g. act like nothing is wrong

JESUS CALMS A STORM

On the evening of that same day Jesus said to his disciples, "Let us go across to the other side of the lake." So they left the crowd; the disciples got into the boat that Jesus was already in, and took him with them. Other boats were there too.
   A very strong wind blew up and the waves began to spill over into the boat, so that it was about to fill with water. Jesus was in the back of the boat, sleeping with his head on a pillow. The disciples woke him up and said,

2. I think the disciples awakened Jesus because they (circle one):
   a. resented anyone sleeping in a time of crisis
   b. were afraid for his life
   c. were afraid for their own lives
   d. wanted a little help from him
   e. expected a miracle

3. Jesus calmed the wind because he wanted to (circle one):
   a. impress the disciples
   b. relieve their anxiety
   c. demonstrate his power
   d. teach them a lesson in faith
   e. show them how to deal with future storms in their lives

GOING DEEPER

1. When I am going through a storm in my life, I usually (circle two):
   a. turn to someone I can trust
   b. withdraw into myself
   c. turn to God
   d. get very touchy and irritable
   e. stay pretty calm and collected
   f. play like nothing is wrong
   g. don't know

2. If I told my family about some of the struggles I am going through right now, they would probably (circle one):
   a. die on the spot
   b. kick me out of the house
   c. reach out to me
   d. try to understand
   e. pour out their love as never before
   f. share some of their struggles with me

3. Somehow I have gotten the feeling that (circle one):
   a. it is not OK to have a problem
   b. it is OK for me to have a problem, but not for some others
   c. it is OK for others to have a problem, but not for me
   d. it is OK to have a problem but not to talk about it
   e. it is OK to have a problem and to talk about it

OVERTIME CHALLENGE

1. If I could compare my own life right now to a storm, I would be (circle one):
   a. floating on smooth waters
   b. feeling just a few ripples
   c. sensing a storm is brewing
   d. going through a storm, bailing water like mad to keep afloat
   e. calling for help
   f. seeing the storm winds subside and the calm return
   g. checking weather reports

2. "Be quiet!"..."Be still!" If Jesus were to speak these words to me today, I would take it to mean (circle one):
   a. settle down
   b. shut up and listen
   c. hang in there
   d. expect a miracle
   e. relax and let God handle this
   f. keep the faith, baby
   g. learn the secret of relying on God's energy
   h. commit your life to God and let him run it
   i. let go and let God

"Teacher, don't you care that we are about to die?"

Jesus got up and commanded the wind, "Be quiet!" and said to the waves, "Be still!" The wind died down, and there was a great calm. Then Jesus said to his disciples, "Why are you frightened? Are you still without faith?"

But they were terribly afraid, and began to say to each other, "Who is this man? Even the wind and the waves obey him!"

MARK 4:35-41 GNFMM

(Share how you would answer the first couple of things and set a pace for real openness. After 15 minutes call time and move on.)

Overtime Challenge / 4's or 8's / 15 min.

(You will have to decide if there is time to share the Overtime Challenge and, if so, whether to use groups of 4 or 8. If you are limited for time, stay with the 4's. If you have plenty of time, have the groups double up to form the same 8's as before.)

Take the first question and go around your group, letting each person explain his answer and the why. Then go around on the second question, etc. *(Explain your answer to the first question and set the pace for honesty.)*

Close-out

In each group, gather together in a football huddle—with your arms over each other's shoulders. If anyone wants to say a short prayer—a word of thanks or a request for help about something in his life—he can do so while we pause. Then I will close with a final prayer. *(Wait about 60 seconds for the groups to pray among themselves. Then break in with a prayer and Amen for all the groups. Pick up the books.)*

PUTTING IT TO THE TEST

WARM-UP

1. **If I had been one of the disciples of Jesus right after his death, I probably would have been** *(circle one)*:
   a. **hiding too**
   b. **brokenhearted**
   c. **terrified**
   d. **totally disillusioned**
   e. **skeptical about everything**
   f. **cynical**

2. **When Thomas said,** *"If I do not see the scars of the nails in his hands, and put my finger on those scars...I will not believe,"* **he meant** *(circle one)*:
   a. **"Prove it"**
   b. **"Show me"**
   c. **"I don't believe it"**
   d. **"You're crazy"**

(continued)

Objective: To discover how your own quest for spiritual truth and certainty and the story of "doubting" Thomas in Scripture are parallel, and to use the insight as the basis for a sharing experience in your support group.

PROCEDURE

The instructions are given in the words you can use in leading the group.

Silent Preparation / 5 to 10 min.
Turn to page 34 in your player's book and fill out the questionnaire.

Warm-up / 4's / 10 min.
Get together with 3 others from your group of 8 and share the Warm-up in the questionnaire with each other. Go around on the first question. Then go around on the second question, etc. *(Take a moment and explain your answer to the first question. Set the pace for gut honesty—especially in this*

e. "I want to believe, but..."
f. "Don't break my heart a second time"

3. Thomas reminds me of a *(circle two)*:
   a. research scientist
   b. politician
   c. spoiled child
   d. honest doubter
   e. college student
   f. myself
   g. know-it-all teacher

GOING DEEPER

1. This whole idea of being open and honest about one's religious doubts strikes me as *(circle one)*:
   a. dangerous
   b. healthy
   c. disrespectful
   d. helpful
   e. part of growing up spiritually
   f. really encouraging to me
   g. childish

2. If I could ask one question of Jesus about my own faith, it would be *(circle one)*:
   a. how do you know when you have "touched" God?
   b. what happens when you don't feel like a Christian?
   c. how do you deal with feelings of doubt and failure?
   d. what about the guys who say that Christianity is a bunch of superstitions?
   e. how can I know for sure that I am in God's will?

OVERTIME CHALLENGE

1. The times in my life when Jesus Christ has made himself especially known to me are *(circle two)*:
   a. Easter
   b. seeing a sunset
   c. during pain and sorrow
   d. meditating on Scripture
   e. at communion
   f. hearing a great piece of music
   g. at the death of a close friend
   h. right now
   i. when I found wonderful fellowship with another Christian
   j. _____

2. In my own quest for religious certainty, I am the kind who relies on *(circle two)*:
   a. a bolt of lightning
   b. scientific verification
   c. emotional peace
   d. simple faith
   e. what others say
   f. the Scripture
   g. feeling good
   h. logic
   i. don't know
   j. Christian friends
   k. pastor/priest

3. The thing that helps me to believe in the resurrection is *(circle two)*:
   a. the fact that the Bible says it
   b. the evidence of daily miracles
   c. the faith of my parents
   d. the historical endurance of the church
   e. experiencing his presence in this support group
   f. my own life-change

JESUS AND THOMAS

One of the twelve disciples, Thomas (called the Twin), was not with them when Jesus came. So the other disciples told him, "We saw the Lord!"

Thomas said to them, "If I do not see the scars of the nails in his hands, and put my finger on those scars, and my hand in his side, I will not believe."

A week later the disciples were together indoors again, and Thomas was with them. The doors were locked, but Jesus came and stood among them and said, "Peace be with you." Then he said to Thomas, "Put your finger here, and look at my hands; then stretch out your hand and put it in my side. Stop your doubting, and believe!"

Thomas answered him, "My Lord and my God!"

Jesus said to him, "Do you believe because you see me? How happy are those who believe without seeing me!"

JOHN 20:24-29 GNFMM

Scripture passage about honesty. *After 10 minutes call time and move on.)*

Going Deeper / 2's / 10 min.
Split into 2's and share your answers to Going Deeper in the questionnaire. *(Share your thoughts about the first question. Let your answer permit other's to feel it is OK to have spiritual doubts. After 10 minutes call time and move on.)*

Overtime Challenge / 4's or 8's / 15 min.
(You will have to decide if there is time to share the Overtime Challenge and if so, whether to use groups of 4 or 8. If time is limited, go back to 4's. If you have plenty of time, use 8's—the same 8's that have been together before.)

Take the first question and go around your group, letting each person explain his answer. Then go around on the second question, etc. *(Explain your answer to the first question. Then turn the groups loose.)*

Close-out
Stand together in a close circle— with your arms over each other's shoulders and spend a time in prayer. Anyone who wants to pray may do so, and I will close. *(Wait just a few moments then break in and pray for all the groups. Collect the books.)*

WARM-UP

1. Personally, I find the whole idea of death *(circle one):*
   a. upsetting
   b. far off
   c. something I don't like to think about
   d. mysterious
   e. part of life
   f. something I need to deal with
   g. haven't thought about it

2. The closest I have come to seeing a person brought back from the dead is *(circle one):*
   a. a drowning person
   b. a heart attack victim
   c. an attempted suicide
   d. my own mental attitude about life
   e. my spiritual life

3. The thing that amazes me about this story is *(circle one):*
   a. the faith that Mary had in Jesus: *"Lord, if you had been here, my brother would not have died."*
   b. the love of Jesus for his friends: *"his heart was touched, and he was deeply moved...Jesus wept."*
   c. the willingness of the friends to do the outrageous: *"They took the stone away."*
   d. the power of Jesus to command a dead person to come back: *"Lazarus, come out."*
   e. the way Jesus called on the friends to help in the healing process: *"Untie him...and let him go."*

Objective: To discover how the people in your group have enabled you to come forth as a new person in Christ, and to use the insight as the basis for a sharing experience.

PROCEDURE
The instructions are given in the words you can use in leading the group.

Silent Preparation/5 to 10 min.
Turn to page 34 in your player's book and fill out the questionnaire.

Warm-up / 4's / 10 min.
Get together in 4's—with others from your group of 8—and share the Warm-up. Go around on the first question. Then go around on the second question, etc. *(Take a moment and explain your answer to the first question. Set the pace for candor and honesty. Remember, your example will set the tone. After 10 minutes call time and move on.)*

THE DEATH OF LAZARUS

A man named Lazarus, who lived in Bethany, became sick....His sisters (Mary and Martha) sent Jesus a message....When Jesus arrived, he found that Lazarus had been buried four days before....Mary fell at Jesus' feet. "Lord," she said, "if you had been here, my brother would not have died!"

Jesus saw her weeping, and the Jews who had come with her weeping also; his heart was touched, and he was deeply moved. "Where have you buried him?" he asked them.

"Come and see, Lord," they answered.

Jesus wept. So the Jews said, "See how much he loved him!"...

LAZARUS BROUGHT TO LIFE

Deeply moved once more, Jesus went to the tomb, which was a cave with a stone placed at the entrance. "Take the stone away!" Jesus ordered.

Martha, the dead man's sister, answered, "There will be a bad smell, Lord. He has been buried four days!"

Jesus said to her, "Didn't I tell you that you would see God's glory if you believed?" They took the stone away. Jesus looked up and said, "I thank you, Father, that you listen to me. I know that you always listen to me, but I say this because of the people here, so they will believe that you sent me." After he had said this he called out in a loud voice, "Lazarus, come out!" The dead man came out, his hands and feet wrapped in grave cloths, and a cloth around his face. "Untie him," Jesus told them, "and let him go."

JOHN 11:1-44 GNFMM

GOING DEEPER

1. If I could compare my own feeling of spiritual freedom to Lazarus' experience, I am right now *(circle one)*:
   a. in the tomb—lifeless
   b. hearing the words of Jesus, *"Come out!"* but that's all
   c. out of the tomb, but tied up in the graveclothes so that I cannot move
   d. feeling a new freedom as the graveclothes are untied
   e. alive and free
   f. someplace inbetween

2. The people in my support group have helped "untie some of the old graveclothes" by *(circle one)*:
   a. letting me share some of my hangups
   b. sharing some of their hangups
   c. accepting me with all of my hangups
   d. telling me it is OK to have hangups
   e. affirming my good points
   f. not letting me dwell on my hangups

OVERTIME CHALLENGE

1. When I feel down, I usually *(circle two)*:
   a. get away from it all
   b. seek out a friend
   c. turn to God
   d. just sit and watch TV
   e. don't want to talk to anybody
   f. take a long walk
   g. cry
   h. never cry
   i. take it out on everybody else
   j. seek out my pastor

2. The idea of opening up and sharing some of my struggles with my support group sounds *(circle one)*:
   a. risky
   b. difficult
   c. dangerous
   d. valuable, but
   e. OK, if everybody else will
   f. just what I'm looking for
   g. like what we're already doing
   h. immature

Going Deeper/2's/10 min.
Divide into 2's and share your answers to Going Deeper. *(Give your thoughts about the first question. Let your answer be the permission to feel OK about spiritual doubts. After 10 minutes call time and move on.)*

Overtime Challenge / 4's or 8's / 15 min.
(You will have to decide if there is time to share the Overtime Challenge and if so, whether to use groups of 4 or 8. If you are limited for time, go back to 4's. If you have plenty of time, move into 8's—the same 8's that have been together before.)
Take the first question and go around your group, letting each person explain his answer. Then go around on the second question, etc. *(Take a moment and explain your answer to the first question. Then turn the groups loose.)*

Close-out
Get together in a football huddle and spend a time in prayer. Anyone that wants to say a prayer may do so while I pause. Then I will close in prayer for all of the groups. *(Wait 60 seconds while the groups pray. Then break in with a final prayer. Pick up all the books.)*

Objective: To discover how your own view of God and grace influences your desire to live a clean life, and to use your insight as the basis for a sharing experience.

PROCEDURE

The instructions are given in the words you can use in leading the group.

Silent Preparation/5 to 10 min.
Turn to page 34 in your player's book and fill out the questionnaire.

Warm-up / 4's / 10 min.
Get together in 4's—with others from your group of 8—and share the Warm-up. Go around on the first question. Then go around on the second question, etc. *(Take a moment and explain your answer to the first question. Set the pace for openness and honesty. After 10 minutes call time and move on.)*

Going Deeper / 2's / 10 min.
Divide into 2's and share your answers to Going Deeper. *(Give*

WARM-UP

1. If I had been the girl who was caught in the act of sexual intercourse and dragged (naked) before Jesus, I would have been *(circle one)*:
   a. furious   d. bitter
   b. terrified   e. dazed
   c. ashamed   f. embarrassed

2. If I had been one of the crowd, I would have *(circle one)*:
   a. looked the other way
   b. blushed
   c. stood up for the girl
   d. joined in with the crowd
   e. probably done nothing

3. The beautiful thing about this story for me is the way Jesus *(circle one)*:
   a. was gentle with the girl
   b. exposed the double standards of the Pharisees
   c. doodled in the sand
   d. put down religious hypocrisy
   e. gave the girl a second chance

GOING DEEPER

1. If I could compare my idea of God to a football system, I would see God as a *(circle one)*:
   a. hard-nosed business manager
   b. rugged, demanding coach
   c. quarterback—calling the plays
   d. scout—checking out the opposition and recommending strategy
   e. owner—sitting in the stands
   f. water boy—ready with some instant energy for the game
   g. trainer—keeping the team in condition

2. In the last sentence Jesus was saying to the girl, "I will accept you..." *(circle one)*:
   a. if you change your ways
   b. whether you change your ways or not
   c. as you are, but I don't want you to stay this way

THE WOMAN CAUGHT IN ADULTERY

[*Then everyone went home, but Jesus went to the Mount of Olives. Early the next morning he went back to the temple. The whole crowd gathered around him, and he sat down and began to teach them. The teachers of the Law and the Pharisees brought in a woman who had been caught committing adultery, and made her stand before them all. "Teacher," they said to Jesus, "this woman was caught in the very act of committing adultery. In our Law Moses gave a commandment that such a woman must be stoned to death. Now, what do you say?" They said this to trap him, so they could accuse him. But Jesus bent over and wrote on the ground with his finger. As they stood there asking him questions, he straightened up and said to them, "Whichever one of you has committed no sin may throw the first stone at her." Then he bent over again and wrote on the ground. When they heard this they all left, one by one, the older ones first. Jesus was left alone, with the woman still standing there. He straightened up and said to her, "Where are they, woman? Is there no one left to condemn you?"*

"No one, sir," she answered.

"Well, then," Jesus said, "I do not condemn you either. Go, but do not sin again."]

JOHN 8:1-11 GNFMM

3. In my own life, the greatest motivation to lead a clean life is *(rank top three 1, 2, 3)*:
   ___ my family—not to disappoint them
   ___ my friends—not to let them down
   ___ my own self-respect—to be true to myself
   ___ my fear of God—not to incur his anger
   ___ my love for God—to please him
   ___ God's love for me—freely given

OVERTIME CHALLENGE

1. The people that accept me with the same unconditional love that Jesus offered to the girl are *(circle two)*:
   a. my family
   b. my friends
   c. my support group
   d. one special person
   e. my relatives
   f. no one that I know of

2. When I blow it in one way or another, I usually *(circle one)*:
   a. crawl into a hole
   b. see my priest
   c. talk to a friend who will listen
   d. try to forget it
   e. turn to God
   f. try to be extra good
   g. punish myself

3. Since being in this support group, I have learned that *(circle one)*:
   a. it is OK to have a problem
   b. everyone has problems
   c. we can help each other by sharing our problems
   d. we are supposed to confess our faults to each other
   e. everyone has blown it at one time or another
   f. there is forgiveness from God and acceptance from his people for anything we have done wrong

your thoughts about the first question. After 10 minutes call time and move on.)

Overtime Challenge / 4's or 8's / 15 min.

(You will have to decide if there is time to share the Overtime Challenge and if so, whether to use groups of 4 or 8. If you are limited for time, go back to 4's. If you have plenty of time, move into 8's—the same 8's that have been together before.)

Take the first question and go around your group, letting each person explain his answer. Then go around on the second question, etc. *(Take a moment and explain your answer to the first question. Then turn the groups loose.)*

Close-out

Get together in a football huddle and spend a time in prayer. Anyone that wants to say a prayer may do so while I pause. Then I will close in prayer for all of the groups. *(Wait 60 seconds while the groups pray. Then break in with a final prayer. Pick up all the books.)*

TURNING

Objective: To discover how your spiritual encounter with Jesus Christ and the encounter of Zacchaeus with Christ are similar, and to use the insight as the basis for a sharing experience with your support group.

PROCEDURE

The instructions are given in the words you can use in leading the group.

Silent Preparation / 5 to 10 min.
Turn to page 36 in your player's book and fill out the questionnaire.

Warm-up / 4's / 10 min.
Get together with 4 people from your group of 8 and share what you put down in the Warm-up—one question at a time. *(Take a moment and explain your answer for the first question. After 10 minutes call time and move on.)*

JESUS AND ZACCHAEUS

Jesus went on into Jericho and was passing through. There was a chief tax collector there, named Zacchaeus, who was rich. He was trying to see who Jesus was, but he was a little man and could not see Jesus because of the crowd. So he ran ahead of the crowd and climbed a sycamore tree to see Jesus, who would be going that way. When Jesus came to that place, he looked up and said to Zacchaeus, "Hurry down, Zacchaeus, because I must stay in your house today."

Zacchaeus hurried down and welcomed him with great joy. All the people who saw it started grumbling, "This man has gone as a guest to the home of a sinner!"

Zacchaeus stood up and said to the Lord, "Listen, sir! I will give half my belongings to the poor; and if I have cheated anyone, I will pay him back four times as much."

Jesus said to him, "Salvation has come to this house today; this man, also, is a descendant of Abraham. For the Son of Man came to seek and to save the lost."

LUKE 19:1-10 GNFMM

WARM-UP

1. If I had been Zacchaeus when Jesus stopped and told him, "Hurry down," I would have been *(circle one):*
   a. flabbergasted
   b. scared spitless
   c. overwhelmed with joy
   d. apprehensive about his motives
   e. embarrassed
   f. excited and afraid at the same time

2. When Jesus called Zacchaeus by name and asked to stay at his house, he probably wanted to *(circle one):*
   a. talk to him about his shady tax collecting
   b. touch him up for a loan
   c. demonstrate to everyone that even the most hated man in town was also worth saving
   d. remind Zacchaeus of his great heritage as a son of Abraham
   e. make a lonely little man feel OK
   f. stay in the nicest house in town

3. The amazing turn-around in Zacchaeus' life probably came about because Jesus *(circle one):*
   a. made this a condition for acceptance
   b. accepted him as he was
   c. made Zacchaeus feel worthwhile
   d. threw down a challenge
   e. let him see what "greatness" looked like

GOING DEEPER

1. In my own life, God's call got through to me by *(circle one):*
   a. showing me a better way
   b. convicting me of wrongdoing
   c. accepting me as I am
   d. lifting my own self-esteem
   e. giving me his own love
   f. coming to me through a caring friend

2. As I honestly consider my own life and purpose right now, I feel *(circle two):*
   a. nervous
   b. frustrated
   c. empty
   d. excited
   e. uncertain
   f. satisfied
   g. contented
   h. fulfilled
   i. foreboding
   j. up-tight

3. The idea of opening up and talking about my life this way strikes me as *(circle two):*
   a. awkward
   b. silly
   c. scary
   d. awful
   e. helpful
   f. easy
   g. dumb
   h. fine, but…
   i. difficult
   j. mature
   k. immature

OVERTIME CHALLENGE

1. If Jesus were to pass my way today, he would probably *(circle one):*
   a. ask me, "Why are you always dodging me?"
   b. give me a bawling out
   c. put his arms around me and hug me
   d. give me a swift kick in the pants
   e. slap me on the shoulder and tell me I'm great
   f. make me whole

2. Down deep inside, I wish I could *(circle one):*
   a. accept myself
   b. accept God
   c. relate more easily to others
   d. have a good friend
   e. have the strength to improve
   f. stand up for what I believe
   g. lead more people to God
   h. share my feelings
   i. get along with my parents

3. If I could give myself a gift right now, it would be a little more *(circle one):*
   a. patience
   b. love
   c. joy
   d. peace
   e. talent
   f. ability
   g. kindness
   h. faith
   i. courage
   j. understanding
   k. trust

Going Deeper / 2's / 10 min.

Split into 2's and share your answers to Going Deeper with each other. *(Share your answer to the first question—how God's call got through to you. Set the pace for real openness. After 10 minutes call time and move on.)*

Overtime Challenge / 4's or 8's / 15 min.

(You will have to decide if there is time to share the Overtime Challenge and if so, whether to use groups of 4 or 8. If time is limited, go back to the 4's. If there is plenty of time, use 8's—the same 8's that have been together all along.)

Take the first question and go around your group, letting each person explain his answer. Then go around on the second question, etc. *(Explain what Jesus would likely do with you. Set the pace for understanding His nature and one's need.)*

Close-out

Stand together in a close circle—with your arms over each other's shoulders and let anyone who wants to volunteer a prayer do so. *(After a few moments offer a word of thanks for the lives the Lord turns around and the love he gives us. Collect the books.)*

JESUS WASHES HIS DISCIPLES' FEET

It was now the day before the Feast of Passover. Jesus knew that his hour had come for him to leave this world and go the Father. He had always loved those who were his own in the world, and he loved them to the very end.

Jesus and his disciples were at supper. The Devil had already decided that Judas, the son of Simon Iscariot, would betray Jesus. Jesus knew that the Father had given him complete power; he knew that he had come from God and was going to God. So Jesus rose from the table, took off his outer garment, and tied a towel around his waist. Then he poured some

Objective: To discover how the persons in your support group have ministered to your needs during this program, and to use the insight as the basis for a sharing experience.

PROCEDURE

The instructions are given in the words you can use in leading the group.

Silent Preparation / 5 to 10 min.

Turn to page 36 in your player's book and fill out the questionnaire.

Warm-up / 4's / 10 min.

Get together with four people from your group of 8 and share what you put down in the Warm-

WARM-UP

1. If I had been one of the disciples when Jesus came to wash their feet, I would have *(circle one)*:
   a. been humiliated
   b. refused
   c. felt like refusing
   d. insisted on washing his feet
   e. cried
   f. considered it a great honor

2. Frankly, I find the idea of washing another's feet *(circle one)*:
   a. degrading
   b. silly
   c. embarrassing
   d. childish
   e. the greatest kind of leadership
   f. what Christianity is all about
   g. what we need more of
   h. old-fashioned
   i. ridiculous

3. In my estimation, the reason why Jesus washed the feet of his disciples was to *(circle one)*:
   a. show his deep love for them
   b. teach them a lesson in servanthood
   c. shame them for being insensitive to each other's needs
   d. show them real leadership
   e. give them a new model for their lives together

GOING DEEPER

1. The reason why we do not see more genuine footwashing in Christian relationships today is because we *(circle one)*:
   a. don't need each other
   b. don't know we need each other
   c. don't know each other's needs
   d. don't want to know each others' needs
   e. don't want others to know our needs

water into a washbasin and began to wash the disciples' feet and dry them with the towel around his waist....

After he had washed their feet, Jesus put his outer garment back on and returned to his place at the table. "Do you understand what I have just done to you?" he asked. "You call me Teacher and Lord, and it is right that you do so, because I am. I am your Lord and Teacher, and I have just washed your feet. You, then, should wash each other's feet. I have set an example for you, so that you will do just what I have done for you."

JOHN 13:1-15 GNFMM

3. If I were serious about "footwashing," I would have to start in my home *(fill in the blanks with the service you would perform for each):*
   a. with my mom by _____
   b. with my dad by _____
   c. with my brother/sister by _____

OVERTIME CHALLENGE

How has each one in your group "washed your feet"? *(In the circles write the names of your support group and beside each name, jot down a service that each has performed for you.)*

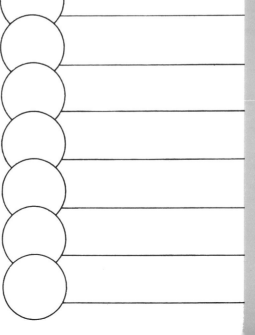

2. If Jesus were to step into our support group to "wash our feet" in a meaningful way, I think he would probably *(circle one):*
   a. give us a good pat on the back
   b. tell us he was proud of us
   c. put his arms around us and give each one of us a great big hug
   d. wash our feet just like he did for his disciples

up—one question at a time. *(Take a moment and explain your answer for the first question. After 10 minutes call time and move on.)*

Going Deeper/2's/10 min.

Divide into 2's and share your answers to Going Deeper. *(Take a moment and explain your answer to the first question. Set the pace for real openness. After 10 minutes call time and move on.)*

Overtime Challenge / 4's or 8's / 15 min.

(You will have to decide if there is time to share the Overtime Challenge and, if so, whether to use groups of 4 or 8. If you are limited for time, go back to the 4's. If you have plenty of time, move into 8's —the same groups that have been together all along.)

Ask one person in your group to sit in silence while the others explain how he has ministered to their needs during the program. Then move to the next person and go around again, etc., until everyone has been covered. *(Choose one person you know well and share how he has ministered to you.)*

Close-out

In your group, join in a football huddle and let anyone who wants to volunteer a prayer do so while I pause. Then I will close with a prayer for the whole group. *(Wait about 60 seconds while the groups pray. Then break in with a final prayer. Pick up all the books.)*

WARM-UP

1. If I had been one of the disciples when Jesus suggested that they feed the crowd, I would have *(circle one)*:
   a. fainted on the spot
   b. quietly slipped away
   c. found some excuse to put off the problem
   d. passed the buck
   e. referred it to a committee
   f. reacted just as the disciples did

Objective: To discover how you respond to human need situations in view of the disciples' reactions when the 5,000 were fed, and to use your insight as the basis for a sharing experience.

PROCEDURE

The instructions are given in the words you can use in leading the group.

Silent Preparation / 5 to 10 min.
Turn to page 36 in your player's book and fill out the questionnaire.

Warm-up / 4's / 10 min.
Get together with four people from your group of 8 and share what you put down in the Warm-up—one question at a time. *(Take*

JESUS FEEDS THE FIVE THOUSAND

The apostles came back and told Jesus everything they had done. He took them with him and they went off by themselves to a town named Bethsaida. When the crowds heard about it they followed him. He welcomed them, spoke to them about the Kingdom of God, and healed those who needed it.

When the sun had begun to set, the twelve disciples came to him and said, "Send the people away so they can go to the villages and farms around here and find food and lodging, because this is a lonely place."

But Jesus said to them, "You yourselves give them something to eat."

They answered, "All we have is five loaves and two fish. Do you want us to go and buy food for this whole crowd?" (There were about five thousand men there.)

Jesus said to his disciples, "Make the people sit down in groups of about fifty each."

The disciples did so and made them all sit down. Jesus took the five loaves and two fish, looked up to heaven, thanked God for them, broke them, and gave them to the disciples to distribute to the people. They all ate and had enough; and the disciples took up twelve baskets of what the people left over.

LUKE 9:10-17 GNFMM

2. The thought of my having special gifts to contribute to the world's needs makes me feel *(circle two)*:
a. sort of responsible
b. kinda funny
c. scared
d. guilty
e. like doing something
f. never thought about it

3. My favorite way of avoiding my own responsibility is usually to *(circle one)*:
a. say the problem is too large
b. blame somebody else
c. insist that someone else go first
d. put off the decision
e. confess how inadequate I am
f. decide that nothing can be done about the situation, so why bother

OVERTIME CHALLENGE

1. If my support group had been the disciples of Jesus at the time of this crisis, we would probably *(circle one)*:
a. still be trying to decide what to do
b. have organized a committee among ourselves
c. still be running (in the other direction)
d. jumped at the chance to do something

2. If our support group had to come up with five loaves and two fishes among ourselves, I think we would be able to offer a lot of *(circle two)*:
a. caring for people
b. commitment to Christ
c. loyalty to one another
d. Bible knowledge
e. strong spiritual leadership
f. dedication to be God's men in our world

3. Our support group might be lacking a bit in *(circle one)*:
a. enthusiasm
b. commitment
c. desire
d. follow-through
e. know-how
f. clear-cut objectives
g. courage
h. confidence
i. teamwork

2. I see this story primarily as a lesson in *(circle two)*:
a. frustration
b. ecology
c. faith
d. crowd psychology
e. food conservation
f. human resourcefulness
g. spiritual power
h. discipleship training
i. compassion
j. exhibitionism
k. who Jesus is

GOING DEEPER

1. When faced with an overwhelming need like the one that the disciples of Jesus faced, I tend to *(circle two)*:
a. panic
b. rise to the occasion
c. feel totally inadequate
d. take charge
e. shy away from responsibility
f. get involved in any way I can
g. cave in
h. get interested in something else

a moment and explain your answer for the first question. After 10 minutes call time and move on.)

Going Deeper / 2's / 10 min.
Divide into 2's and share your answers to Going Deeper. *(Take a moment and explain your answer to the first question. Set the pace for real openness. After 10 minutes call time and move on.)*

Overtime Challenge / 4's or 8's / 15 min.
(You will have to decide if there is time to share the Overtime Challenge and, if so, whether to use groups of 4 or 8. If time is limited, stay with the 4's. If there is plenty of time, move into 8's.)
Take the first question and go around your group, letting each person share his position. Then go around on the second question, etc. *(Share your position on the first question, but leave the door open for others to differ.)*

Close-out
In your group, join in a football huddle and let anyone who wants to volunteer a prayer do so while I pause. Then I will close with a prayer for the whole group. *(Wait 60 seconds while the groups pray among themselves. Then break in with a prayer and Amen for all the groups. Pick up the books.)*

179

Objective: To discover how your commitment to Jesus Christ and the challenge that Jesus put to his disciples coincide, and to use the insight as the basis for a sharing experience with your support group.

PROCEDURE

The instructions are given in the words you can use in leading the group.

Silent Preparation / 5 to 10 min.
Turn to page 38 in your player's book and fill out the questionnaire.

Warm-up / 2's / 5 min.
Get together with someone from your group of 8 and share your Warm-up with one another. *(Take a moment and explain your*

WARM-UP

1. When I compare my own life to the standard laid down in this passage for a "follower of Jesus," I feel like *(circle one):*
   a. getting involved
   b. erasing my past
   c. rethinking where I am
   d. starting all over again
   e. going for broke
   f. ducking
   g. yawning

2. If Jesus were to ask the same question of me that he asked Peter, *"Who do you say I am?"* I would have to say he is *(circle two):*
   a. my friend
   b. a great teacher
   c. an embarrassment
   d. the Son of God
   e. love
   f. Savior
   g. someone I want to know
   h. a mystery
   i. don't know

3. *"If anyone wants to come with me, he must forget himself, take up his cross every day, and follow me."* This sounds like *(circle two):*
   a. a commercial
   b. a Sunday School lesson
   c. an appeal for help
   d. something worth giving my life to
   e. getting back to fundamentals
   f. a father-son or mother-daughter talk

PETER'S DECLARATION ABOUT JESUS

One time when Jesus was praying alone, the disciples came to him. "Who do the crowds say I am?" he asked them.

"Some say that you are John the Baptist," they answered. "Others say that you are Elijah, while others say that one of the prophets of long ago has come back to life."

"What about you?" he asked them. "Who do you say I am?"

Peter answered, "You are God's Messiah."

JESUS SPEAKS ABOUT HIS SUFFERING AND DEATH

Then Jesus gave them strict orders not to tell this to anyone, and added, "The Son of Man must suffer much, and be rejected by the elders, the chief priests, and the teachers of the Law. He will be put to death, and be raised to life on the third day."

And he said to all, "If anyone wants to come with me, he must forget himself, take up his cross every day, and follow me. For whoever wants to save his own life will lose it; but whoever loses his life for my sake will save it. Will a man gain anything if he wins the whole world but is himself lost or defeated? Of course not!

LUKE 9:18-25 GNFMM

GOING DEEPER

1. If I could compare my own Christian life to a football game, I would be right now *(circle one)*:
   a. suiting up
   b. waiting for the game to start
   c. sitting on the bench
   d. playing "catch up"
   e. at half time
   f. on the injured list
   g. worn out
   h. giving it all I've got

2. My favorite way of dodging the issue of Christian discipleship is by *(circle one)*:
   a. claiming I don't understand
   b. saying nobody else is serious
   c. just ignoring it
   d. putting it off until next week
   e. asking somebody else to go first

3. My biggest fear in going further in my Christian commitment is the fear of being *(circle one)*:
   a. laughed at by my friends
   b. considered anti-intellectual
   c. cramped in my lifestyle
   d. a failure
   e. "too" emotional
   f. called a sissy
   g. asked to give up something important

OVERTIME CHALLENGE

1. If God could deal with me right now like a principal, he would probably *(circle two)*:
   a. chew me out
   b. suspend me
   c. make me stay after school
   d. give me extra work
   e. be patient with my mistakes
   f. put his arm around me and say he is proud of me
   g. give me a swift kick in the pants
   h. put me in charge of something

2. An attitude I need to transfer from athletic training into my spiritual training is *(rank top three 1, 2, 3)*:
   _____ absolute dedication
   _____ knowledge of the game
   _____ team loyalty and support
   _____ day-to-day training
   _____ a good mental attitude
   _____ desire to win
   _____ ability to bounce back from a loss
   _____ long-range strategy
   _____ team spirit
   _____ concentration on the basics
   _____ _____
   _____ _____

answer to the first question. Then turn the groups of 2 loose. After 5 minutes call time and move on.)

Going Deeper / 4's / 10 min.

Take your partner and get together with 2 others from your group of 8 and share Going Deeper—one question at a time around the group. (Explain your answer to the first question. Then turn the groups loose. After 10 minutes call time and move on.)

Overtime Challenge / 8's / 15 min.

Regather your group of 8—the same that have been together before—and share the Overtime Challenge with one another. (Explain your answer to the first question and set the pace for openness and honesty.)

Close-out

Stand together in a close circle—with your arms over each other's shoulders. Anyone who wants to say a prayer—a few words of thanks or a request concerning a problem or need—can do so while we wait. Then I will close. (After about 60 seconds break in with a brief prayer. Collect the books.)

Objective: To discover how you would respond to the question that Jesus asked Peter, "Do you really love me?" and to use the insight as the basis for a sharing experience.

PROCEDURE

The instructions are given in the words you can use in leading the group.

Silent Preparation / 5 to 10 min.

Turn to page 38 in your player's book and fill out the questionnaire.

Warm-up / 2's / 5 min.

Get together with someone from your group of 8 and share the Warm-up. *(Take a moment and explain your answer to the first*

WARM-UP

1. If I had been Peter when Jesus asked three times: *"Do you love me?"* I think I would have *(circle one):*
   a. burst out in tears
   b. blown my top
   c. refused to answer
   d. been deeply hurt
   e. gotten mad
   f. wondered what was wrong

2. I think Jesus put the question three times to Peter in order to *(circle one):*
   a. get him to listen
   b. rub it in
   c. shame Peter with his past failure
   d. impress Peter with the importance of the answer
   e. _____

3. When Jesus said, *"Take care of my sheep,"* I think he was saying *(circle one):*
   a. settle down to the job of spreading the Gospel
   b. cut out the Mickey-Mouse stuff
   c. people are more important than anything else
   d. watch your priorities
   e. quit fooling around
   f. _____

GOING DEEPER

1. If Jesus were to ask me, *"Do you love me more than all else?"* I would have to say *(circle one):*
   a. yes—all of the time
   b. yes—most of the time
   c. yes—some of the time
   d. yes—when I am thinking of it
   e. huh?
   f. I wish you hadn't asked right now

2. Since being in this support group, my greatest growth has been in the area of my *(rank top three 1, 2, 3):*
   ____ personal discipline
   ____ moral development
   ____ spiritual development
   ____ mental attitude
   ____ self-acceptance
   ____ Bible understanding
   ____ willingness to share myself
   ____ concern for others
   ____ attitude about school
   ____ family relationships

OVERTIME CHALLENGE

1. Right now, I feel that I am living up to *(circle one):*
   a. all that I know is God's call for my life
   b. all that I am willing to know of God's call for my life
   c. less than what I know is God's call for my life
   d. just what's possible—I can't do anymore
   e. what I want to do. Please don't bother me with God's call

2. Frankly, if I were to take this matter of Christian commitment seriously, I would have to *(circle one):*
   a. change a few things
   b. overhaul my priorities—decide what is really important
   c. give up some of my own desires
   d. clear up a few of my sour relationships
   e. start all over again

3. If I decided to do something about committing my whole life to God, I would need *(circle two):*
   a. some support from my friends
   b. a good kick in the pants
   c. a little more self-confidence
   d. a greater spiritual commitment
   e. all of the love I can get
   f. an awareness of what God wants

JESUS AND PETER

After they had eaten, Jesus said to Simon Peter, "Simon, son of John, do you love me more than these?"

"Yes, Lord," he answered, "you know that I love you."

Jesus said to him, "Take care of my lambs." A second time Jesus said to him, "Simon, son of John, do you love me?"

"Yes, Lord," he answered, "you know that I love you."

Jesus said to him, "Take care of my sheep." A third time Jesus said, "Simon, son of John, do you love me?"

Peter became sad because Jesus asked him the third time, "Do you love me?" and said to him, "Lord, you know everything; you know that I love you!"

Jesus said to him, "Take care of my sheep."

JOHN 21:15-17 GNFMM

---

question. Then turn the groups loose. After 5 minutes call time and move on.)

Going Deeper/4's / 10 min.

With your partner get together with another pair from your group of 8 and share Going Deeper — one question at a time around the group. *(Explain your answer to the first question. After 10 minutes call time and move on.)*

Overtime Challenge / 8's / 15 min.

Regather your group of 8—the same group that has been together before—and share the Overtime Challenge with one another. *(Explain your answer to the first question and set the pace for openness and honesty.)*

Close-out

In your group join together in a football huddle and let anyone who wants to say a prayer—of thanksgiving or about a problem or need—do so while I wait. Then I will close in prayer for the entire group. *(Wait about 60 seconds. Then break in with a final prayer for all the groups. Collect all the books.)*

Turn to page 38 in your player's book and fill out the questionnaire.

Objective: To discover how you respond to challenges that involve personal risk, and to use your insight as the basis for a sharing experience in your group.

PROCEDURE

The instructions are given in the words you can use in leading the group.

Silent Preparation / 5 to 10 min.

WARM-UP

1. If I had been Peter when Jesus invited him to step out of the boat and walk on the water, I probably would have *(circle one):*

   a. shrunk back in horror
   b. made some excuse
   c. asked someone else to go first
   d. explained I was just kidding
   e. jumped at the chance

JESUS WALKS ON THE WATER

Then Jesus made the disciples get into the boat and go ahead of him to the other side of the lake, while he sent the people away. After sending the people away, he went up a hill by himself to pray. When evening came, Jesus was there alone; by this time the boat was far out in the lake, tossed about by the waves, because the wind was blowing against it. Between three and six o'clock in the morning Jesus came to them, walking on the water. When the disciples saw him walking on the water they were terrified. "It's a ghost!" they said, and screamed with fear.

Jesus spoke to them at once. "Courage!" he said. "It is I. Don't be afraid!"

2. When it comes to doing something new, I am *(circle two)*:
   a. just plain scared
   b. very cautious
   c. daring
   d. afraid that someone will laugh
   e. willing to try anything once
   f. afraid of failing
   g. a follower, not a leader

GOING DEEPER

1. To me, the Christian life is like *(circle one)*:
   a. a wild roller-coaster ride
   b. a smooth sailing ship
   c. a trapeze artist—letting go of one bar to reach for another
   d. fourth down and goal to go
   e. locked in by accident in a department store
   f. fire escape in a "towering inferno"
   g. swimming the English Channel after seeing "Jaws"
   h. _____

2. If I could count on the support of the others in my group, I would like to *(circle one)*:
   a. make a new commitment of my life to Christ
   b. find out what God wants with my life
   c. go deeper with Christ
   d. stand up for what I believe
   e. get involved in some kind of action

3. Before I do anything, I must deal with my *(circle one)*:
   a. fear of failure
   b. family relationships
   c. spiritual bankruptcy
   d. crippling thought-life
   e. sense of inadequacy
   f. inconsistency
   g. intellectual doubts
   h. fear of standing alone
   i. impulse to rush into things before counting the cost

OVERTIME CHALLENGE

1. The area in my life where I have experienced the greatest growth lately is my *(rank 1, 2, 3)*:
   ___ spiritual life
   ___ relationships with people
   ___ self-acceptance
   ___ attitude toward the church
   ___ ability to take action
   ___ personal discipline

2. If God could deal with me right now as a teacher or boss, he would probably *(circle one)*:
   a. chew me out
   b. be patient with my mistakes
   c. work me extra hours
   d. tell me to go home and|rest
   e. give me a good kick in the pants
   f. put his arm around me and tell me that he was proud of me
   g. _____

Then Peter spoke up. "Lord," he said, "if it is really you, order me to come out on the water to you."

"Come!" answered Jesus. So Peter got out of the boat and started walking on the water to Jesus. When he noticed the wind, however, he was afraid, and started to sink down in the water. "Save me, Lord!" he cried.

At once Jesus reached out and grabbed him and said, "How little faith you have! Why did you doubt?"

They both got into the boat, and the wind died down. The disciples in the boat worshiped Jesus. "Truly you are the Son of God!" they exclaimed.

MATTHEW 14:22-33 GNFMM

Warm-up / 2's / 5 min.

Get together with someone from your group of 8 and share the Warm-up. *(Take a moment and explain your answer to the first question. Then turn the groups loose. After 5 minutes call time and move on.)*

Going Deeper / 4's / 10 min.

With your partner get together with another pair from your group of 8 and share Going Deeper— one question at a time around the group. *(Explain your answer to the first question. After 10 minutes call time and move on.)*

Overtime Challenge / 8's / 15 min.

Regather your group of 8—the same group that has been together before—and share the Overtime Challenge with one another. *(Explain your answer to the first question and set the pace for openness and honesty.)*

Close-out

In your group join together in a football huddle and let anyone who wants to say a prayer—of thanksgiving or about a problem or need—do so while I wait. Then I will close in prayer for the entire group. *(Wait about 60 seconds. Then break in with a final prayer for all the groups.)*

Notes

Scripture Heavies is another term for motivational Bible study, an approach to permit a person to "take inventory" of his life and behavior while studying Scripture. This approach is especially useful with the teachings of Jesus in the Gospels or with the Epistles.

Each questionnaire has three parts: (a) Warm-up—for group members to dig into the Scripture and measure their responses in a simple testing or rating scale, (b) Going Deeper—to evaluate what they have discovered, and (c) Overtime Challenge—to clarify their positions or decide on the actions they need to take.

At the close of each questionnaire, deeper reflection is called for. The student is led to think about the ultimate questions to deal with moral questions in light of the larger spiritual values.

Of the four tracks, this is the most straightforward. While no particular position is taken in the questionnaires on any moral values or conduct, the choice of Scripture and the analytical treatment of the material will have its own "moralizing" effect.

The sharing of the questionnaires in small groups, in turn, will have the effect of forcing a person to "take a stand," to weigh his behavior and do something about it. When the material to be shared is particularly personal, we always use groups of two. When a discussion is called for, we use groups of four. And when there is a need for affirmation or wrap-up, we usually recommend groups of eight. However, if you are pressed for time reduce the size of the groups so everyone can participate.

Hopefully, the student will come up with a mature, responsible, deeply spiritual philosophy of life.

Scripture Heavies

STRUCTURED SESSIONS

YOU-AND THE BIG TEN

WARM-UP

How do you see yourself in connection with the Ten Commandments? *(Read over the Scripture. Then rank your conduct on each commandment from 1 to 10—1 being very low and 10 being very*

Objective: To take inventory of your moral values in light of the Ten Commandments and to use your insight as the basis for a sharing experience.

PROCEDURE

The instructions are given in the words you can use in leading the group.

Silent Preparation / 5 to 10 min.

Turn to page 42 in your player's book and fill out the questionnaire.

Warm-up / 4's / 15 min.

Get together in groups of 4, with 3 others from your group of 8. Give each one in your group a chance to share how he ranked himself on two commandments: (a) the one on which he ranked

THE TEN COMMANDMENTS

Then God spoke all these words. He said, "I am Yahweh your God who brought you out of the land of Egypt, out of the house of slavery.

"You shall have no gods except me.

"You shall not make yourself a carved image or any likeness of anything in heaven or on earth beneath or in the waters under the earth; you shall not bow down to them or serve them. For I, Yahweh your God, am a jealous God and I punish the father's fault in the sons, the grandsons, and the great-grandsons of those who hate me; but I show kindness to thousands of those who love me and keep my commandments.

"You shall not utter the name of Yahweh your God to misuse it, for Yahweh will not leave unpunished the man who utters his name to misuse it.

"Remember the sabbath day and keep it holy. For six days you shall labour and do all your work, but the seventh day is a sabbath for Yahweh your God. You shall do no work that day, neither you nor your son nor your daughter nor your servants, men or women, nor your animals nor the stranger who lives with you. For in six days Yahweh made the heavens and the earth and the sea and all that these hold, but on the seventh day he rested; that is why Yahweh has blessed the sabbath day and made it sacred.

"Honour your father and your mother so that you may have a long life in the land that Yahweh your God has given to you.

"You shall not kill.

"You shall not commit adultery.

"You shall not steal.

"You shall not bear false witness against your neighbour.

"You shall not covet your neighbour's house. You shall not covet your neighbour's wife, or his servant, man or woman, or his ox, or his donkey, or anything that is his."

EXODUS 20:1-17 NEB

high. For instance, on the first commandment, you might circle "8" because you feel you have given first place to God in your life but you still need to give some areas of your lifestyle to God.)

You shall have no God except me

I have given God first place in my life. God is more important to me than popularity, money, friends, winning in sports, or any relationship that competes with God. Every part of my life has been surrendered to God—my time, my priorities, my values, my lifestyle.

1 2 3 4 5 6 7 8 9 10

You shall not misuse God's name

When I use the name of God or Christ, I use it with honor and respect, out of love and thanksgiving for what they mean to me. I cherish the name of God.

1 2 3 4 5 6 7 8 9 10

Remember the Lord's day

I set aside time in my schedule to be with God regularly; to slow down and let God speak to me; to share with God's people in worship and praise.

1 2 3 4 5 6 7 8 9 10

Honor your father and mother

I respect and cherish my parents and recognize their authority over me as from God. I try to make their responsibility easier for them. I tell them out loud how much I appreciate them.

1 2 3 4 5 6 7 8 9 10

You shall not kill

I have a reverence for life as from God. I share God's concern for the oppressed and unprotected peoples in the world.

1 2 3 4 5 6 7 8 9 10

You shall not commit adultery

I recognize that sexual relationship is the sacred heart of marriage—not to be engaged in with any other person after marriage. I am willing to discipline my sexual desires—to keep myself for the person God has for me.

1 2 3 4 5 6 7 8 9 10

You shall not steal

I do not take what does not belong to me. I work for what I get. I respect and protect the property of others. I refuse to go along with mischief that destroys the property of others.

1 2 3 4 5 6 7 8 9 10

You shall not bear false witness against your neighbor

I endeavor to tell the truth about my conduct and to reserve judgment about others until I know the facts. I refuse to engage in gossip. I try to stand up for someone who is falsely blamed, even at the risk of a few friends.

1 2 3 4 5 6 7 8 9 10

You shall not covet your neighbor's wife

I am not jealous for relationships that are already sealed with marriage. I will not engage in sexual competition, nor permit myself to be involved in something I know is wrong.

1 2 3 4 5 6 7 8 9 10

You shall not covet your neighbor's goods

I am content with what God has given me, both talents and possessions. I can honestly affirm my own unique gifts and opportunities and do not feel that someone else "got all the breaks."

1 2 3 4 5 6 7 8 9 10

GOING DEEPER

1. I found this check-up on my life in terms of the Ten Commandments to be (circle two):
   a. fascinating
   b. sobering
   c. challenging
   d. heavy
   e. confusing
   f. helpful
   g. awful
   h. valuable
   i. painful
   j. disturbing
   k. convicting

2. In the crowd that I associate with, living according to the Ten Commandments is (circle two):
   a. ridiculous
   b. out of date
   c. expected
   d. impossible today
   e. unnecessary
   f. just for religious people
   g. pooh-poohed
   h. OK, but...
   i. the Christian thing to do

3. Frankly, I find that my commitment to God influences my moral values (circle one):
   a. a lot
   b. a little
   c. not at all
   d. not as much as I would like
   e. huh?

himself the highest and (b) the one on which he ranked himself the lowest. *(Share the commandments on which you ranked yourself the highest and lowest. Set the pace for openness. After 10 minutes call time and move on.)*

Going Deeper / 2's / 15 min.

Split into 2's and share with one another your answers to Going Deeper. *(Explain your answer to the first point and set the pace for a deep discussion about influence upon moral values.*

Close-out

Stand together in a close circle and pray for the person on your right either silently or out loud. This can be a prayer of thanks for what this person means to you, or a prayer about some need that this person has shared with your group. After a few moments I will pray. *(Wait a bit, then break in and close with a prayer and "Amen" for all of the groups. Pick up all of the books.)*

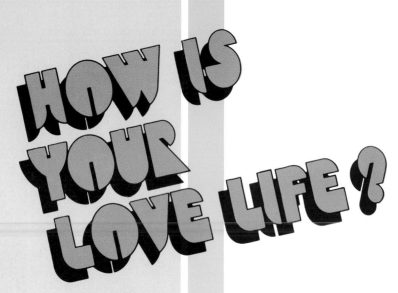

HOW IS YOUR LOVE LIFE?

Objective: To take inventory of your "love life" in light of the Love Chapter, and to use your insights as the basis for a sharing experience in your support group.

PROCEDURE

The instructions are given in the words you can use in leading the group.

Silent Preparation / 5 to 10 min.
Turn to page 42 in your player's book and fill out the questionnaire.

Warm-up / 4's / 10 min.
Get together in groups of 4, with others from your group of 8. Each of you share how you ranked your-

WARM-UP

How is your "love life" with your family, your neighbors and friends? *(Read the Scripture passage. Then in each aspect rank yourself from 1 to 10—1 being very weak and 10 being very strong. For instance, on "patience" you might circle 3 because you lose your temper a lot, but you are not as bad as you used to be! Be honest. Be very honest.)*

Love is patient: I keep my cool when people get on my back. I am slow to get angry with those I love. I rarely yell at people or lose my temper.

1   2   3   4   5   6   7   8   9   10

Love is kind: I really try to be thoughtful of those around me. I am willing to praise the success of others. I share my time and concern when it's needed, and I'm always on the lookout to "build up" others.

1   2   3   4   5   6   7   8   9   10

Love is not jealous: I'm not upset when others perform better than I do or get promoted ahead of me, even when it's undeserved. I am not

threatened by other's talents. When I'm overlooked, I don't punish people with my moods.

1   2   3   4   5   6   7   8   9   10

Love is not conceited: I don't hog the spotlight in the group. I avoid focusing glory on myself. I strive to make others look good, and never

LOVE IS...

Love is patient and kind; love is not jealous, or conceited, or proud; love is not ill-mannered, or selfish, or irritable; love does not keep a record of wrongs; love is not happy with evil, but is happy with the truth. Love never gives up; its faith, hope, and patience never fail.

I CORINTHIANS 13: 4-7 GNFMM

tell exaggerated stories about my accomplishments.

1 2 3 4 5 6 7 8 9 10

Love is not proud: I know my limitations and work within them. I don't need special attention or favors to get me to cooperate. I don't go around putting people down.

1 2 3 4 5 6 7 8 9 10

Love is not ill-mannered: I avoid making any crude or sarcastic comments to others or about others. Instead, my conversation is polite and supportive and my approach to others is sincere and friendly.

1 2 3 4 5 6 7 8 9 10

Love is not selfish: I am not self-centered. I avoid making others fit my expectations. I am not possessive of my friends. I don't always insist on my way. I want to learn others' ways of doing things.

1 2 3 4 5 6 7 8 9 10

Love is not irritable: I am not touchy, cranky, defensive or super-sensitive. I don't lay my bad moods on others. I am approachable, warm, open and easy-to-get along with.

1 2 3 4 5 6 7 8 9 10

Love keeps no record of wrongs: I am quick to forgive those who have hurt me. I don't fight back or seek revenge when jumped on by someone. I forget mistakes others make and avoid holding grudges.

1 2 3 4 5 6 7 8 9 10

Love is not happy with evil: When someone is proven wrong, I avoid self-satisfaction. I never take delight in another's failure, even if it has made me look good. When anyone slips up, I am there with encouragement instead of an "I told you so."

1 2 3 4 5 6 7 8 9 10

Love is happy with the truth: I welcome honesty and justice, even when it shows my weaknesses. I am willing to give credit and praise wherever it is due. I live my commitment to God honestly, and am willing to admit my mistakes.

1 2 3 4 5 6 7 8 9 10

Love never gives up: When my relationship with someone is a struggle, I keep sharing. I never miss an opportunity to help someone. There is no rejection or failure that can make me give up my commitment to love.

1 2 3 4 5 6 7 8 9 10

GOING DEEPER

1. After taking this Inventory, I feel like (circle one):
   a. crawling into a hole
   b. giving up
   c. trying harder
   d. starting all over again
   e. crying for help
   f. shouting
   g. _____

2. For me, loving as Christ loved is (circle two):
   a. impossible
   b. beautiful
   c. hard, but worth trying
   d. a nice ideal, but
   e. something I'll need help on
   f. something I'm really committed to
   g. what it's all about

3. If I am going to do anything about this, I need a little more (circle two):
   a. guts
   b. faith in Christ
   c. support from those close to me
   d. confidence in myself
   e. grounding in the Scripture
   f. determination/commitment
   g. direction
   h. _____

self on two of the phrases: (a) the one on which you marked yourself the highest, (b) the one on which you marked yourself the lowest. *(Take a moment and share the two phrases—the ones you marked highest and lowest. Set the pace for openness. After 10 minutes call time and move on.)*

Going Deeper / 4's / 15 min.

Stay with your group of 4 and move on to Going Deeper in the questionnaire. Take the first question and go around your group, letting each person explain his answer. Then go around on the next question, etc. *(Explain your answer to the first question and set the pace for a deep sharing experience. After 15 minutes move on to the Close-out.)*

Close-out

In your groups of 4, spend a few moments in prayer for one another. Mention any needs that have been shared. After a couple minutes I will break in and close with prayer for the whole group. *(Pause for two or three minutes. Then offer a closing prayer. Pick up the books.)*

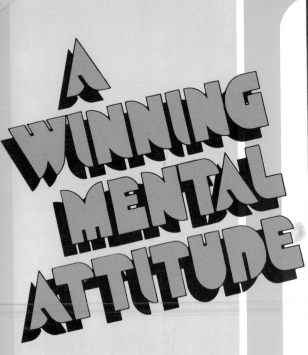

A WINNING MENTAL ATTITUDE

Objective: To take inventory of your life and lifestyle in light of the Beatitudes, and to use your insight as the basis for a sharing experience in your support group.

PROCEDURE

The instructions are given in the words you can use in leading the group.

Silent Preparation / 5 to 10 min. Turn to page 42 in your player's book and fill out the questionnaire.

TRUE HAPPINESS

"Happy are those who know they are spiritually poor; the Kingdom of heaven belongs to them!
"Happy are those who mourn; God will comfort them!
"Happy are the meek; they will receive what God has promised!
"Happy are those who greatest desire is to do what God requires; God will satisfy them fully!
"Happy are those who are merciful to others; God will be merciful to them!
"Happy are the pure in heart; they will see God!
"Happy are those who work for peace among men; God will call them his sons!
"Happy are those who are persecuted because they do what God requires; the Kingdom of heaven belongs to them!"

MATTHEW 5:3-10 GNFMM

WARM-UP

How do you stand in relation to the Beatitudes? *(Read over the Scripture passage. On each of the Beatitudes rank your life from 1 to 10—1 being very weak and 10 being very strong. For instance on the first Beatitude, you might circle number 8 because you know that you are far from perfect but that God accepts you anyway.)*

Happy are those who know they are spiritually poor: Are you ready to admit to yourself and others that you don't have all the answers? That you have needs? That you need God and others? Are you able to let others know where you are "spiritually poor" so they can help?

1   2   3   4   5   6   7   8   9   10

Happy are those who mourn: Are you sensitive enough to other people to help them when they are hurting? Are you able to show your feelings—and to let others show their feelings without your feeling like a sissy? Are you able to let others unload and to really enter into their pain?

1   2   3   4   5   6   7   8   9   10

Happy are the meek: Are you the kind of person who will let the other person carry the ball? Are you quiet enough inside yourself to hear what God and others are saying? Are you mellow enough to lead by listening, allowing others to have their say?

1   2   3   4   5   6   7   8   9   10

Happy are those whose greatest desire is to do what God requires: Is God number one in your life? Do you let him call the plays? Do you know the difference between his will and your will? In the tough choices of your personal life do you honestly seek to put God first?

1   2   3   4   5   6   7   8   9   10

Happy are those who show mercy to others: Are you a "caring" kind of person who warms up other people's lives? Are you quick to respond to need? Do you give without thought of getting something back? In short, are you a grace-giver—like Christ?

1   2   3   4   5   6   7   8   9   10

Happy are the pure in heart: Can you be your *real* self? Are you the same person in school that you are in church? Are you free to let others know you? Are you open and honest, letting God show through?

1   2   3   4   5   6   7   8   9   10

Happy are those who work for peace among men: Are you able to heal broken relationships through your caring and understanding? Are you a bridge builder—accepting others who differ with you—without giving up your own convictions? Do you bring harmony?

1   2   3   4   5   6   7   8   9   10

Happy are those who suffer persecution because they do what God requires: Are you able to take criticism from those near you without reacting defensively? Are you willing to let others know you are a Christian, even if it is unpopular? Can you "take the heat" and come back smiling?

1   2   3   4   5   6   7   8   9   10

GOING DEEPER

What Beatitudes are especially meaningful to you right now? *(Below are a series of statements adapted from the Beatitudes. Rank them 1, 2, 3, etc., in the order of their importance to you.)*

_____ God accepts me as I am. I don't have to have it all together.

_____ Jesus wept. Feelings are a part of life. It is OK to cry.

_____ Gentleness is a mark of strength. A person who is really strong does not have to prove it.

_____ God made us for his fellowship. The soul of man will be restless until it finds its rest in God.

_____ God showed his love for us by giving his life. We show our love for God by giving our lives for others.

_____ God made himself known through Christ. Christ makes himself known through us.

_____ Christ is the bridge over troubled waters for us. We are the bridge over troubled waters for the world.

_____ Obedience to God cost him his life. His followers were asked to follow in his steps.

Warm-up / 4's / 10 min.

Get together in 4's—with others from your regular group—and share two of the Beatitudes: (a) the one in which you ranked yourself the highest—closest to 10, (b) the one in which you ranked yourself the lowest—closest to 1. *(Take a moment and share the two Beatitudes in which you ranked yourself—the highest and the lowest. After 10 minutes call time and move on.)*

Going Deeper / 4's / 15 min.

Stay with your group 4 to share Going Deeper. Let each person explain the top three statements he checked on his list and explain why they are important to him at the moment. *(Share the top three statements you picked and explain why. Set the pace for real soul-searching by your own sharing. After 15 minutes call time and move on to the Close-out.)*

Close-out

In your groups of 4 spend a few moments in prayer for one another. Mention any particular needs that have been shared. After a couple minutes I will break in and close with prayer for the whole group. *(Pause for two or three minutes. Then break in with a closing prayer. Pick up the books.)*

BACK TO BASICS

WARM-UP

How do you see your spiritual growth in relation to 2 Peter? *(Read over the Scripture. Then rank your growth in each of the qualities—after reading the description—by circling a number between 1 and 10. 1 is very weak and 10 is very strong. For instance, you might circle "7" under faith because you feel that your faith is pretty strong, but not as strong as it could be.)*

Faith

I am totally committed to Christ and his church. I am willing to go all the way with Christ—regardless of the cost. Christ is top priority in my life. I am ready for the risky, scary adventure of living with Christ.

1   2   3   4   5   6   7   8   9   10

Goodness

I am trying to live every day as Christ would live it; to clean up my life; to change the bad habits; to check out my priorities, values and lifestyle. I am willing to let God make me into the person he wants.

1   2   3   4   5   6   7   8   9   10

GOD'S CALL AND CHOICE

God's divine power has given us everything we need to live a godly life through our knowledge of the one who called us to share his own glory and goodness. In this way he has given us the very great and precious gifts he promised, so that by means of these gifts you may escape from the destructive lust that is in the world, and come to share the divine nature.

For this very reason do your best to add goodness to your faith; to your goodness add knowledge; to your knowledge add self-control; to your self-control add endurance; to your endurance add godliness; to your godliness add brotherly love; and to your brotherly love add love.

These are the qualities you need, and if you have them in abundance they will make you active and effective in your knowledge of our Lord Jesus Christ. But whoever does not have them is so shortsighted that he cannot see, and has forgotten that his past sins have been washed away.

2 PETER 1:3-9 GNFMM

Objective: To take inventory of your spiritual development in light of the teaching in 2 Peter 1, and to use your insights as the basis for a sharing experience.

PROCEDURE

The instructions are given in the words you can use in leading the group.

Silent Preparation / 5 to 10 min.
Turn to page 44 in your player's book and fill out the questionnaire.

Knowledge

I am giving priority to learning more about God and what he wants with my life. I spend time daily in prayer and in the study of Scripture. I am open to God's will for my life and willing to pay the price to follow it.

1 2 3 4 5 6 7 8 9 10

Self-control

I am taking seriously the lordship of Jesus Christ over my whole being, putting aside my own selfish interests and desires. I am willing to "get in shape" and "stay in shape" spiritually—whatever the cost.

1 2 3 4 5 6 7 8 9 10

Endurance

I am learning how to "hang in there" when the going gets tough. I can stand up under pressure; to take the heat; to stand up for what I believe and know is right, even if it means standing alone.

1 2 3 4 5 6 7 8 9 10

Godliness

I am as conscientious about my spiritual development as my physical and mental development, making my spiritual growth a daily discipline. I am not ashamed to let others know that I am a Christian. No matter where I am, I try to make my life count for God.

1 2 3 4 5 6 7 8 9 10

Brotherly love

I go out of my way to help my family, my friends. I am willing to take the initiative in clearing up misunderstanding; to go the second mile when there is a need; to build up others by affirming the good things; to always be on the lookout for ways to help.

1 2 3 4 5 6 7 8 9 10

Love

I am being an instrument of God's love, reaching out, touching, giving, sharing his grace in the same way that he gave up his life for me.

1 2 3 4 5 6 7 8 9 10

GOING DEEPER

1. After measuring my spiritual growth against this Scripture passage, I want to (circle two):
   a. throw in the towel
   b. try harder
   c. start all over again
   d. cry for help
   e. get with it
   f. give up
   g. do something, but I don't know what

2. It would sure help if I had (circle two):
   a. some support
   b. a better situation
   c. more time
   d. a great big kick in the pants
   e. an understanding friend
   f. love
   g. a little more peace of mind

Warm-up / 2's / 15 min.

Get together with someone from your support group and share how you ranked yourself on each of the qualities, one at a time. (Explain how you ranked yourself on the first quality. Then turn the groups loose. After 15 minutes call time and move on.)

Going Deeper / 4's / 15 min.

With your partner get together with 2 others from your group.

Take the first question and go around your group, letting each person share his position. Then go around on the second question, etc. (Share your position on the first question, but leave the door open for others to differ.)

Close-out

Stand together in a close circle and pray for the person on your right either silently or out loud. This can be a prayer of thanks for what this person means to you, or a prayer about some need that he has shared with your group. (Wait about 2 minutes to give everyone an opportunity to pray. Then break in and close in prayer for all the groups. Collect the books.)

HOW IS YOUR EQUIPMENT?

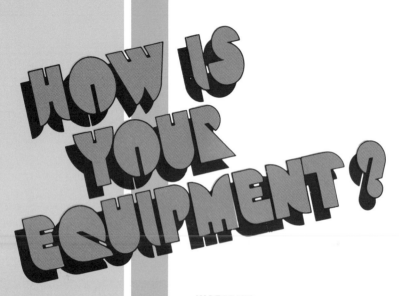

Objective: To take inventory of your spiritual equipment in light of the check list in Ephesians 6, and to use your insights as the basis for a sharing experience in your support group.

PROCEDURE

The instructions are given in the words you can use in leading the group.

Silent Preparation / 5 to 10 min.
Turn to page 44 in your player's book and fill out the questionnaire.

Warm-up / 2's / 15 min.
Get together in 2's—with someone from your support group—and share how you ranked yourself on each part of your spiritual equip-

WARM-UP

How are you spiritually equipped right now? *(Read over the Scripture passage. Then on each point below rank yourself from 1 to 10—1 being very weak and 10* *being very strong. For instance, for "truth" you might circle 8, because you are pretty firm in your Christian convictions but you could improve.)*

THE WHOLE ARMOR OF GOD

Finally, build up your strength in union with the Lord, and by means of his mighty power. Put on all the armor that God gives you, so that you will stand up against the Devil's evil tricks. For we are not fighting against human beings, but against the wicked spiritual forces in the heavenly world, the rulers, authorities, and cosmic powers of this dark age. So take up God's armor now! Then when the evil day comes, you will be able to resist the enemy's attacks, and after fighting to the end, you will still hold your ground.

So stand ready: have truth for a belt tight around your waist: put on righteousness for your breast-plate, and the readiness to announce the Good News of peace as shoes for your feet. At all times carry faith as a shield; with it you will be able to put out all the burning arrows shot by the Evil One. And accept salvation for a helmet, and the word of God as the sword that the Spirit gives you. Do all this in prayer, asking for God's help. Pray on every occasion, as the Spirit leads. For this reason keep alert and never give up; pray always for all God's people.

EPHESIANS 6:1-18 GNFMM

196

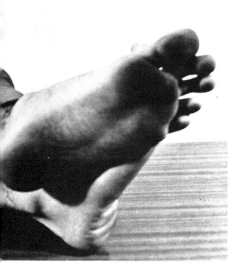

Truth

I am prepared to stake my life on the fact that Jesus Christ is the Son of God. I have thought through what I believe, and I am willing to take a stand.

1   2   3   4   5   6   7   8   9   10

Righteousness

I am prepared to put my life where my mouth is—in clean and right living—with genuine integrity—as Christ did. I am serious about being God's man/woman.

1   2   3   4   5   6   7   8   9   10

Readiness to announce the Good News

I am willing to publicly affirm my faith in Christ—at school or work. I find it easy to talk about my personal faith.

1   2   3   4   5   6   7   8   9   10

Faith

I am prepared to step out with Christ—to risk my life, my fortune and my future to him whatever the cost or consequences. I am willing to build my whole life around God's will.

1   2   3   4   5   6   7   8   9   10

Salvation

I know that I am part of the family of God because of Jesus Christ. I have a strong inner peace because I am at peace with God.

1   2   3   4   5   6   7   8   9   10

Word of God

I actively seek to know more about God and his will for my life through an ongoing study of his guidebook, the Bible. I discipline myself to study daily.

1   2   3   4   5   6   7   8   9   10

Prayer

I set aside time regularly to talk with God and to let him speak to me. I consciously try to submit every decision in my life to God.

1   2   3   4   5   6   7   8   9   10

GOING DEEPER

1. If I were thrown into a tough spiritual contest today, I would probably *(circle one)*:
   a. collapse before the game even started
   b. tire out before the first quarter was over
   c. barely make it through
   d. find reserves I didn't know I had
   e. rise to the occasion

2. From my own experience, I seem to grow in my spiritual life when *(circle one)*:
   a. the pressure is on
   b. I am around others who are serious
   c. I have plenty of time to devote to it
   d. I am away from home
   e. I am really serious about it
   f. someone is checking up on me

3. In my own personal habit of Bible study and prayer, the hardest thing for me is *(circle two)*:
   a. getting time alone
   b. consistency
   c. concentration
   d. desire
   e. getting to bed the night before
   f. finding some privacy at home
   g. knowing how to get something out of the Bible
   h. keeping from falling asleep
   i. ...what habit?

ment in the Warm-up. Take the first part and both share your responses and why. Then take the second part and explain how you checked yourself, etc., through the series. *(Explain how you ranked yourself on the first part "truth." Then ask each person to explain his answer to his partner. After 15 minutes call time and move on.)*

Going Deeper / 4's / 10 min.

With your partner get together with another pair from your group of 8. Go around, each one giving his answer to the first question in Going Deeper and explaining why. If there is time, go around on the next question, etc. *(Explain your answer to the first question and set the pace for real soul-searching in the support groups. After 10 to 15 minutes call time and move on to the Close-out.)*

Close-out

In your groups of 4, spend a few moments in prayer for one another, mentioning in particular any needs that have been shared. After a couple of minutes I will break in and close with a prayer for the whole group. *(Pause two or three minutes. Then break in with a closing prayer. Pick up the books.)*

Objective: To take inventory of your personal conduct in your relationships in light of the Sermon on the Mount, and to use your insights as the basis for a sharing experience in your support group.

PROCEDURE

The instructions are given in the words you can use in leading the group.

Silent Preparation / 5 to 10 min.

Turn to page 44 in your player's book and fill out the questionnaire.

Warm-up / 2's / 15 min.

Get together in 2's—with someone from your support group—and share how you ranked yourself on each question in the Warm-up. Take the first question and let each person explain his answer. Then

TEACHING ABOUT ADULTERY

"You have heard that it was said, 'Do not commit adultery.' But now I tell you: anyone who looks at a woman and wants to possess her is guilty of committing adultery with her in his heart."

TEACHING ABOUT REVENGE

"You have heard that it was said, 'An eye for an eye, and a tooth for a tooth.' But now I tell you: do not take revenge on someone who does you wrong. If anyone slaps you on the right cheek, let him slap your left cheek too.... when someone wants to borrow something, lend it to him."

LOVE FOR ENEMIES

"You have heard that it was said, 'Love your friends, hate your enemies.' But now I tell you: love your enemies, and pray for those who persecute you, so that you will become the sons of your Father in heaven. For he makes his sun to shine on bad and good people alike, and gives rain to those who do good and those who do evil. Why should God reward you if you love only the people who love you? Even the tax collectors do that!"

MATTHEW 5:27-46 GNFMM

WARM-UP

If you were to ask yourself the following questions, how would you answer? *(Read over the Scripture passage. Then on each line put a dot somewhere between the two extremes*

Adultery

1. **Am I willing to live a clean life sexually?**
   not willing _____ very willing

2. **Is my talk about the opposite sex dirty or clean?**
   dirty _____ clean

3. **How strong is my self-discipline when it comes to sexual opportunities?**
   very weak _____ very strong

4. **Do I seek in my relationships God or self-satisfaction?**
   self _____ God

Revenge

1. **When someone is mean to me and tries to hurt me, do I seek revenge or turn the other cheek?**
   revenge _____ turn cheek

2. **Do I use my moods to punish people?**
   punish _____ never punish

3. **Do I protect myself from hurt by threatening others?**
   threaten _____ never threaten

4. **Do I seek punishment of those who are wrong as my job or God's?**
   my job _____ God's job

Love for enemies

1. **Do I go out of my way to reach people who are not my close friends?**
   no reach out _____ reach out

2. **Is my relationship with others as important as my relationship with Christ?**
   as important _____ not as important

3. **When I see people I don't like, do I reject them or try to understand them?**
   reject _____ understand

4. **Do I enjoy the failure of enemies or offer them support and encouragement?**
   enjoy their failure _____ support

GOING DEEPER

1. **Who or what influences the decisions you make every day?** *(Place one or more of the following symbols beside each category to indicate who/ what has the most influence in your decisions. For instance, in the area of "clothes," you might put an "F" because your friends are the biggest influence.)*

   P pals   **S** school
   F family   **TV** television
   C church   **EX** experience

   _____ clothes—what to wear
   _____ time/leisure—how to use it
   _____ money—how to spend it
   _____ grades—their importance
   _____ reading matter—what to read
   _____ sex/love—what is OK
   _____ engagement/marriage—when and how
   _____ family/children—their importance
   _____ work/job—what to do
   _____ success—what it means to you
   _____ happiness—what it is to you

2. **From this exercise, I discovered that the most important influences in my life are** *(rank 1, 2, 3, etc., in order of importance):*
   _____ pals   _____ school
   _____ family   _____ television
   _____ church   _____ experience

take the next question, etc., through the Warm-up. *(Explain how you marked yourself on the question, "Am I willing to live a clean life sexually?" Then ask each person to explain his answer to his partner. After 15 minutes call time and move on.)*

Going Deeper / 4's / 10 min.

With your partner get together with another pair from your original group. Go around and share how you marked the second part of Going Deeper, telling who influences your conduct most —and why. If there is time, go back to the individual items and share your answers, beginning with who influences your decisions on clothes. *(Take a moment and tell who or what you ranked as the most important influences in your life. Explain why. Then turn the groups loose. After 10 minutes call time and move on to the Close-out.)*

Close-out

In your same groups. spend a few moments in prayer for one another, mentioning in particular any needs that have been shared. After a couple minutes, I will break in and close with prayer for the entire group. *(Wait a bit. Then pray for the group. Pick up the books.)*

THE GOOD LIFE

Objective: To take inventory of the qualities of your life in the light of the fruits of the Spirit, and to use your insights as the basis for a sharing experience.

PROCEDURE

The instructions are given in the words you can use in leading the group.

Silent Preparation / 5 to 10 min.

(Have the groups of 8's sit together so that they can see each other while completing the questionnaire.)

Turn to page 46 in your player's book and fill out the questionnaire.

WARM-UP

How would you evaluate the positive qualities in your life? *(Read over the Scripture passage. Then rank yourself on each of the fruits of the Spirit by circling a number from 1 to 10—1* *being very weak and 10 being very strong. For instance, for the fruit of love, you might circle "8" because you feel you are sensitive and caring, but you could do even better.)*

THE SPIRIT AND HUMAN NATURE

What human nature does is quite plain. It shows itself in immoral, filthy, and indecent actions; in worship of idols and witchcraft. People become enemies, they fight, become jealous, angry, and ambitious. They separate into parties and groups; they are envious, get drunk, have orgies, and do other things like these. I warn you now as I have before: those who do these things will not receive the Kingdom of God.

But the Spirit produces love, joy, peace, patience, kindness, goodness, faithfulness, humility, and self-control. There is no law against such things as these. And those who belong to Christ Jesus have put to death their human nature, with all its passions and desires. The Spirit has given us life; he must also control our lives. We must not be proud, or irritate one another, or be jealous of one another.

GALATIONS 5:19-26 GNFMM

THE FRUIT OF THE SPIRIT

Love
I am quick to sense the needs of my friends, classmates and family, and I respond—just as Christ would.

1 2 3 4 5 6 7 8 9 10

Joy
I can celebrate life even in the midst of pain and confusion because of deep, spiritual reservoirs.

1 2 3 4 5 6 7 8 9 10

Peace
I have a quiet, inner confidence in God's care of my life that keeps me from feeling uptight and anxious.

1 2 3 4 5 6 7 8 9 10

Patience (endurance)
I have a staying power that helps me to handle frustration and conflict without blowing my stack.

1 2 3 4 5 6 7 8 9 10

Kindness
I act toward my friends, classmates and family as I want them to act toward me—warm, considerate, generous with praise—always trying to see the best in others.

1 2 3 4 5 6 7 8 9 10

Goodness
I have a real desire to live a clean life, to set a good example by my conduct wherever I am. I want to be God's man!

1 2 3 4 5 6 7 8 9 10

Faithfulness (fidelity)
I stick to my word; I stand up for my friends; I can be counted on to stay firm in my commitment to God and others.

1 2 3 4 5 6 7 8 9 10

Humility (gentleness)
I have an inner strength that permits me to be gentle in my relationships; open; aware of my own abilities without having to make a show of them.

1 2 3 4 5 6 7 8 9 10

Self-control
I am learning to discipline my time, energy and desires to reflect my spiritual values and priorities.

1 2 3 4 5 6 7 8 9 10

GOING DEEPER

What qualities do you appreciate most in the members of your group? *(In the circles write the names of your support group. Then go back to the list of fruit of the Spirit and jot down a fruit beside each name—the one most appropriate for each person. For instance, beside Tom's name you might jot down "peace" because you have observed an inner peace in his life lately—even in the midst of storms.)*

Warm-up / 2's / 15 min.
Get together with one other person from your group of 8 and share the Warm-up. Take the first fruit and each of you explain how you ranked yourself and why. Then take the next fruit and do the same, etc., until you have covered them all. *(Share how you ranked yourself on the first fruit. Set the pace for painful honesty. After 10 minutes call time and move on.)*

Going Deeper / 8's / 15 min.
Regather your group of 8. While one person remains silent the others explain the fruit they feel is the strongest in this person's life. Repeat the process for each person in the group. *(Choose one person and explain the fruit you would put down for him and why. Set the pace for beautiful, sincere affirmation. Then turn the groups loose.)*

Close-out
Stand together in a close circle and have a time of prayer for each other. After a couple minutes I will close in prayer for all of the groups. *(Wait about 2 minutes. Then break in and give a short prayer. Pick up the books.)*

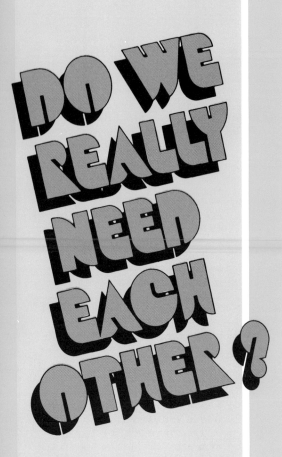

DO WE REALLY NEED EACH OTHER?

Objective: To take inventory of the qualities in your life in light of the spiritual gifts mentioned in Romans 12, and to affirm the qualities you have observed in your support group.

PROCEDURE

The instructions are given in the words you can use in leading the group.

WARM-UP

To what degree do you feel strong or weak in the various spiritual gifts?
(Read over the Scripture passage. Then rank yourself from 1 to 10 on each of the spiritual gifts—1 being very weak and 10 being very strong. For instance, on the gift of "speech" you might circle number 3 because you feel that you are rather weak in communicating the Gospel verbally.)

Speak God's message (speech)
God has given me a gift for communicating the Gospel. When I explain the Good News, God seems to use my words to bring insight and understanding about his grace.

1 2 3 4 5 6 7 8 9 10

Serve (service)
God has given me a special knack for helping out when a need arises. I am sensitive to other people and find it easy to respond to their needs.

1 2 3 4 5 6 7 8 9 10

Teach (teaching)
God has given me a skill for helping others to learn. I am good at getting other people motivated.

1 2 3 4 5 6 7 8 9 10

Encourage others
God has given me the disposition to see the best in others. I find it easy to compliment people—to point out their strengths, to "call forth" their best.

1 2 3 4 5 6 7 8 9 10

Generosity
God has given me a freedom to share myself with others. I find it easy to give, to reach out, to touch and care whenever there is a need.

1 2 3 4 5 6 7 8 9 10

Authority (leadership)
God has given me a gift for organization. I can get things done. I find it easy to

LIFE IN GOD'S SERVICE

"...Do not think of yourselves more highly than you should. Instead, be modest in your thinking, and each one of you judge himself according to the amount of faith that God has given him. We have many parts in the one body, and all these parts have different functions. In the same way, though we are many, we are one body in union with Christ and we are all joined to each other as different parts of one body. So we are to use our

take responsibility and direct others.

1 2 3 4 5 6 7 8 9 10

Kindness

God has given me the ability to be compassionate—warm and tender—whenever someone is in trouble or needs help. I can enter into people's pain—feel with them—and minister.

1 2 3 4 5 6 7 8 9 10

GOING DEEPER

1. **What gifts have the members of your group shown during these sessions?** *(In the circles write the names of the people in your group. Then think over the list of "gifts" and jot a gift beside each name. For instance for Tom you might put down "speech," because with his explanation you really understand the Gospel. For Bea you might put down "encouragement," because he has been the one to call forth the best in you.)*

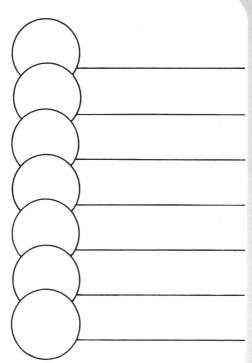

2. **If God were to grade you on the use you have made of his gifts, what would he probably give you?** *(Circle one.)*
   a. A+   c. B+   e. C   g. F
   b. A-   d. B-   f. D-

3. **When it comes to "affirming your own gifts," what do you tend to do?** *(Circle one.)*
   a. think I have no gifts
   b. downgrade my gifts
   c. overestimate my gifts
   d. pooh-pooh the whole idea of spiritual gifts
   e. shy away from thinking about it

different gifts in accordance with the grace that God has given us. If our gift is to speak God's message, we must do it according to the faith that we have. If it is to serve, we must serve. If it is to teach, we must teach. If it is to encourage others, we must do so. Whoever shares what he has with others, must do it generously; whoever has authority, must work hard; whoever shows kindness to others, must do it cheerfully."

ROMANS 12:3-8 GNFMM

Silent Preparation / 5 to 10 min.

(Ask the groups of 8 to sit together so that they can see each other while filling out the questionnaire.)
Turn to page 46 in your player's book and fill out the questionnaire.

Warm-up / 4's / 10 min.

Get together in 4's—with others from your support group—and share two of the gifts of the Spirit: (a) the gift on which you ranked yourself the highest, (b) the gift on which you ranked yourself the lowest. *(Take a moment and explain the gifts on which you ranked yourself highest and lowest. After 10 minutes call time and move on.)*

Going Deeper / 8's / 15 to 20 min.

Regather your group of 8. Have one person remain silent while the others share the gifts they would give him and why. After everyone is through, he tells how he answered the last two questions in the questionnaire and explains why. Repeat the procedure until everyone in your group has had a turn. *(Pick out one person and explain to everyone the gift you have observed in this person. Then let the groups proceed.)*

Close-out

Stand together in a close circle and have a time of prayer for each other. Remember the high points of our time together. *(Wait a few moments to give everyone an opportunity to pray. Then break in with thanks to God for his many blessings.)*

Objective: To take inventory of your family life in light of the teachings of Jesus about criticism "murdering your brother," and then to find out from those in your support group what they appreciate most about you.

PROCEDURE

The instructions are given in the words you can use in leading the group.

Silent Preparation / 5 to 10 min.

(Ask the groups of 8 to sit together so that they can see each other while filling out the questionnaire.)

Turn to page 46 in your player's book and fill out the questionnaire.

Warm-up / 4's / 10 min.

Get together in 4's—with people from your support group—and share the Warm-up in the questionnaire. Go around on the first question, each one explaining his

TEACHING ABOUT ANGER

"You have heard that men were told in the past, 'Do not murder; anyone who commits murder will be brought before the judge. But now I tell you: whoever is angry with his brother will be brought before the judge; whoever calls his brother 'You good-for-nothing!' will be brought before the Council; and whoever calls his brother a worthless fool will be in danger of going to the fire of hell. So if you are about to offer your gift to God at the altar and there you remember that your brother has something against you, leave your gift there in front of the altar and go at once to make peace with your brother; then come back and offer your gift to God."

MATTHEW 5:21-24 GNFMM

WARM-UP

After reading the Scripture how would you complete the following?

1. Murder is defined in the Scripture passage as *(circle one)*:
   a. killing your brother
   b. slandering your brother
   c. tearing down your brother's self-worth
   d. making it difficult for your brother
   e. not giving in to your brother

2. According to the passage God expects *(circle one)*:
   a. the person who has done wrong to go to God and make it right
   b. the person who has been wronged to go to God and make it right
   c. the person who has done wrong to go to the person and make it right
   d. the person who has been wronged to go to the person and make it right

3. If I were to describe my relationship with each person with whom I live now, I would use the following symbols. *(Write the names of the people on the lines Then beside each name place one of the symbols.)*

○ Our relationship is completely affirming. I build this person up and he builds me up. We help each other to win.

◑ Our relationship is half affirming. I try to build this person up but he refuses to build me up.

◑ Our relationship is half affirming in the other direction. This person tries to build me up, but I do not know how to build him up.

◉ Our relationship is mutually destructive. I tear this person down and he tears me down, We are destroying each other.

GOING DEEPER

What do you appreciate most about each member of your group? *(Write the names of your group in the circles. Then beside each name write what you appreciate most about him—or his "most outstanding strength." For instance, for Tom you might put: "warmth" or "moral courage." Be honest. Here is your chance to do what the Scripture passage is all about.)*

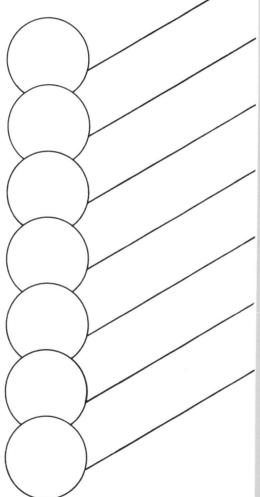

answer and why. Then go around on the next question, etc. *(Take a moment and explain your answer to the first question. Then turn the groups loose. After 10 minutes call time and move on.)*

Going Deeper / 4's or 8's / 15 min.

(You will have to decide whether to use groups of 4 or 8, depending upon the time available. If there is plenty of time, move into groups of 8. If not, stay with groups of 4 so the participation can be greater.)

This is what might be called a "strength bombardment" experience. Let one person sit in silence while the others explain what they appreciate most about him—or what they feel is his most outstanding strength. When everyone is finished, let the person finish the sentence. "The thing I would most like to change about myself is..."

Then another person remains silent while the others share what they appreciate most about him, etc., until everyone in your group has been covered. *(Choose a person and explain in all honesty the thing you appreciate most about him. By your own example set the pace for deep sharing. When all of the groups are through, call time and move on to the Close-out.)*

Close-out

Spend a few moments in prayer for one another mentioning particular needs that have been shared. After a few minutes I will break in and close with a prayer for the whole group. *(Wait a bit. Then pray for the entire group. Collect the books.)*

THE LIFE THAT WINS

Objective: To take inventory of your personal attitudes and life-style in light of the creed for the personal behavior of a Christian as suggested in Romans 12, and to use your insights as the basis for a sharing experience.

PROCEDURE

The instructions are given in the words you can use in leading the group.

Silent Preparation / 5 to 10 min.
Turn to page 48 in your player's book and fill out the questionnaire.

Warm-up / 2's / 15 min.
Get together with someone from your group of 8 and share the Warm-up—one phrase at a time. Take the first phrase and explain to each other how you rated your life. Then take the next phrase and each explain his rating, etc. *(Honestly share how you ranked*

WARM-UP

Where do you stand in view of Romans 12? *(Read over the Scripture. Then measure your life against the passage —phrase by phrase—by circling a number between 1 and 10—1 being very weak and 10 being very strong. For instance for "love must be completely sincere," you might circle "4" because you find you're likely to play that you love a person when you really don't.)*

Love must be completely sincere
I am able to really give myself to other Christian brothers and sisters, not in some phony way, but with real meaning.

1   2   3   4   5   6   7   8   9   10

Hate what is evil, hold on to what is good
I am learning to stand up for my convictions; to say no to something I know is wrong and yes to God's thing.

1   2   3   4   5   6   7   8   9   10

Love one another warmly as brothers in Christ...and show respect for one another
I am learning how to reach out and hug my Christian brothers and sisters warmly—in the right way—and for purely spiritual reasons.

1   2   3   4   5   6   7   8   9   10

Work hard and do not be lazy
I have a deep desire to pitch in at home and school and at work without having to be asked.

1   2   3   4   5   6   7   8   9   10

Serve the Lord with a heart full of devotion
I am eager and enthusiastic to do anything I can for Christ because my heart is full of gratitude for what he did for me.

1   2   3   4   5   6   7   8   9   10

Let your hope keep you joyful
I am experiencing a new freedom that overflows in praise because I know that God is in control.

1   2   3   4   5   6   7   8   9   10

Be patient in your troubles
Problems don't get me down any more. I can take the heat. Under pressure I can stay cool.

1   2   3   4   5   6   7   8   9   10

LIFE IN GOD'S SERVICE

Love must be completely sincere. Hate what is evil, hold on to what is good. Love one another warmly as brothers in Christ, and be eager to show respect for one another. Work hard, and do not be lazy. Serve the Lord with a heart full of devotion. Let your hope keep you joyful, be patient in your troubles, and pray at all times. Share your belongings with your needy brothers, and open your homes to strangers.

Ask God to bless those who persecute you; yes, ask him to bless, not to curse. Be happy with those who are happy, weep with those who weep. Have the same concern for all alike. Do not be proud, but accept humble duties. Do not think of yourselves as wise.

If someone does evil to you, do not pay him back with evil. Try to do what all men consider to be good. Do everything possible, on your part, to live at peace with all men. Never take revenge, my friends, but instead let God's wrath do it. For the scripture says, "I will take revenge, I will pay back, says the Lord."

Instead, as the scripture says: "If your enemy is hungry, feed him; if he is thirsty, give him a drink; for by doing this you will heap burning coals on his head." Do not let evil defeat you; instead, conquer evil with good."

ROMANS 12:9-21 GNFMM

Pray at all times

I have learned to turn over every need to Christ and to share every decision I have to make with him. I have learned to "wait on God" and let him work things out.

1 2 3 4 5 6 7 8 9 10

Share your belongings with the needy ...open your homes to strangers

I have learned that my possessions, my time, my whole being, belongs to God— to be shared with those in need.

1 2 3 4 5 6 7 8 9 10

Ask God to bless those who persecute you

I have learned to respond with kindness to those who put me down—and to pray on their behalf. I am no longer defensive about my life.

1 2 3 4 5 6 7 8 9 10

Be happy with those who are happy, weep with those who weep

I have learned to roll with the punches; to celebrate life when the occasion is right, and to grieve openly when the occasion demands. I am not afraid to show my feelings.

1 2 3 4 5 6 7 8 9 10

GOING DEEPER

1. If this passage is a picture of what a Christian ought to be, then I am (circle one):
   a. really in trouble
   b. a poor specimen
   c. moving in the right direction
   d. doing OK, but...
   e. going to have to change some things
   f. _____

2. Since being in this program, I feel that in my Christian life I have (circle one):
   a. slipped back
   b. started to move
   c. only just begun
   d. come a long way
   e. really grown
   f. a long way to go
   g. changed

3. The greatest change in my Christian life since starting in this program has been in my (circle two):
   a. sense of freedom
   b. feeling of what is important
   c. own self-acceptance
   d. personal devotional habits
   e. desire to clean up my life
   f. feeling of really belonging to God's family
   g. commitment to follow God's will

yourself on the first phrase. Then turn the people loose. After 15 minutes call time and move on.)

Going Deeper / 4's / 15 min.

With your partner get together with 2 others to form a group of 4. Go around and explain your answer on the first point in Going Deeper. Then go around on the second question, etc. *(Explain your answer to the first question and set the pace for openness and honesty.*

Close-out

Stand together in a close circle and have a time of prayer for each other. Remember the high points of our time together. *(Wait a few moments to give everyone an opportunity to pray. Then break in with thanks to God for his many blessings.)*

ARE YOU WINNING THE RACE?

Objective: To take inventory of your life during the time you have been in this program, and to share the results with your support group.

PROCEDURE

The instructions are given in the words you can use in leading the group.

GOD OUR FATHER

As for us, we have this large crowd of witnesses around us. Let us rid ourselves, then, of everything that gets in the way, and the sin which holds on to us so tightly, and let us run with determination the race that lies before us. Let us keep our eyes fixed on Jesus, on whom our faith depends from beginning to end. He did not give up because of the cross! On the contrary, because of the joy that was waiting for him, he thought nothing of the disgrace of dying on the cross, and is now seated at the right side of God's throne.

HEBREWS 12:1-2 GNFMM

WARM-UP

How have you progressed while in this program? *(Read over the Scripture passage. Then rank your progress. Circle a number between 1 and 10—1 being very low and 10 being very high. For instance, for the first one you might circle number 3 because you have made a little progress but you still have a long way to go.)*

In my prayer life
1   2   3   4   5   6   7   8   9   10

In my regular study of Scripture
1   2   3   4   5   6   7   8   9   10

In sorting out my priorities
1   2   3   4   5   6   7   8   9   10

In understanding God's will for my life
1   2   3   4   5   6   7   8   9   10

In developing my own value system
1   2   3   4   5   6   7   8   9   10

In standing up for what I believe
1   2   3   4   5   6   7   8   9   10

In disciplining my leisure for the best use
1   2   3   4   5   6   7   8   9   10

In controlling my temper
1   2   3   4   5   6   7   8   9   10

In my own inner peace of mind
1   2   3   4   5   6   7   8   9   10

In my personal habits
1   2   3   4   5   6   7   8   9   10

In my determination to do what is right
1   2   3   4   5   6   7   8   9   10

In appreciating what Jesus has done for me
1   2   3   4   5   6   7   8   9   10

In sharing the Gospel
1   2   3   4   5   6   7   8   9   10

In submitting wholeheartedly to God
1   2   3   4   5   6   7   8   9   10

In realizing God's love
1   2   3   4   5   6   7   8   9   10

In being sensitive to other people
1   2   3   4   5   6   7   8   9   10

In using my energy for God
1   2   3   4   5   6   7   8   9   10

In resisting temptation to waste myself
1   2   3   4   5   6   7   8   9   10

In determining to use the gifts God has given me
1   2   3   4   5   6   7   8   9   10

GOING DEEPER

In what areas do you have strong feelings? *(Below are a series of statements. Choose five that really mean something to you. Rank them in the order of their importance in your life right now. For instance you might rank "Pain has meaning" number 1, because God has taught you something special through a painful experience.)*

_____ Those who give themselves will receive God.
_____ Caring for others is caring for God.
_____ God's love is unearned.
_____ We should obey authority, but not imitate those in authority.
_____ Pain has meaning.
_____ Death has no permanent hold over us.
_____ God makes up the difference in my efforts.
_____ Knowing God is different from knowing about God.
_____ I need to be quietly receptive to God's speaking to me.
_____ God dispenses his power to us to use.
_____ Through Jesus, God is made visible in people like us.
_____ I can do anything through Jesus Christ.
_____ Nothing can separate me from the love of God.
_____ We should do everything to the glory of God.
_____ No temptation that we have, need overcome us.

Silent Preparation / 5 to 10 min.
Turn to page 48 in your player's book and fill out the questionnaire.

Warm-up / 2's / 10 min.
Get together in 2's—with someone from your support group—and share how you ranked yourself in the Warm-up. Take the first point and let each person explain how he ranked himself and why. Then take the second, etc. *(Take a moment and explain how you ranked yourself on the first point. After 10 minutes call time and move on.)*

Going Deeper / 8's / 15 to 20 min.
Get together with your entire support group and share your answers to Going Deeper. Take the first point and go around, letting each person explain his answer and why. If there is time, go around on the second question, the third, etc. *(Explain your answer to the first question and set the pace for real depth sharing. At the close call time and move on to the Close-out).*

Close-out
In your support groups, spend a few moments in prayer for one another, mentioning the particular needs that have been shared. After a couple minutes I will break in and close with prayer for the entire group. *(Wait two or three minutes. Then break in with a closing prayer.)*

Objective: To take inventory of your life during the time you have been in this program, and to share the results with your support group.

PROCEDURE

The instructions are given in the words you can use in leading the group.

Silent Preparation / 5 to 10 min.

Turn to page 48 in your player's book and fill out the questionnaire.

Warm-up / 2's / 10 min.

Get together in 2's—with someone from your support group—and share how you ranked yourself in the Warm-up. Take the first point

WARM-UP

How have you progressed while in this program? *(Read over the Scripture. Then in each area rank your spiritual progress from 1 to 10—1 being very low and 10 being very high. For instance, for your "prayer life" you might circle number 3, because you don't have much of a prayer life but you have more than when you started this program.)*

In living out my commitment to Christ

1 2 3 4 5 6 7 8 9 10

In reshaping my lifestyle around spiritual values

1 2 3 4 5 6 7 8 9 10

RUNNING TOWARD THE GOAL

I do not claim that I have already succeeded or have already become perfect. I keep going on to try to win the prize for which Christ Jesus has already won me to himself. Of course, brothers, I really do not think that I have already won it; the one thing I do, however, is to forget what is behind me and do my best to reach what is ahead. So I run straight toward the goal in order to win the prize, which is God's call through Christ Jesus to the life above.

All of us who are spiritually mature should have this same attitude. If, however, some of you have a different attitude, God will make this clear to you. However that may be, let us go forward according to the same rules we have followed until now."

PHILIPPIANS 3:12-16 GNFMM

In working for justice for all peoples

1 2 3 4 5 6 7 8 9 10

In thinking of my long-range goals

1 2 3 4 5 6 7 8 9 10

In experiencing God's inner peace

1 2 3 4 5 6 7 8 9 10

In discovering my own special gifts

1 2 3 4 5 6 7 8 9 10

In dealing with feelings of insecurity and inadequacy

1 2 3 4 5 6 7 8 9 10

In dealing with sexual hangups

1 2 3 4 5 6 7 8 9 10

In experiencing God's forgiveness

1 2 3 4 5 6 7 8 9 10

In believing in myself

1 2 3 4 5 6 7 8 9 10

GOING DEEPER

1. **Five years from now, I will probably look back upon the time in this program as** *(circle one)*:
   a. a waste of time
   b. the beginning of my spiritual life
   c. the first time I really got serious about God
   d. a time of fun and laughter with people who really came to mean a lot to me
   e. a beautiful experience, but...
   f. _____

2. **If I had to put my finger on one thing in this program where God "touched" me, it would be** *(circle one)*:
   a. the prayer time
   b. the sharing of our problems
   c. getting into Scripture for myself
   d. _____

3. **The challenge in the Scripture to "forget what is behind me" and run "straight toward the goal" in Jesus Christ, strikes me as** *(circle one)*:
   a. almost impossible
   b. what I am already doing
   c. what the Christian life is all about
   d. separating the men from the boys

In putting my money where my mouth is

1 2 3 4 5 6 7 8 9 10

In developing a daily devotional habit

1 2 3 4 5 6 7 8 9 10

In keeping thoughts under control

1 2 3 4 5 6 7 8 9 10

In standing up for what I believe

1 2 3 4 5 6 7 8 9 10

In controlling my temper

1 2 3 4 5 6 7 8 9 10

In dealing with family relationships

1 2 3 4 5 6 7 8 9 10

In managing my time for best use

1 2 3 4 5 6 7 8 9 10

In sharing my faith with my friends

1 2 3 4 5 6 7 8 9 10

and let each person explain how he ranked himself and why. Then take the second, etc. *(Take a moment and explain how you ranked yourself on the first point. After 10 minutes call time and move on.)*

Going Deeper / 8's / 15 to 20 min.

Get together with your entire support group and share your answers to Going Deeper. Take the first point and go around, letting each person explain his answer and why. If there is time, go around on the second question, the third, etc. *(Explain your answer to the first question and set the pace for real depth sharing. At the close call time and move on to the Close-out).*

Close-out

In your support groups, spend a few moments in prayer for one another, mentioning the particular needs that have been shared. After a couple minutes I will break in and close with prayer for the entire group. *(Wait two or three minutes. Then break in with a closing prayer.)*

Notes

Special Group Activities

HOW TO
Celebrate Your Differences

by Paul and Nellie Tournier

Dr. Tournier: It is our conviction that God has a plan for every person, and that the meaning of life is to seek God's will in order to carry out this plan.

If He has a plan for me and a plan for Nellie, then it follows that He must have a plan for both of us. But inevitably each of us sees God from his own point of view, so that the search for God can become a source of real harmonization between the two of us.

That is not easy. There are Christians who say, "Only believe, and problems disappear." However, that is not what we've found, and indeed we feel that the hard work which the difficulties of life make of the search for God has caused us to mature.

The will of God is not easy to know. The most terrible wars have been religious wars, precisely because both sides were convinced that God was on their side. I've also seen religious wars in families. How tragic it is to see the cruelty with which a believer can treat his spouse! A certain pastor who brought his sick wife to me remarked, "You see, Doctor, I have the Holy Spirit and she doesn't." I immediately thought, *That attitude in itself would be enough to make his wife sick!* And that if he did have the Holy Spirit, the Spirit could tell him to rethink his attitudes!

We laugh at such an extreme example, but all of us tend to think that God is of our opinion rather than our neighbor's. Little by little I have learned that God speaks to everybody — men and women, adults and children, blacks and whites, the rich and the poor. To discover the will of God, you must listen to Him in all men. Of course I prefer to have God speak directly to me, rather than through my wife, and yet in truly seeking His will I must be persuaded that He speaks as much through her as through me; to her as much as to me.

Then God becomes a voice which is neither my voice nor her voice, but one which can unite us. Neither my wife nor I possess God. We seek Him together, and to seek Him together there must be oneness between us. Conjugal communion, even in the best of marriages, is difficult.

My wife intimidates me, even after more than forty years of marriage. And timidity is a real hindrance to human encounter. At the moment I am working on a book, and when Nellie says, "Would you like to read a bit of it to me?" I'm intimidated. I could read the manuscript to a thousand persons with less effort than it takes to read her a single passage. How important it is to be able to feel free and relaxed with each other!

Mme. Tournier: When Paul asked me to

215

marry him, what an explosion in my life! He was a great intellectual, and I was not even a good student. All through my youth I had considered Tournier far above other people. I certainly did not think of myself as his equal.

Dr. Tournier: I tried to give her good reasons to help her find a sense of equality: psychological, theological, philosophical, etc. The more reasons I gave, the more she felt inferior to me. Even in matters of faith this was a difficulty. We wanted to make ours a Christian home, so from time to time we took the Bible and I read from it. Then I commented on the Scripture passage and my wife listened, passive and silent. It wasn't very lively, and often we would give up trying.

Then we would say, "No; we must have devotions together," and the whole thing would begin again. I played preacher and Nellie was my flock.

Mme. Tournier: I clearly sensed that if I could get to the point where I could pray just once in my husband's presence, I would be freed from my feelings of inferiority. Finally I did so by selecting a hymn and praying the words. Later I was able to pray using words of my own.

Dr. Tournier: We had a long way to go to become a real couple. I lived in the intellectual world, and she had the simplicity of faith. Slowly, we were able to bring together a union of my complexity and her simplicity. Such a union is extremely important, for simplicity without thought turns maudlin, while religious thought without faith's simplicity becomes empty theology.

A decisive event on the path we travelled turned out to be our discovery of silence. In 1932 I met a man who told me of the importance silent meditation played in his life. The next day I attempted an hour of silent meditation in God's presence. At the same time, unknown to me, my wife was trying the same thing.

Neither of us dared speak of this experiment to the other. When at last we admitted what we were doing, we began to wait upon God silently together.

Both of us felt ill at ease. During those periods of meditation it would have been easy for me to fall back into my pattern of abstract thought, but there was no question of that for the subject was my life and what God was saying to me, personally, about it. As verbalizing had always been an obstacle between Nellie and me, silence became for us an open door.

Mme. Tournier: Once when I said something to my husband which I had sensed during our common silence, he began to enlarge on it. I found the strength to say, "I'm talking now about something I feel God is trying to bring us to understand. There's no need for you to embroider it."

Dr. Tournier: Our temperaments are quite different, and a lot of work had to be done in order for our viewpoints to converge. This convergence is the work of God in our marriage.

I'm an optimist and she a pessimist. She thinks of every difficulty, misfortune, and catastrophe that might happen, and I cannot promise her that such things will not happen. But God is neither optimist nor pessimist. The search for Him leads one beyond his own personality and temperament to a path that is neither optimism nor pessimism.

Another difference between us is that

I tend to take the stance of a man who knows no fear, while Nellie is of a rather fearful nature. One night our son had gone someplace in the car and did not return when expected. Both of us were very worried, and suddenly I said to Nellie, "I'm just as upset as you are, though I try to hide it."

She replied, "That makes me feel better," for she was no longer alone in her fear.

Husband and wife tend to accentuate their attitudes in a delicate balance of oppositions. Each becomes a counter-weight to the other. If one shows fear, the other hides it. But in fact all of us are divided between fear and courage. The separation, the frontier, is not between the two spouses, but in each of us.

Still another difference we have had

and placed it in God's hands.

Mme. Tournier: I was injured in that accident and hospitalized. During my convalescence and for several months afterward I suffered the pain of knowing that Paul had killed his uncle — it was not his fault, but the death was a fact. At last I turned to my pastor, who had stood by me throughout the ordeal. He said everything humanly possible to bring me comfort, but none of it spoke to my need. Only as I was leaving did he ask, "Did Christ die on the Cross for a few things or for everything?"

A few nights before Christmas I awakened during the night and heard the word *everything*. I was released. When I thought about the accident, the pain was gone.

Dr. Tournier: If it is true that God has a plan for us, then there must be turning points, moments when we must follow in the direction He seems to indicate.

In 1936 we reached such a turning point. It seemed to me that God wanted me to leave medical practice for evangelism. I began to be less absorbed by my life as a doctor, which seemed commonplace compared to the life of an evangelist. I was very enthusiastic about the new prospect, but Nellie was not at all convinced. Again, our different temperaments played their part: I am an adventurer, and she is prudence itself.

What do a husband and wife do when they are seeking to follow God's will but can't agree on what that is? The only thing to do is wait until God gives more light.

For several months we went through a very difficult period. One day when we were fed up with our endless discussions I actually felt despair. But we kept on

is our attitude toward money. I don't like to earn but I love to spend. My wife is quite content for me to earn, but she doesn't like to spend. Again, we had to converge and find common ground.

Mme. Tournier: The man who raised Paul — my husband was an orphan and his uncle had cared for him — came to me one day and said, "The Tourniers have always spent everything. But I know that in your family you have been taught to count the pennies. I want you to be minister of finance in this household."

This was difficult to suggest to my husband, but because we had those periods of silent meditation, I was able to bring it up. Thereafter he turned over to me all the money he earned, and together we decided what to do with it.

Dr. Tournier: With the children my wife was rather strict, and I very easygoing. We were in fact reacting to each other. One day during meditation I had this thought: *I'm really leaving the whole burden for her to carry. I have to be more aware of my responsibilities, stricter with my children.* Whereupon my wife said, "Then I can be less strict!"

Then there are the severe trials of life.

In 1937 we had an automobile accident. I was driving and my uncle, the man who raised me, was killed. Immediately I realized that something terrible and irrevocable had happened. It could never be undone; all I could do was take my suffering to the foot of the Cross and there be forgiven. There was no legal guilt, but I could not rid myself of the feeling of guilt until I prayed waiting and hoping.

There were also financial implications to the problem: giving up my medical practice meant giving up job security.

Mme. Tournier: I had "charming" friends, even relatives, who said to me, "If you go along with that scheme, don't count on us for help." But our younger son, not yet ten years old at the time, said one day, "Mother, I'll soon be able to go out and earn a living."

At last I really sensed that my husband had received a call to become an evangelist, while remaining in his practice. So I asked a young pastor if I could pray in his presence to accept the prospect that my husband fulfill God's will by becoming a doctor-evangelist.

Dr. Tournier: When I realized that God did not want me to leave medical practice but to put my faith to work in it, I knew it would be necessary to inaugurate a new kind of medicine. I would consecrate myself to the task of discovering to what degree one's spiritual life could influence his health. None of my close friends understood what I was trying to do. I was alone, with only my wife's real understanding.

How I wanted some direct bits of advice from God, but I had only three ideas: to re-read a certain book in order to find out whether there were answers to those questions for which medicine has no answer; to talk things over with six colleagues; and to write a letter to my clients explaining that now I would concern myself with the influence of spiritual life on health.

We went away for two weeks, still waiting for God to give me additional inspiration. It never came, and at last I understood that I must begin with the ideas I had, and God would supply others.

During all the succeeding years our periods of meditation have been the source of the whole direction my professional life has taken. I had to resolve practical questions: how to organize my time, for instance. With patients to see, meetings to attend, books to write, speeches to give, there were always conflicts over how to budget my time. Which invitation should I accept? Which article should I decline to write? We always took up such questions together in meditation.

Now that I'm getting old and must reduce my activities, there are new problems, and each time the working together of two temperaments is necessary. Together we seek the right path according to God's will.

The path is different for each person and for each couple. Don't try to imitate us; follow your own path. Perhaps it will be to speak rather than to remain silent.

What counts is the search for God. Sometimes there are answers. Sometimes you have the definite conviction that God is asking something precise of you. But very often there is only silence, with no answer. Only long afterwards do you discover that God's plan has been carried out without your knowing it was done, and that you have been guided without realizing it.

My wife and I thank God for the way He has led us and for all He has given us. The most important thing is not to have received such-and-such an order, because we're often mistaken about that. No, the most important thing is to enter more and more into intimacy, so that our intimacy as a couple is deepened by our intimacy with God.

Reprinted by permission from "Faith at Work."

DISCUSSION DESIGN
for article by Paul and Nellie Tournier

Instructions: There are three parts: (1) silent preparation — with everyone reading the article and completing the Reflection Questionnaire in approximately 15 minutes, (2) interaction in groups of two, preferably with your husband or wife — sharing Phase One for 15 minutes, (3) interaction in groups of six to eight — sharing Phase Two for 30 minutes.

REFLECTION QUESTIONNAIRE *for "Celebrate Your Differences."*

1. The openness that Dr. and Mme. Tournier have about their differences makes me feel (circle one):

a. envious

b. better   d. embarrassed

c. hopeful   e. guilty

2. The Tourniers mention five areas in which they are different or disagree. On the lines below, put an "x" for yourself and an "o" for your spouse to indicate where each of you stands on these issues.

ON FAITH

complex, intellectual ——————————— simple

ON TEMPERAMENT

optimist ——————————— pessimist

ON MONEY

sprendthrift ——————————— skinflint

ON CHILDREN

easygoing ——————————— strict

ON VOCATION

adventurer ——————————— cautious

3. From your own experience, how do you feel about the following statement by Dr. Tournier:

"Husband and wife tend to *accentuate* their attitudes in a delicate balance of oppositions. Each becomes the counterweight to the other. If one shows fear, the other hides it. But in fact all of us are divided between fear and courage. The separation, the frontier, is not between the two spouses, but in each of us."

a. agree   b. disagree

1. The first time my wife (or husband) and I had a major conflict in our marriage it was over the issue of (finish the sentence):

2. I generally deal with conflict in marriage by (circle one):

a. pouting

b. screaming

c. the silent treatment

d. sharing my feelings calmly

e. trying to see it my partner's way

f. ignoring the whole thing

3. "To discover the will of God, you must listen to Him in all men. Of course, I prefer to have God speak directly to me, rather than through my wife, and yet in truly seeking His will I must be persuaded that He speaks as much through her as through me; to her as much as to me."

I find the statement above (circle one):

a. hard to accept

b. easy to accept but hard to practice

c. easy to accept and easy to practice

4. In the delicate balance of our marriage relationship, my greatest weakness is (finish sentence):

To offset this weakness, my spouse is able to contribute (finish this sentence):

HOW TO
Have a Turned-on Church

Purpose: For the pastor and board members to evaluate their personal and church lifestyle. Do not attempt this session unless you are committed to spend a block of time together — in complete openness to each other.

Setting: A retreat atmosphere.

Time: At least four hours.

PROCEDURE

The session is divided into three parts: (1) silent preparation — with everyone on his own, (2) sharing — in groups of five or six, (3) commissioning — with everyone together.

Silent preparation (30 minutes)

1. Read the article.

2. Fill out the questionnaire as thoughtfully as you can. Please do not discuss your answers with anyone during this time.

Sharing (3 hours)

1. Get together in groups of five or six.

2. Start with the first category on the worksheet and let everyone share his answer and explain. Feel free to explain *why* you feel as you do.... Be open. Be honest.

3. After 25 or 30 minutes, move on to the next category and go around a second time, etc., until you have completed each part.
   If you want to take a break for coffee in the middle of the sharing, this is fine, but do not have any activity that would take your mind off the subject.

Commissioning (30 minutes)

Based on the hopes, dreams, goals and strategies that grow out of the sharing experience, create a commissioning service that celebrates the hopes you have established.

Our family once participated in a moving experience. A little boy in our neighborhood suffered brain damage in an automobile accident. The only hope for him to walk and run and play again was through what the doctors called a

by Lloyd Ogilvie

repatterning of his brain.

For several hours each week many of the children in the neighborhood, including our own, would take turns working the little boy's legs and arms. The doctor told us new grooves were being formed in the brain that would eventually enable the boy to use his limbs again.

I'll never forget the excitement we all felt when that boy began to regain his ability to walk and play. And as I watched the process I realized what the task of the contemporary churchman is. It is to discover how to repattern the mind of the church so the people of God can walk and run on a two-legged Gospel — one of deep commitment to the living Christ and of dynamic action in the world.

Several principles undergird our involvement. First, nothing can happen through us that hasn't happened to us. Second, we can only communicate that which we are in the process of learning. Third, people will support only those things they share in discovering. And fourth, only as we become the vulnerable, open people God wants us to be will we be able to participate in the reproduction of what we find in the churches we serve.

I believe we need a new picture of what the church needs to be in our generation. The institutions of which we are a part are in the process of becoming what we envision them to be. So we need a new vision of the purpose of the parish, of its program and of its leadership. Only as we see clearly why we exist as an institution can we repattern the program to meet its purpose.

The church exists not for itself but for the world. But for the past 20 years we have been sending people into the world to be something for which they have neither the power nor the personal experience. We have made people conscious of racial issues, of segregated neighborhoods, of poverty and confusion. We've talked about the isolated and the lonely, and every Sunday morning we have pressed our people out into the world to do something they have not had the kind of experience they need together to do.

Let's picture the kind of people who could make a difference in our society — people who would outcare and outdare the world, whose experience of Jesus Christ would make them so warm and accepting and forgiving that they would become ingrained in the wounds of the world. As contagious agents they would be able to share their faith with others, attack the evil in the structures of society and make a difference.

One of the great needs before us is the recovery of intimacy. Perhaps the most impersonal place in society is the local parish. It is not impersonal; it is nonpersonal. We do not produce people who love themselves, accept themselves, forgive themselves and are able to reproduce themselves in the world.

Most of us as Christian leaders live in two worlds: our own personal world

and the world of our leadership. And there's a strong membrane between what is happening in our lives and what we share in our leadership. The institutions of which we are a part, therefore, become impersonal and incapable of helping people share the love and forgiveness of God in the world.

To love God is to let God love you. To love people is to let them love you. And to let them love you is to let them know you. This calls for a new quality of vulnerability.

I believe the greatest gift we have to share with our parish is what God is doing with the down-to-earth everyday raw material of our own lives. It's because we share ideas and thoughts and theories and creeds rather than the fresh and vital things that God is doing with our lives that people in our parishes go into the world with a confused misunderstanding of the theories and creeds of the faith and are not able to reproduce them either

with individuals or with the complex problems that exist within the institutions of society.

What happens to us as leaders is that we feel we have to be the super-saints of the parish. As a result we climb the ladder of our self-justifying, self-propelled adequacy rather than share with our people the things that God is doing each day in our marriages, in our homes with our kids, with our own image, with our money, with our future, with the deep fears and anxieties and frustrations that face us.

In Los Angeles, the greatest social problem is loneliness. And yet in many of the churches of Los Angeles the greatest problem is loneliness. We sing our hymns and pray our prayers and go through the rituals of our institutionalized Christianity and don't touch down into the deep inner needs of people. We are the lonely people and we're reproducing a lonely institution that is not meeting the profound needs of a lonely world.

When I was called to First Presbyterian Church of Hollywood, I had a decision to make. I have to make it again and again. It was whether I was going to allow the leadership of that church to know me as I really was. The temptation was to try and project an image of adequacy.

I refused to preach the first weekend and instead asked the officers to take a three-day retreat with me. I tried to share with them what God was doing in the down-to-earth experiences of my own life — the pilgrimage Mary Jane and I have been on discovering how to love each other, the failures that I knew in trying to be the kind of husband who would meet her needs. I talked about my role as a father, and how I often fail. I talked to them about my own needs for security, affirmation and encouragement. And one

after the other of them came up to me and said, "We can't imagine this is true. Why, you face the same kinds of problems we face. And we thought you had it all put together. But, you know, we feel differently about being the elders of the church now."

As they got together in small clusters and began talking with each other about their greatest dream for themselves and their church, about the implications of the faith for their deeply personal problems which they'd never talked with each other about before, suddenly there was a new warmth among them. And after three days of this openness and honesty and freedom, there was a new sense of daring and adventure. Then we asked the question, "If you knew you couldn't fail, where would you like to be five years from now and where would you like this church to be?"

Little by little, dreams were formed. Then we put it all together and that became the five-year plan for the church. And they came up with the realization that they wanted the church to be what they had experienced together. "We want our church to be a worshiping congregation," they said; "a healing communion, an equipping center and a deployment agency."

We were then able to take those four basic things, divide them into smaller categories and make task forces to achieve those four basic elements in the life of the church. The things that I've seen happen during this past year

have all come out of the experience of the session. We've met together in small groups, and they now want small groups in the life of the church as a whole. Because we've had times of caring for each other and hearing each other out and praying for each other, they now want the church to be a healing center, and a healing ministry has begun. On Sunday evenings we gather together for a service of praise and thanksgiving and then specific prayers, with the laying on of hands for lonely people in our own parish.

Reuel Howe says that the curriculum for our ministry is written out of the things that God teaches us. There's an edge on which each of us is living. Those needs are the place where God is going to begin to work with us so that we'll be able to minister with new sensitivity, new openness, new tenderness, new grace, to be able to be the Gospel that we proclaim with such agility. The healing of the church and its repatterning must begin with us if we are to be the kind of church to meet the loneliness of our world.

There are five questions I ask myself which are the basis of my understanding of how to repattern the church:

1. What are the kind of people the church exists to deploy in the world?

2. What kind of a church makes possible that kind of a person?

3. What kind of team of officers makes possible that kind of a local church?

4. What kind of pastor or leadership-enabler makes possible that kind of a church in order to deploy in the world that quality of life?

5. What kind of a relational experience, what kind of authenticating, liberating experience, must happen in the life of a pastor to make him that kind of an enabler to set free that kind of officer to dare to develop that kind of a church in order to put out into the world that kind of a person?

I find the times of retreats and conferences give one a long, deep experience in order to be able to share the quality of life that I'm talking about. I've found that it's impossible to dare to branch out into this new style of life without a team of people who are willing to share with me.

I have a group in southern California that I meet with once a month. We meet early in the morning until late at night. And that is the most exhausting day of my month. We are committed to help each other. Each man is given about an hour. In that hour he is encouraged, enabled and empowered to do the thing that he most needs to do. We laugh with some and cry with others. But our total energy is combined together to help that man in that hour. Then we move on to the next man. I couldn't do what I'm called to do if I didn't have that experience once a month.

Mary Jane and I are a part of a couples' group that meets every other week where we're accepted, not as pastor and wife, but as people. We are as free to have needs there as anyone else and to be prayed for.

I wouldn't dare to do what I'm called to do without a consistent fellowship of which I was a part.

We have to make a choice. Either we go the route of a traditional ministry that is non-relational and that doesn't reach

people's deepest needs; or, if we choose a relational ministry, we need a small band of people who love us utterly, with whom we can sort things out. It is sheer arrogance and contrary to the New Testament to think we can make it otherwise.

About the author: Lloyd Ogilvie is senior pastor of First Presbyterian Church, Hollywood, California, and Chairman of the Board of Directors for Faith at Work. Reprinted by permission from "Faith at Work" magazine, August, 1973.

REFLECTION QUESTIONNAIRE
for "Have a Turned-on Church."

Basic elements in the life of the church

Lloyd Ogilvie gives four goals of
his church. How does your church
program rank in these areas?
(circle a number for each area):

very poor / weak / average / above average / excellent

A WORSHIPPING COMMUNITY
(where worship in-depth takes
place) — 1 2 3 4 5

A HEALING COMMUNION
(where the whole person is
ministered to) — 1 2 3 4 5

AN EQUIPPING CENTER
(where laymen are prepared
for their ministry) — 1 2 3 4 5

A DEPLOYMENT AGENCY
(where laymen are sent forth
into the world) — 1 2 3 4 5

Basic assumptions behind the ministry

Lloyd Ogilvie gives four basic principles that underlie
his philosophy of the ministry. Rank the way you
would agree or disagree on each principle —

1. Nothing can happen through us that hasn't happened to us.

   Total agreement 5 4 3 2 1 Neutral 1 2 3 4 5 Total disagreement

2. We can only communicate that which we are in the process
   of learning ourselves.

   Total agreement 5 4 3 2 1 Neutral 1 2 3 4 5 Total disagreement

3. People will support only those things they share in
   discovering.

   Total agreement 5 4 3 2 1 Neutral 1 2 3 4 5 Total disagreement

4. Only as we become the vulnerable, open people God wants
   us to be will we be able to participate in the reproduction
   of this in the church.

   Total agreement 5 4 3 2 1 Neutral 1 2 3 4 5 Total disagreement

The pastor's openness

**Below is a quote from the article. Think about it
and respond to the category that fits you.**

"I believe the greatest gift we have to share with our parish
is what God is doing with the down-to-earth, everyday raw
material of our own lives....As leaders, we feel we have to
be the super-saints of the parish. As a result we climb the
ladder of our own self-justifying, self-propelled adequacy
rather than share with our people the things that God is
doing each day in our marriages, in our homes, with our
kids, with our own image, with our money, with our future,
with the deep fears and anxieties and frustrations that
face us."

**FOR PASTORS: With my people, I would like to
share more of my personal struggles, but
(circle one):**

a. I don't think a minister should

b. I am afraid to

c. I am afraid my people would not accept me if I did

d. I do not think my people want me to be open
   about my own needs

e. I don't know where to begin

**FOR BOARD MEMBERS: If my pastor shared some
of his personal struggles with us, I would
(circle one):**

a. think less of him

b. feel closer to him

c. be threatened by him

d. be more honest about some of my own struggles

e. feel that the Gospel was being diminished

Loneliness in the church

Lloyd Ogilvie said that the church as an institution is as lonely as the secular world. To evaluate the statement below in your own experience, assume for a moment that you have a *pressing* personal problem. Then — with the appropriate letter — indicate on the line below *how far* you would go in sharing this problem with the following individuals:

your... **Spouse**
      Best Friend
      Minister
      Boardmembers
      Church Members

For instance, if you feel quite hesitant about talking to the Boardmembers, put B close to *Tell nothing*.

Tell everything _____ *Tell nothing*

Sharing groups

Lloyd Ogilvie belongs to three sharing groups in his community. Read the summary for each one and indicate your fellowship needs: NO, if you can do without it; OK, if you would like to belong to it; YES! if you desperately need it.

NO OK YES!

___ ___ ___ *Couples' Group:* **meets every other week in the evening — with other couples in the church — to share and care for each other.** "We are free to have needs there as anyone else and to be prayed for."

___ ___ ___ *Pastors' Group:* **meets once a month for the whole day — with other pastors — one hour for each person to debrief, be encouraged, enabled and empowered. A depth, no-holds barred fellowship.** "We laugh with some and cry with others. But our total energy is combined together to help that man."

___ ___ ___ *Board Members' Group:* **meets once in a while for an entire week to share failures, needs, problems, dreams, hopes and the future strategy of the church.** "After three days of this openness and honesty and freedom, there was a sense of daring and adventure we had never known before....We came to the realization that we wanted the church to be what we had just experienced together."

Five questions for goal-setting

Lloyd Ogilvie gives five questions that he uses in establishing goals for himself and his ministry. Read each question. Then, jot down how you would respond to each question with two words or statements of your own. For instance, for the first question, you might jot down: *fearless; well versed in doctrine.*

1. **What kind of people does the church want to deploy into the world?** _____
_____

2. **What kind of a church makes possible that kind of person?** _____
_____

3. **What kind of team of officers makes possible that kind of church?** _____
_____

4. **What kind of a pastor makes possible that kind of a team of officers?** _____
_____

5. **What must happen in the life of a pastor to make him that kind of person?** _____
_____

In all honesty

Lloyd Ogilvie closed his article with the statement below. Check the responses you would make:

"We have to make a choice. Either we go the route of a traditional ministry that is non-relational and that doesn't reach people's deepest needs; or, if we choose a relational ministry, we need a small band of people who love us utterly, with whom we can sort out things. It is sheer arrogance and contrary to the New Testament to think we can make it otherwise."

1. **I would be willing to take the risk and belong to such a community if I knew (circle one):**

a. **others would join me**

b. **others would accept me**

c. **I could get out anytime I wanted to**

d. **it was going to be for real**

2. **My own dream for the church is that it be a place where (finish the sentence):**

*Stop
for an evening
midway through the course
and enjoy the social
described here —
and possibly invite
a few friends
to share
some of the experiences
you have had together
as a small group.*

A Serendipity Party

Purpose: To give the groups a chance to share what they have learned in the sessions or to reach out to other friends and involve them in some of the experiences of the course.

Setting: A casual party atmosphere where the group can sit at card tables or in small clusters of four to six.

Time required: Two hours...plus an open-ended period at the close for those who wish to keep going in their small groups.

Materials required: Any materials that are needed for playing the games or for creative experiments you decide to use, plus the refreshments.

SUGGESTIONS FOR THE PLANNING CABINET

1. The Planning Cabinet should perform or delegate to others in preparation for the social three tasks:
(a) Program...what to do at the social, (b) Refreshments...what to serve at the social, and (c) Invitations...who to invite to the social.

2. For the program, select two or three of the small-group games or exercises that were found most meaningful in your own experience as a group — one to break the ice, one to build small-group relationships, and one to

bring a sort of catharsis or fulfillment in the small-group experience.

3. The refreshments can be anything from a snack to a full-course dinner — at a restaurant or at one of your homes. If you go-for-broke on a dinner, have the dishes removed and the second cup of coffee served before you start on the group exercises.

4. If there are guests at the social, you will want to visit with them after the program. You can ask them what they thought about the games, and lead from there into conversations about the background of the group.

5. Invitations for this social should be extended to two circles of people: church-related friends and unchurched friends. Sometimes, the best response in a social like this is from the least likely types — the raunchy, gutsy guys that will have nothing to do with church or God. (Don't tell them this.)

6. If anybody asks what the social is all about, call it "A Serendipity" — a fun fair of interpersonal relationships that are profoundly entertaining and entertainingly profound." If they want to know more, tell them to come and see.

7. Separate husbands and wives, close friends, and church cliques when they start to sit down. People tend to be more open and honest at first if they are with strangers — some husbands feel a little goosey around their wives.

8. If you are going to say anything by way of introduction or explanation about the exercises, speak in very personal terms...and as gutsy as possible. Don't telegraph the experience beforehand by telling them what they are going to find out about themselves in the exercises. Let them discover it for themselves.

9. Before you start the last exercise, explain that each small group should dismiss themselves when they are through and help themselves to refreshments quietly, without disturbing the other groups that are still going.

10. After everyone is through, you may want to get the entire group back together — around another cup of coffee.

11. If this social is a howling success, think about a second one. Ask the friends who attended the first one to invite some of their friends. In this way, you may find yourselves naturally evolving into a mission team...reaching out in this unique way to minister in the name of Jesus Christ to the hurts of others. Read over the suggestions in *Groups in Action* for an ongoing mission outreach.

12. Don't be surprised if you are called on by other groups, both religious and secular, to put on a similar social at one of their meetings. People are starved for meaningful relationships and the word travels quickly!

Experimental Worship

Worship

If this course is being used as the program for a week-long conference where you have the extra resource personnel and the facilities for a creative worship experience at the close of the week, an Experimental Worship Service would be an excellent style of service. Keep the various elements of worship, but change the forms to permit a lot of participation from the audience.

The atmosphere for this service could be anything from the chancel of a church to a rustic, outdoor campfire.

To develop a program, simply take the traditional form of worship service that you are familiar with and rewrite a contemporary liturgy for each part. For instance instead of the traditional "Call to Worship," you might insert a ballad that someone in your group has written. Instead of the traditional confession, you might insert a poem or confession from one of your group.

Keep in mind as you write that the word "liturgy" means "the people work." Try to involve the entire audience by asking for their participation in every phase of the worship service.

You may want to ask the Art Workshop to develop a special art exhibit or a backdrop for the service.

For the close, you may want to employ some of the elements from the other worship services suggested.

Quaker Service

Commissioning Service

Communion Service

The simplest form of service to conclude this course experience on a retreat is the Quaker Service…a service of silence in which any person who feels led of the Spirit can break the silence and say something.

The atmosphere should be very, very informal…with the entire group sitting on the floor or in chairs in a semicircle, facing a fire, an altar, or a worship center.

Begin the service by explaining a little about the Quaker tradition and the importance of being in silence and letting God speak to us before we speak to Him or to others. Explain further that after a period of quiet, there will be a bell, or a hymn, or something to indicate the transition…and that afterwards, anyone who would like to say something can get up and say it.

To introduce the period of silence, lead the group in singing together a meditative hymn or chorus to focus their attention upon Christ.

This type of service is especially appropriate at the close of a weekend retreat or week-long conference at which there has been a lot of talking in groups, and everyone is just about talked-out.

If you are at a camp where you can precede the service with a quiet walk on the grounds and everyone can have an hour to think over the experience of the weekend alone, it would be very good. You may want each one to find something that symbolizes his feelings… and bring it to the Quaker Service as a way of sharing what the conference has meant to him. Possibly, at the close, he could place it on the altar as his offering to God.

At the close of a weekend retreat or week-long conference, it would be appropriate to hold a Commissioning Service.

This service is best carried out in small-group clusters where each person has a chance to say what he is going to face when he gets home and what he needs in the way of support from the group.

Then, one by one, each person kneels or sits in the middle of his group and each one in the group lays his hands on the person and prays for his task back home.

Then, when everyone has been commissioned, the group members can join together in a football huddle and celebrate their experience together.

Some groups will want to exchange addresses with each other in order to correspond. Other groups may want to write letters to themselves about their commitments…and designate one person in the group to mail the letters a year later.

If a small group has been together throughout the entire program, this dedication is doubly meaningful…because the community of love will support each person even after he gets back home.

Following the Commissioning Service, the small groups may want to take communion together, following the procedure suggested in that service. You may want to give each small group a hard roll and a common cup and let them serve each other in the name of Christ.

After the service, you may want to join all the groups together in one large circle for a final celebration…and let each person pass the "kiss of peace" to the person on his left and his right… in whatever way he wishes. And in closing, everyone can sing together, "We are one in the Spirit; we are one in the Lord."

Possibly the most meaningful service the group could participate in at the close of the course would be Communion. It could take many forms, depending upon the tradition of the group and the facilities. One possibility is to administer communion in the traditional way, but around a central table where the administering priest serves the bread and the wine informally.

Another possibility would be to partake in the same small groups that you were in during the regular sessions of the course…where you have really established relationships on a deep level. In this way, the priest would come to the group and administer the elements to each person…or each person would be the priest to the person on his right and administer the elements to this person in the name of Christ.

Another possibility would be to give everybody a small hard roll and ask him to go to anybody that he would like to break bread with and give him a piece, telling him why he wanted to break bread with him. Then, for the wine, everyone would share a common cup as a symbol of unity through the person of Christ.

Whatever form you use, keep in mind the integrity of the ordinance itself. This is not a game…and whatever you do must bring to mind the presence of Christ and celebrate His death with great, great meaning.

At the close, it would be fitting to celebrate the experience together in some way. One way would be to pass the "kiss of peace" to the person on your left and on your right…in whatever way you like. Another way would be to send each other forth with the words, "May the peace of Christ go with you" …and let the other person respond, "And with you."

Another way would be to join hands in a giant circle and sing together, "We are one in the Spirit; we are one in the Lord."

Notes

Index

U

V

W

X

Y

Z

Notes

get books

kids put a dollar down

Notes

Peter Graber

Wayne Shearier
604 N. John Beers Rd
Stevensville, Mi 49127
616/429-5356

Aron Valleskey
718 Bellevue
Ypsilanti, MI 48197
313/482-3552

Al Aubert
2080 Pauline Apt. 2A
Ann Arbor, Mich. 48103
(313) 668-8517
   or 994-1478

Dave Hales
1236 Green acre ct
Wabash, In
   219-563-1035

Elizabeth Reis, SSJ
Nazareth Center
Nazareth, Mi-49074
(616) 381-6290

Therese Miller
23889 Strywin Rd
Battle Creek, Mich
   965-6735   49014

James Kunz
RR#7 Greensburg
Ind 47240
   812-663-5449